THE SACREDNESS OF THE PERSON

THE SACREDNESS OF THE PERSON

A New Genealogy of Human Rights

Hans Joas

Alex Skinner, Translator

Georgetown University Press / Washington, DC

Library of Congress Cataloging-in-Publication Data

Joas, Hans.
The sacredness of the person : a new genealogy of human rights / Hans Joas.
pages cm
Includes bibliographical references and index.
ISBN 978-1-58901-969-0 (pbk. : alk. paper)
1. Human rights—History. 2. Human rights—Religious aspects. I. Title.
JC571.J563 2013
323.09—dc23
2012037547

⊛ This book is printed on acid-free paper meeting the requirements of the American National Standard for Permanence in Paper for Printed Library Materials.

15 14 13 9 8 7 6 5 4 3 2
First printing

Printed in the United States of America

To
Bettina Hollstein
Matthias Jung
Wolfgang Knöbl

CONTENTS

PREFACE

Readers may understand this book better if they know something about its lengthy genesis. The basic idea was directly inspired by the two books I wrote in the second half of the 1990s (*The Genesis of Values* and *War and Modernity*). I wished to test out the theory presented in the first of these books, which centers on the genesis of value commitments of all kinds, by examining a specific value system. I wanted this to be a value system that has been influenced by and has itself exerted an influence on the history of violence, to which the second book was dedicated. The history of human rights seemed an ideal choice for such a project.

But as I set about implementing this plan I found myself confronted with a problem that caused me far greater trouble than I had expected. Familiarizing myself with the extensive historical literature and getting to grips with a wide range of philosophical and theological contributions to the justification of human rights proved not just unavoidable but extremely time-consuming. This came as no great surprise. But it became increasingly unclear how, in a positive sense, I should conceive of my own contribution—which I envisaged neither as history, philosophy, nor theology. The individual chapters of the present book certainly draw extensively on major sociologists and their theories: chapter 1 on Max Weber, chapter 2 on Émile Durkheim, and chapters 5 and 6 on Talcott Parsons. But my central aim is not just to explain historical processes of value change through the prism of social science, but to link such explanation with a discussion of the justification of these values. This approach is so far from being self-evident that it requires detailed explanation. I therefore had to supplement the historical-sociological sections with a methodological chapter. Here one author emerged as crucial, an author who has done more than anyone else to think through the problems lying at the intersection of a sociologically informed historical science and a philosophical-theological discussion of values: Protestant theologian Ernst Troeltsch, who might also be said to have pioneered the historical sociology of Christianity. I was, however, increasingly concerned that these studies were becoming unmanageable and impossible to integrate into a whole.

A number of invitations to present my ideas and discuss them with others proved extremely useful to the progress, and ultimately to the successful conclusion, of this program of study. I am truly grateful for all these opportunities, but can mention only the most important here.

At an early stage I was aided by an invitation from Susanna Schmidt, then director of the Catholic Academy in Berlin, to give the Guardini Lectures at Humboldt University of Berlin in 2002; this allowed me to impose an initial order on my ideas. I am greatly indebted to her and the discussants of the four lectures (Wolfgang Huber, Herfried Münkler, Michael Bongardt, and Wilhelm Schmidt-Biggemann). An invitation from the Forschungsinstitut für Philosophie Hannover in February 2009 to teach a so-called master class in philosophy on the topic of this book played an important role. I would especially like to thank its then director, Gerhard Kruip, and the young scholars who attended this course for this opportunity to sharpen up my arguments. Important to the book's final form was an invitation from the Berkley Center for Religion, Peace, and World Affairs at Georgetown University, Washington, DC, to hold a series of public lectures on the topic in autumn 2009. This allowed me to streamline a project that risked becoming hopelessly unwieldy. Thanks are due here to the directors of the center, Thomas Banchoff and José Casanova. In certain chapters of the book I draw on some of the ideas already set out in published essays; this is indicated throughout.

Over the last few years I have had the privilege of being invited to take up fellowships at the Swedish Collegium for Advanced Study, Uppsala, the Berlin Wissenschaftskolleg (Institute for Advanced Study), and the Stellenbosch Institute for Advanced Study (South Africa). As well as working on other book projects, I used these fellowships to advance the present work. I am deeply grateful to the directors of these institutions and the other fellows for the excellent working atmosphere.

Bettina Hollstein, Wolfgang Knöbl, and Christian Polke read the entire manuscript and made helpful comments. It's wonderful to have such friends and colleagues. I dedicate this book to three of them with whom I enjoyed a particularly productive association during my years as director of the Max Weber Center for Advanced Cultural and Social Studies at the University of Erfurt. I am grateful also to all my other colleagues at the Max Weber Center for our time together there. Eva Gilmer at Suhrkamp Verlag has supervised the production of the original German version of this book (Frankfurt am Main: Suhrkamp Verlag, 2011) with great care and attention; my thanks to her too. I would like to thank Ella Müller and Jonas Lindner, who carefully proofread the manuscript and compiled the index following my move to the Freiburg Institute for Advanced Studies (FRIAS). And finally many thanks again to Alex Skinner, my translator, for all his efforts.

INTRODUCTION

This book deals with the history of human rights and the problem of their justification. But it provides neither a comprehensive intellectual or legal history nor a new philosophical justification for the idea of universal human dignity and the human rights based upon it. Anyone harboring such expectations will be disappointed. This is not for essentially trivial reasons, such as the fact that—despite all the impressive preparatory work that has been done—further in-depth research is needed for any comprehensive history of human rights. Nor is it because any of the existing philosophical justifications, those put forward by Kant, Rawls, or Habermas, for example, have rendered any new effort of this kind superfluous. The approach I am taking here is characterized by a specific way of linking justificatory arguments and history, a linkage not found in this form in histories of human rights or in philosophical treatises, a linkage moreover that these approaches do not usually seek to achieve. The ambitious philosophical attempts to justify human rights make do without history. They construct their arguments in light of the (alleged) character of practical reason and of moral oughts, the preconditions found in thought experiments on the establishment of political order, or the characteristics of an idealized discourse. A strangely tense relationship inevitably exists between such constructions and history. From this perspective it must appear strange that the timelessly valid has so rarely been recognized as such in the history of humankind. Here, the history of ideas merely presents the steps on the way to the real discovery. It becomes a prehistory consisting of tentative and imperfect efforts. Empirical history, meanwhile, becomes the mere process of moving closer toward or farther away from an ideal, unless a model of progress enables us to think in terms of gradually moving closer to this ideal in the past and continuing to realize it in the future.

Consciously or unconsciously, the writing of history is in turn often pervaded by philosophical justifications; it may also include a history of the various philosophical, political, and religious arguments and debates on human rights and human dignity. As science, however, this history must limit its aspirations to the empirical level of an appropriate reconstruction of historical processes. Through their division of labor, then, the disciplines of history and philosophy reinforce the distinction between genesis and validity, which many consider to be one of the foundations of any genuine engagement with normative questions. On this model, we are concerned either with the validity claims of normative statements or with their historical origins; historical knowledge cannot help us reach a conclusion about normative validity claims, at least not in any definitive way.

In this book, I attempt a fundamentally different approach. Perhaps historically oriented sociology, on which I repeatedly draw, can overcome this gulf between philosophy and history. The first reason for taking this approach is a negative one. I do not believe in the possibility of a purely rational justification for ultimate values. This way of putting things itself seems to me to be self-contradictory. If we are really talking about ultimate values, what exactly might any rational justification refer back to? What could lie deeper than these ultimate values and yet itself have a value-like character? Or are we to derive ultimate values from facts? These questions provide, of course, no more than a very rough indication of why I am so skeptical about philosophical attempts to justify values; I do not claim to do justice here to the great intellectual edifices aimed at the rational justification of a universalist morality. Even those, however, who share the skepticism I have expressed may shy away from its consequences because they assume that doing without rational ultimate justifications opens the door to a historical or cultural relativism or a (supposedly) postmodern arbitrariness. Human rights and universal human dignity are, however, such a sensitive topic that a shoulder-shrugging or playful stance is surely out of the question. But does giving up rational ultimate justifications really force us to embrace relativism? This concern is also inspired by the notion that genesis and validity are clearly separable. And it is this notion that I vigorously challenge here. If issues of genesis and validity cannot be separated so sharply with respect to values, then I may also state my intentions here in positive terms. On this premise, we may construct the history of the genesis and dissemination of values in such a way that narrative and justification are interwoven within this history in a specific way. As a narrative, such an account makes us aware that our commitment to values and our notion of what is valuable emerge from experiences and our processing of them; this shows them to be contingent rather than necessary. Values no longer appear as something pregiven that we merely have to discover or perhaps reestablish. But by making us aware that our values are historical individualities, such a narrative by no means inevitably weakens and corrodes our commitment to these values. Unlike Nietzsche, I do not assume that discovering the genesis of values removes the scales from our eyes to reveal the false gods and idols we have believed in. If, with Nietzsche, we want to do justice to the interleaving of genesis and validity through a genealogy, then we can certainly produce an *affirmative genealogy* as opposed to a destructive history of origins.

This book, then, aims to provide an affirmative genealogy of the universalism of values. As objections can be raised to such a project at every stage, in the middle of this book (chapter 4) I say more about the reasons for taking this approach in some intermediate methodological reflections. It is vital to explain the idea that there are such things as universal values, what a genealogy in general and an affirmative genealogy in particular is, and much more besides. For now, all we need to know is that the concept of the "genesis of values"—developed in a previous book whose ideas the present work attempts to apply in a historically concrete way—is equally distant from the concept of "construction" and that of "discovery." While the concept of discovery implies a preexisting realm of values or an objectively given natural law, that of construction is redolent of deliberate creation, which could scarcely engender commitment; at any rate, such commitment could be no more than a choice. The concept of genesis, meanwhile, aims to identify the genuine historical innovation represented by human rights *as* innovation, while at the same time preserving the self-evident character that such innovation may also exhibit for those involved. For those who feel bound to values, they obviously represent the good. This is not because these individuals have made a decision or come to an agreement. The metaphor of birth might be another appropriate way of expressing how something historically new may take on an unconditional quality. It is in this sense that I am concerned with the "birth," with the "genesis," of a central complex of universalist values and its legal codification.

Since the end of the nineteenth century at the latest, the genesis of this value complex has been subject to constant and heated debate.

One of the most common, though unproductive, debates revolves around whether the origins of human rights lie in the religious or secular-humanistic sphere. One conventional view, found not so much in the academy as among the general public, assumes that human rights emerged from the spirit of the French Revolution, which is in turn considered a political expression of the French Enlightenment; this was allegedly at least anticlerical if not openly anti-Christian or antireligious. From this perspective, human rights are clearly not the fruit of any religious tradition, but rather the manifestation of resistance to a power alliance linking state and (Catholic) church, or to Christianity as a whole.

There is a kind of elective affinity between this conventional view and a secular humanism, as there is between the convictions of Christian, chiefly Catholic, thinkers of the twentieth century and an alternative master narrative. The exponents of this latter view concentrate on long-term religious and intellectual traditions. For them, the path to human rights was paved by the understanding of the human person imparted by the Gospels, and by the philosophical elaboration of this religious inspiration in connection with a personalist concept of God since the days of medieval philosophy. This narrative emerged when, in the course of the twentieth century, the Catholic Church repudiated its original condemnation of human rights as a form of liberal individualism and began instead to vigorously defend them.

Of course, these two views of history are not the only ones, just as there is no simple opposition between secular humanism and a self-satisfied or triumphalist understanding of Catholic Christianity. There is also a compromise position. This asserts that while the Enlightenment may have seen itself as anti-Christian, its deepest motives were in fact a consequence of the Christian emphasis on individuality, sincerity, and love of neighbor (or compassion). But my aim here is not to list further nationally or confessionally imbued variations on this theme. It is instead to set out along a new path, one that takes us beyond these unproductive debates. Such a path is not only necessary because the exchange of opinions in this field has so far led to very few modifications of the original arguments on either side. More important is the fact that neither of the above positions is tenable. The conventional secular-humanist narrative is untenable for empirical reasons. This will become apparent in this book in a number of different ways. While this narrative distorts the historical reality above all of the eighteenth century, it at least has the merit of attempting to explain a cultural innovation in light of the historical period in which it occurred. The alternative history, meanwhile, cannot convincingly explain why a particular element of Christian teaching that for centuries proved compatible with the broadest range of political regimes, none of which were founded on the idea of human rights, should suddenly have become a dynamic force in the institutionalization of such rights. Maturation across centuries is not a sociological category, and even if we switch from the listing of intellectual forerunners to the level of institutional traditions, where this thesis sounds more plausible, we must keep in mind that traditions do not perpetuate themselves but are sustained through the actions of individuals. Even if we concede, at least retrospectively, that human rights may to some extent be considered a modern rearticulation of the Christian ethos, we must be able to explain why it took seventeen hundred years for the Gospel to be translated into legally codified form in this regard. I am also highly skeptical about the above-mentioned compromise position. It looks a bit like sleight of hand when something is claimed as an achievement of one's own tradition despite its having been condemned by representatives of that same tradition when it first emerged.

The message of this book is that there is a fundamental alternative to this mélange of narratives. The key term here is "sacrality" or "sacredness." I propose that we understand the belief in human rights and universal human dignity as the result of a specific process of sacralization—a process in which every single human being has increasingly, and with ever-increasing motivational and sensitizing effects, been viewed as sacred, and this understanding has been institutionalized in law. The term "sacralization" should not be understood as having an exclusively religious meaning. Secular content may also take on the qualities characteristic of sacrality; namely, subjective self-evidence and affective intensity. Sacredness may be ascribed to new content. It may migrate or be transferred; indeed, the entire system of sacralization that pertains within a culture may undergo revolution. The key idea of this book, then, is that the history of human rights is a history of sacralization—the history of the sacralization of the person.

We have now identified the book's two basic and intertwined motifs ("sacralization" and "affirmative genealogy"). They are intertwined because a specifically genealogical argument is necessary if justifications are to be adequate to the phenomenon of sacrality. If a commitment to values does not grow out of rational considerations, purely rational arguments may perhaps unsettle value commitments or prompt the reinterpretation of existing concepts of self and world, but they cannot themselves generate the force inherent in value commitments. This requires an affirmative genealogy.

The book begins with three historical-sociological chapters. The first explores the genesis of the first declaration of human rights in the late eighteenth century. Here I scrutinize the conventional view of "Enlightenment" origins, but especially Max Weber's thesis that human rights are a case of the "charismatization" (or sacralization) of reason. In light of the abolition or widespread repression of torture in eighteenth-century Europe, the second chapter sets out an alternative to the typical Enlightenment—and Foucauldian—account; namely, the sacralization of the person. This chapter also explains in more depth precisely what this means.

The genesis of human rights, and above all their subsequent dissemination and the increasing commitment to them, should not be understood as a process of cultural diffusion. Human rights might have emerged and then disappeared again. We might now be scoffing at them as a curiosity of the eighteenth century—rather like mesmerism. The third chapter deals with one segment of this history; namely, the significance of experiences of violence to the maintenance and dissemination of human rights. The historical case that I draw on here is the (American) antislavery movement of the nineteenth century. Certainly, this movement—in light of which I propose a model of the transformation of experiences of violence into mobilization to achieve universal values—and experiences of violence in general represent just one piece of the puzzle. But in the context of the sacralization of the person, we must consider not only how positive experiences that are constitutive of values may lead to a commitment to universal values, but how negative, distressing, traumatizing experiences of our own and others' suffering may do so as well.

The historical-sociological chapters are followed by a chapter of methodological self-reflection. Here I provide detailed justification for what is merely asserted in this introduction: When it comes to fundamental values, there is no philosophical justification that may make unconditional, universal claims independently of all history, but this does not force us to adopt a relativistic perspective from which all values are merely the subjective suppositions of individuals or cultures. What I am defending here, drawing extensively on the "existential historicism" of Ernst Troeltsch, is an alternative to Kant and Nietzsche, to put it in formulaic terms, but also to Hegel, Marx, and Max Weber.

These intermediate methodological reflections bring us to a turning point in my account. If the focus so far was on the main features of an affirmative genealogy of human rights as the sacralization of the person, our attention now turns to two basic elements of the Christian (mostly Judeo-Christian) tradition, elements often claimed to have paved the way for human rights and to be essential to sustaining them. These two elements are the idea of the immortal soul of every human being as her or his sacred core, and the notion of the life of the individual as a gift that incurs obligations, which limit our right to self-determination. I do not, however, introduce these two elements as the historical "progenitors" of human rights; as the historical-sociological chapters show, the relationship between Christianity and human rights is significantly more ambiguous than rose-tinted retrospectives tend to suggest. This chapter aims to examine how, in the name of human rights and on contemporary intellectual premises in general, we might lend new credibility to these two elements of the Christian view of humanity. Such an endeavor is a prime example of the task of rearticulating a religious tradition in light of dramatic value change.

This also lays the ground for the concluding chapter. If human rights do in fact draw on cultural traditions such as Christianity, but also demand that these traditions be articulated in novel ways, then values such as universal human dignity and rights such as human rights are not confined to a particular tradition. They are also approachable in light of other traditions and under new conditions, to the extent that these traditions manage to creatively reinterpret themselves in the same kind of way that the Christian tradition has undoubtedly done. Such religious or cultural traditions may therefore discover new areas of common ground without abandoning their unique perspectives. This is the idea behind the concept of value generalization to be discussed in this chapter, which comes from the sociological theory of social change but is applied here to a more philosophical subject matter. With the help of this concept I conclude by portraying the emergence of the UN Declaration of Human Rights of 1948 as a successful process of value generalization.

All of this will flesh out the affirmative genealogy of human rights that I seek to develop. In order to demonstrate the plausibility of a particular approach, I consider two "declarations" of human rights developed over brief spans of historical time—toward the end of the eighteenth century and after the Second World War—and two long-drawn-out processes of the abolition of phenomena that contradict the sacredness of the person—torture and slavery. This approach, and thus the structure of this book, entails the interleaving of argument and historical narrative. Pure narration or pure argument would be an easier undertaking. But logically and even aesthetically the affirmative genealogy compels us to construct neither an entirely chronological nor purely logical form. It is, however, only by putting it into practice that we can discover how persuasive this program really is.

1

THE CHARISMA OF REASON

The Genesis of Human Rights

If we look at the vast literature on the prehistory and history of human rights, the defining impression is that "success has many parents." The triumphal march of human rights is undoubtedly one of the great success stories in the realm of values and norms. Even those inclined toward skepticism in light of the many conspicuous cases of empty human rights rhetoric or the cynical, legitimizing misuse of the term will be able—to quote an old dictum—to discern in such cant a compliment to morality and its central importance. The triumphal march of human rights gives the lie to claims that the present era, or processes of modernization in general, involve only a decline in values or the loss of shared values. This very triumph, however, turns the spotlight on older "visions," on the seeds or roots of human rights in specific (or in all) religious and cultural traditions. Efforts have therefore been made to collate emphatic statements on the dignity of human beings—all human beings—and on the duty to help the suffering whoever they may be, in all major religions—Hinduism, Judaism, Buddhism, Confucianism, Christianity, and Islam—and to declare these statements the origin of human rights.[1] All of these so-called world religions, at least, do in fact contain statements on the sacredness of human life, an ethos of love and universal respect. In the present era, each of these traditions has produced thinkers and activists—we need think only of Mahatma Gandhi or the Dalai Lama—who, motivated by this ethos, have intervened in modern-day struggles and striven to give contemporary expression to their religious beliefs.

But it is easy to contrast such well-meaning efforts, which make human rights appear as the historical goal toward which religious history has always been headed, with an equally plausible conspectus demonstrating a persistent tendency to limit morality and notions of human dignity to the internal life of religious or political communities. There is no lack of statements to be found within religious traditions that imply that these noble principles are not to be applied to "other tribes, barbarians, enemies, or unbelievers, to slaves or manual workers," either not at all or at least not at present.[2] The Christian religion as well, which is particularly frequently claimed to have laid the ground for human rights over the centuries, is still far from immune either to such limitation of its universalist potential or instrumentalization to political ends.

If we find universalist potential and particularist limitation in all these traditions, a general debate comparing these traditions is unlikely to get us anywhere. What we need to do is radically narrow down the historical explanandum; otherwise, anything and everything can all too easily be proved with cleverly selected quotations. In considering the genesis of human rights, our temporal focus must clearly be on the late eighteenth century. It was then that the first solemn declarations of human rights were made in France and, earlier, in North America. This temporal limitation to the emergence of the first codified declarations of human rights is linked with a spatial and to some extent cultural limitation. The question here is which motives and cultural traditions we might identify to explain the French and North American declarations. Few of the religions mentioned above are then of any relevance in this respect, perhaps none of them, if we believe that secular humanism played the lead role here, as is generally implied by the many references to the "Enlightenment" or to long-term philosophical or legal forerunners and precursors of human rights. In line with what I have already said, however, I emphasize that this does not mean that we must privilege a specific tradition, let alone identify all other religions and worldviews as having limited potential in this regard. It is simply the case that the innovation of a legally momentous declaration occurred for the first time within a very specific set of historical circumstances, and that if we wish to examine the genesis of human rights, we must therefore focus on this case. This takes nothing away from later cases; but these presumably always have something to do with the reception of this first case. In this sense, the specific cultural conditions for the adoption of human rights ideas come strongly into play.

In mentioning France *and* North America we have already touched on a problem that emerges as unavoidable however radically we narrow down the question of genesis. How do we explain these two cases? What role was played by religious or antireligious motives in these particular circumstances? I cited the conventional answer in the introduction primarily because it is more or less the antithesis of the view I adopt in this book. In a nutshell, my thesis is that, far from their origins lying in France, human rights emerged in North America; that while the spirit of the Enlightenment was significant to their genesis, it was by no means necessary in the sense of an antireligious enlightenment; and that Kant's philosophy does not represent the inevitable rational justification of human rights but is instead the perhaps most impressive expression of a cultural change, though his philosophy articulates this change in highly problematic ways. To justify these countertheses and explain the emergence of human rights, I draw mainly on a debate that has been going on for more than one hundred years. This is necessary in order to reveal the problems involved in any view of the history of human rights derived from the idea of the *charisma of reason*.[3]

There are two good empirical reasons for believing that the conventional understanding does not provide an appropriate picture of the historical reality of the eighteenth century. The first prerequisite for correcting this picture is that we free ourselves from the myth that the French Revolution was antireligious; the second is that we pay more attention to the North American case and its particular characteristics.

HUMAN RIGHTS AND THE FRENCH REVOLUTION

The myth of the antireligious character of the French Revolution, along with the supporting notion that the Revolution was inspired by a philosophy amounting to "a modern paganism"—as in the subtitle of Peter Gay's well-known book—has become a constituent feature of the secular-humanist worldview.[4] Yet the origins of this view probably lie in the polemics against the Revolution produced by reactionary clerics, aristocrats, and allied intellectuals.

In the early stages of the Revolution—and this is when the Declaration of the Rights of Man and of the Citizen was made—it was certainly not anti-Christian in character. As one writer has vividly expressed it, in the early stages of the Revolution "it seemed that no meeting could take place without invoking heaven, that every success had to be followed by a Te Deum, that any symbol which was adopted had to be blessed."[5] The all-too-close ties between throne and altar were first loosened and then cut by the Revolution; but this does not mean there was any decrease in religious intensity. Attendance at church services seems to have increased rather than decreased during the first few years of the Revolution, as a new connection between the Revolution and the altar began to take hold: "The Festival of the Federation marking the anniversary of the fall of the Bastille, continued to be framed with religious ceremonial. Traditional Catholic feast days and processions were also widely celebrated in both Paris and the provinces, at least through the summer of 1793. Indeed, before that date, efforts by certain radicals to halt processions in Paris were roundly opposed by the population itself."[6]

Of course, this changes nothing about the fact that the French Revolution led to the first state-sponsored assault on Christianity in Europe since the time of the early Roman Empire.[7] If this differs from the revolutionaries' original motives to a far greater extent than the conventional view implies, what might have brought about this escalation? Alexis de Tocqueville made the crucial point here as early as 1856, when he wrote in his retrospective of the ancien régime and the Revolution,

> It was far less as a religious faith than as a political institution that Christianity had stirred these uncontrolled loathings. It was not that priests claimed to regulate the affairs of the other world but that they were landowners, lords of the manor, exactors of tithes and administrators in this world; not that the Church was unable to find a place in the new order of society about to be created but because it occupied at that time the most privileged and most powerful place in the old society which people were concerned to reduce to dust.[8]

The close connection between throne and altar in the prerevolutionary order was in fact crucial to what came next. This connection was not just political and cultural, in the sense that the state protected the Church from religious competitors, while the Church reciprocated with educational services. It was also straightforwardly economic. In some parts of France the Church was the largest landowner, and the revenue raised was vital to the chronically underfunded state. The Church offered young aristocrats privileged career options and an easy income. By the eighteenth century, these realities, which can only be described as abuses, particularly from the perspective of the Christian faith, had led to tensions between the lower and higher clergy and to various forms of popular anticlericalism, which must of course be clearly distinguished from hostility to Christianity.

The first steps of the Revolution in ecclesiopolitical terms involved the complete elimination of the compulsory church tax ("tithe")—without restitution—and of the Church's manorial rights. These measures were extremely popular among the people and were also backed by the many deputies in the National Assembly who were members of the lower clergy. A few months later, mainly for economic reasons, the Assembly passed legislation facilitating the confiscation of Church property, which was implemented after some delay. The prohibition and dissolution of religious orders also appear to have been carried out primarily for economic reasons. In retrospect, the introduction of state regulation of clerical affairs and, above all, of an oath of political loyalty for priests appears as the first stage in a religious policy that degenerated into religious repression. The background to these encroachments was, first of all, the fact that without Church property the clergy had to be funded in some other way. Guided by the vision of the nationalization of the Catholic Church, the revolutionaries saw this as an opportunity to link the state payment of priests and bishops with provisions regarding their selection by parishes and rejection of the role of Rome. There was no respect here for canon law and Church traditions; the idea of national sovereignty outweighed any notion of institutional autonomy. This greatly strained the loyalty to the Revolution of both clergy and believers. The Church was split by the requirement for an oath of loyalty that, moreover, was to be taken in public after Mass and whose correctness was to be certified by local parishes. The clergy was divided among those who were prepared to swear this oath of loyalty to the nation and those who saw it as a violation of their priestly vows. The numbers in each camp differed greatly in different regions, dependent on the religious situation before the Revolution and the people's attitude to the Revolution in general. Oath refusers were increasingly the target of revolutionary activists' hostility. This hostility intensified when the so-called refractors disputed the validity of the sacraments administered by priests loyal to the Revolution. These ecclesiopolitical conflicts were one of the key reasons why the Revolution escalated to the point of terrorism; it is not the case that religion was simply affected by this escalation.[9] In wartime (from 1792 on) hostility toward the oath refusers often took on a lethal character, as they were assumed to be accomplices of the external enemy (Austria), elevating the hatred felt toward them to hysterical heights. Refractors were now banished from their parishes, arrested and executed or forced to emigrate. Churches were closed and cult objects desecrated or destroyed, while reforms aimed to eliminate every hint of Christianity from the calendar. Even basically loyal priests were forced to marry and harassed in a variety of ways. While the Catholic Church was the main focus of these revolutionary activists' hatred, Protestant ministers and church buildings were no more spared than were rabbis and synagogues.[10]

There is no consensus about which actors were behind this generally unpopular violence. Local militants undoubtedly played a role, but it seems to have been largely the work of itinerant revolutionaries and government agents.[11] What is certain is that it took the inflamed quasi-millenarian passions of wartime for "certain aggressively anti-religious or atheistic positions, positions advocated by a marginal fringe of eighteenth century philosophers and by a tiny minority of Parisian intellectuals early in the Revolution, [to acquire] for a time a substantially larger following."[12] Tocqueville himself already stated of these activists that we can understand their rage and zeal for conversion only if we see their convictions as a kind of new religion, "barely formed, it is true. Godless, without ritual or an afterlife but which, nevertheless, like Islam, has flooded all the Earth with its soldiers, apostles and martyrs."[13]

Religious life continued even at the height of the campaign of de-Christianization, though it was forced underground. Mass was celebrated without priests, baptisms were performed by believers, and religious literature was traded illegally. Women in particular defended churches and cult objects against those who sought to destroy them. The defense of religion was increasingly a unifying force for all those who felt threatened by the excesses of the Revolution. This applied all the more in the French borderlands and in those neighboring states invaded by the revolutionary armies, and was one of the key reasons for popular resistance to the reforms implemented by the French. In French society in particular, this pitted Catholic Christianity against the values of the Revolution, a polarizing development that continued to have an impact long after the collapse of the most extreme form of revolutionary rule. One of the tragic results of this escalating spiral was the intervention in the conflict by Pope Pius VI following a lengthy period of hesitation. But he no more invoked the value of religious freedom than did the French revolutionaries. Instead, in his brief titled *Quod aliquantum* of March 10, 1791, he condemned the Revolution in its entirety and the principles it proclaimed, including human rights, as blasphemous, heretical, and schismatic. This polarization triggered attempts by both sides to enhance their legitimacy through historical narratives; these were based on a fundamental opposition between faith and Revolution not found in the real history of the Revolution. This escalation and polarization were largely contingent. The antireligious campaign of 1793/4 should not be seen, either in a positive or negative sense, as representative of the Revolution and all its different stages, such as the Declaration of the Rights of Man.

But if this escalation was contingent and if the dynamics of the Revolution are best explained not in light of a closed worldview but in terms of economic and political motives and concatenations of actions, then the next stage in the correction of what I call the conventional view of history becomes far less significant. It is enough, therefore, to examine very briefly whether the Enlightenment was in fact antireligious and whether a bitter conflict between Enlightenment and Christianity paved the way ideologically for the intense religious struggles of the Revolution. The more scholars have considered the Enlightenment in countries other than France over the last few decades, the more skeptical they have become about the notion of the Enlightenment's constitutive areligiosity or antireligiosity.[14] What has emerged is that in most European countries the Enlightenment is better understood as a movement of religious reform than as an attempt to overcome or destroy religion. If we learn to understand key motifs of the intellectual and religious history of the eighteenth century without assuming a fundamental hostility to religion, these motifs emerge as aspects of a learning process internal to Christianity or Judaism, in light of which a scattered group of thinkers identified reasons for rejecting these religious traditions altogether.

But the contingency of the ecclesiopolitical escalation characteristic of the French Revolution not only changes how we perceive the Enlightenment. It also sheds a different light on the history of Christianity in eighteenth-century France than if we view this history merely as laying the ground for the Revolution. French Catholicism before the Revolution then appears "more like the harvest of the goals and ideals of reform Catholicism than a decline announcing revolution that turned anti-Catholic."[15] In many respects, the eighteenth century emerges as an age in which, particularly in rural areas, the religious knowledge of clergy and simple believers attained unprecedented levels and the internalization and individualization of religion advanced. While the alliance between throne and altar was important to the political fate of Christianity during the Revolution, there is much more to the religious dynamics of the period before, during, and after the Revolution than this political aspect.

The Declaration of the Rights of Man and of the Citizen of August 26, 1789, is unmistakably a product of the earliest phase of the Revolution. This text, which has had such a huge historical impact, was in fact discarded during the more radical phases and replaced with a different one on a number of occasions. On sober reflection it is clear that the genesis of the existing version, which has increasingly taken on an aura of transhistorical validity, involves numerous contingencies. The debates on the text were broken off after a few days without having come to any real conclusion. Even now, this invites speculation about what else would have been included in the catalog of rights, such as social rights, had the debates continued as planned. The elevation of this text to the status of "spiritual center at which all the various tendencies toward a moral renewal and toward a political and social reform meet and in which they find their ideal unity" is not, therefore, entirely plausible.[16]

Even superficial study of the wording shows that the thrust of the text was not antireligious, which is the key question for us here. The preamble not only includes the statement that the National Assembly recognizes and declares the human and civil rights subsequently listed in detail "in the presence and under the auspices of the Supreme Being."[17] Human rights as such are described as "sacred"; in Article XVII, property in particular is described as a "sacred and inviolable right." Just one of the existing articles relates to the guaranteeing of religious freedom, though in a rather indirect way. Article X declares that "no one should be disturbed on account of his opinions, even religious, provided their manifestation does not upset the public order established by law." This brief provision, which makes religious freedom a subordinate aspect of freedom of expression, neither excludes the possibility of a state church nor guarantees religious communities specific rights. But this stipulation certainly cannot be interpreted as antireligious.

The true core of this declaration is the affirmation of natural, inalienable, and sacred human rights, with the aim of establishing a timeless yardstick for the evaluation of state institutions and actions, "in order that the acts of the legislative power, and those of the executive power, may at each moment be compared with the aim of every political institution and thereby may be more respected." This aim of every political association is in turn described (in Article II) as "the preservation of the natural and imprescriptible rights of man," which are listed as "liberty, property, security and resistance to oppression." The notion of rights that precede and are superordinate to the state had a long and substantial prehistory, both in philosophy and in the political discourse of the ancien régime. In the absence of this previous history, the members of the National Assembly would surely have struggled to compose the declaration in just a few days. What is crucial, though, is not the prehistory. It is the fact that philosophically sophisticated reflections, and spontaneous or traditional articulations of perceptions of injustice, not only gave rise to a coherent whole, but undergirded the aspiration to refound the state itself. For many, it is this aspiration that puts the epoch-making character of this document of political history beyond all doubt.

Things are more complicated than this, however, in two respects. Some researchers do not simply accept the document as something complete but reconstruct the discussions that led to its specific phrasing.[18] They make it abundantly clear that the Rousseauist pathos that derives sovereignty exclusively from the nation, as Article III declares—in other words the notion that "no body, no individual can exercise authority that does not proceed from it in plain terms"—arose from a specific situation. This centered on a legislative body that wished to assert its own legitimacy without questioning (in a practical sense) the monarch, who after all continued to reign, or questioning (in a theoretical sense) the ongoing possibility of a monarchist executive. This was precisely the problem: how to assert individual liberties at the same time as the legitimacy of one's own role. Without considering its context, the text tends to be seen as far more radical than it was intended to be. Its authors did not write it as an attack on dynastic authority, but as a moderate modus vivendi.[19] The text lists a number of norms, but it does not pin down how they should be applied to reality. The language of natural rights was ideally suited to the abolition of aristocratic and clerical privileges; the concurrent emphasis on a single sovereignty left room for a monarchical executive to represent this role symbolically.

But, and this is the second complicating factor, this built into the Declaration of the Rights of Man and of the Citizen a virtually indissoluble tension between the founding of sovereignty in the nation and the protection of individual liberties, which includes protecting them against the sovereign. It may have seemed to the authors of the declaration that they had found an entirely coherent solution to this problem. On the one hand, they underlined that people could do anything they wanted that was not against the law, and that the law could only prohibit that which was damaging to society; on the other, however, they declared that all citizens must obey the law unconditionally and—as stated in Article VII—would render themselves liable to prosecution by resisting arrest and so on. It is no coincidence that it was the experience of twentieth-century totalitarianisms that increasingly caused intellectuals, especially French ones, to question the coherence of this solution.[20] The idea of the inalienability of individual rights gives rise to a more fractured conception of sovereignty than the French declaration implies. Individuals, but also pre- and extrastate associations of individuals, do not obtain their legitimacy as a gift from the sovereign, not even if this sovereign justifies his actions in light of the general will of the citizenry. But in the declaration "the individual" and "the nation" appear as the two highest values, as if no fundamental conflict were possible between them.

The historical impact of the Declaration of the Rights of Man and of the Citizen has much to do with the open-ended and unclear way in which it identifies rights and their bearers. An increasing number of groups invoked the declaration while the Revolution was still going on, in ways its authors neither wanted nor anticipated, in order to express their ideas and interest in the form of demands. Protestant Christians, Jews, free blacks and slaves in the colonies, the propertyless, women, occupational groups excepted from full legal status such as actors and executioners—all demanded recognition as human beings in the spirit of the declaration.[21] All these demands had their opponents; some—such as the abolition of slavery—were bitterly resisted, implemented for a time but quickly reversed; others—such as full rights for women—were viewed, even by the most radical universalists, partly as preposterous, and partly as a danger to the life of society. What happened in this regard during the Revolution was a harbinger of disputes that continued throughout the whole of the nineteenth and twentieth centuries, making a document that might otherwise have faded into obscurity a universal point of reference.

There is one significant aspect of the genesis of the Declaration of the Rights of Man we have not yet considered; namely, the huge importance of North America as role model for the French revolutionaries. The French Revolution and the struggle of Great Britain's North American colonies for independence were linked in a variety of ways. France even provided the American revolutionaries with military support in order to hurt Great Britain, its main political rival on the world stage. The financial consequences of this support were one of the main causes of the fiscal crisis that helped trigger the French Revolution. Because of this support, the censors tolerated translations of American writings and travelers' accounts of the events in North America. Frenchmen fought alongside Americans; some of the most important leaders of the American Revolution such as Thomas Jefferson and Benjamin Franklin lived in Paris for a number of years and were involved in its intellectual and political life. The model for a formal "declaration" itself lay on the other side of the Atlantic. The proposal to compose such a declaration was first put forward by the Marquis de Lafayette, one of the most important military leaders and greatest heroes of the American War of Independence. We even know that he discussed his plan with the American ambassador in Paris—none other than Thomas Jefferson.[22] On the day when the declaration was adopted, a number of deputies met with Jefferson in his residence to clear up remaining differences of opinion. None of this is meant to imply that the declaration was a mere copy. The political situations differed in many ways, and some French revolutionaries wanted their declaration to surpass the American prototype and serve as role model for all other peoples. But there can no longer be any doubt that America played a massive role—contested in the details, but indisputable overall—as model for the French Declaration of the Rights of Man.

It was vital to demonstrate this point here in such detail because there has often been a failure to recognize it. We shall come to the second historical reason why the conventional secular-humanist narrative is untenable as soon as we take a closer look at the role of North America.

HUMAN RIGHTS AND THE AMERICAN REVOLUTION

The point of departure for the discussion that follows is Georg Jellinek's book *The Declaration of the Rights of Man and of Citizens: A Contribution to Modern Constitutional History* (*Die Erklärung der Menschen- und Bürgerrechte: Ein Beitrag zur modernen Verfassungsgeschichte*). First published in 1895, this book is widely regarded as the seminal text that initiated work on this subject.[23] It advances four intriguing hypotheses.[24] One of the most important constitutional historians and legal theoreticians of the time, Jellinek begins by arguing that the declaration of human and civil rights in the French Revolution did not represent the ultimate wellspring of codified human rights, as widely assumed at the time. Rather, he argues, this declaration was directly influenced by, or even modeled on, the American Declaration of Independence, and the various "bills of rights" proclaimed in Virginia, Pennsylvania, and other newly independent North American states in 1776. Jellinek also contested the claim—dominant in his time—that Rousseau's "Contrat social" was the model for the French declaration. In addition, and this is the third point, he stressed that we should not overestimate the continuity between natural law and human rights, since the concepts of natural law could never have led to the institutionalization of human rights in or by themselves. There must have been a driving force behind this development, and Jellinek's fourth thesis is that this was provided by the struggles of Protestant dissenters for religious freedom in North America. With these propositions, Jellinek shifted the credit for the first declarations of human rights away from the French Enlightenment, which was seen to be skeptical or even hostile toward religion, tracing them back instead to Christian roots. He thereby provided the inspiration for a much more famous text: Max Weber's *The Protestant Ethic and the Spirit of Capitalism* (*Die protestantische Ethik und der Geist des Kapitalismus*). Weber was deeply impressed by Jellinek's argument, and especially by his "demonstration of religion's relevance to the genesis of 'human rights'" insofar as it contributed to "the investigation of the scope of religious influences in general, even in areas where one would not expect to find them."[25]

To what extent can Jellinek's hypotheses be maintained given our current state of knowledge? In answering this question, we must constantly bear in mind three different time periods. The first period is the late eighteenth century, when declarations of human rights were proclaimed in North America and France. The second is the time around 1900, when the question of the Christian, and specifically Protestant, roots of modernity more generally became a key subject of intellectual debate. And the third time period is, of course, the present day, from which we look back over the development of human rights and the effects of their changing historical interpretations (*Wirkungsgeschichte*). The middle period continues to be important because we are concerned here not just with historical details and facts, but also with the interpretation of the historical process that produced human rights. For any such interpretation, disputes over the status of human rights as part of modernity, such as those that occurred around 1900, are still of the utmost importance.

Jellinek's book became the subject of a heated national and international debate immediately upon publication. It was translated into numerous languages, including Russian and Chinese. Its reception in France was to prove particularly significant. French critics perceived it as a perfidious attempt to deny France's contribution to one of the most significant achievements of modernity.[26] One can still sense a certain degree of resistance even in Marcel Gauchet's 1989 book on the origin of the French declaration of human rights, where he concedes that "German scholarship" has shown the influence of the American declarations to have been decisive.[27] In Germany, Jellinek's thesis was an important point of reference for all those who wished to separate the question of human rights from the constitutional traditions of France, Germany's "historical enemy," traditions that were usually looked upon with skepticism and resentment. Here, however, Jellinek's text provoked the ire of Catholic critics, who vehemently contested any claims of Protestant superiority with respect to the historical development of freedom and tolerance. Jellinek felt that his intentions and his book were misunderstood in many respects. And indeed such petty, nationalistic, and confessional suppositions surely miss the point. Instead, it seems to me that Jellinek's work must be interpreted as an effort to move beyond the dead-end debate between historicism and the theory of natural law.[28] Like the historicists, Jellinek did not believe that binding metanorms for the regulation of positive law could be derived from any philosophy, not even from natural law or Kant. In this sense he remained a proponent of unlimited state sovereignty. But in contrast to many German historians of his time, especially antiliberal and nationalistic ones, he did not hold conceptions of natural law to be "idle dreams," but sympathized with the notion of a state that limited itself by law and through the positivization of individual rights and freedoms.[29] So he had to try to find a place for such rights within his historicist approach. In this sense, his text marks the point where historicism, becoming aware of the dangers of being turned into relativism, seeks to transcend itself. This is hardly foreign to us today. If the question of the historical roots of inalienable individual rights is not conceived of simply as a question of genesis that is completely independent of the question of their grounding and validation, then this marks a crucial point. We must then find out whether it is fundamentally possible to advance universal validity claims while remaining aware that the genesis of values is historically contingent.[30]

Despite all the objections that were and are raised against it, much of Jellinek's argument can now be regarded as well confirmed. He was correct not only in his emphasis on the chronological priority of the American declarations of human rights and their influence on the French declaration (though the latter was certainly no mere imitation of the American declarations). He was also correct to point out that there is a difference between theories of natural law and the legal codification of specific individual rights intended to hold for all people and removed from legislative authority. "The assertion of objective moral and legal limits to all worldly powers," writes Hasso Hofmann, agreeing with Jellinek, does not itself equate with "a theory of subjective rights. The idea of constitutional freedom and security against *illegal* tyranny is not equivalent to the human rights idea of basic, individual freedoms and protection against *legal* tyranny."[31] We must also agree with Jellinek when he rejects the view that the English legal tradition, with its codification of rights and freedoms, led directly to the declarations of human rights of the late eighteenth century, since these guarantees only applied to the traditional rights of the subjects of the English king and by no means to all people. This is not to deny entirely the influence of this legal tradition, but as the universalization of these rights is the crucial step in need of clarification, it is not enough merely to refer to this influence.

More difficult to evaluate is Jellinek's view that Rousseau's influence was not of constitutive significance. It would in fact be absurd to dispute that Rousseau played a role for some of the most important initiators of the French declaration, such as Sieyès. For Jellinek, Rousseau was out of the question as author of the idea of inalienable liberties that must be respected by the state because he had argued against any limiting of popular sovereignty by legislatures. But it might also be argued that Rousseau's work itself already features the unresolved tension between collectivism and individualism mentioned above with respect to the French declaration. Rousseau, after all, is not just the author of *The Social Contract*, which is what Jellinek clearly had in mind, but also—as in the "Profession of Faith of the Savoyard Vicar" in his pedagogical novel *Émile*—the defender of an undogmatic religiosity, which by no means points in the same direction as the idea of a state-oriented civic religion. Some have deduced from this that it is quite possible to claim Rousseau as defender of religious freedom against an omnipotent sovereign. Against this, however, "the space left by Rousseau for citizens' positive religions is determined in light of these religions' capacity to support citizens' 'moral aptitude.' . . . Clearly, this proviso, which amounts to the functionalization of religion to political ends, cannot form the basis for freedom of conscience and religion."[32] All these points are disputed by one author or another. If it is nonetheless correct to state that there is now a broad consensus that Jellinek was right, then the debate revolves solely around the last, though boldest, hypothesis in his book, that of the religious roots of the American declarations of human rights.

The utmost caution is necessary here. We must first demonstrate that we are not simply dealing with an intellectual background. Of course, Jellinek was aware that the belief in the dignity of all human beings had deep roots in the centuries-old Judeo-Christian tradition—though this tradition cannot be treated as an unbroken process of maturation that gave rise to modern ideas, especially when one considers how often its universalism was violated, when Jews, heretics, or native peoples were denied these same rights. The intellectual roots of human rights in Renaissance humanism, the Reformation, or late Spanish Scholasticism are generally of less help in understanding our problem than the dynamics of their sudden institutionalization. And it is here that Jellinek saw the struggle for religious freedom of American Protestants, especially (Calvinist) Congregationalists, as decisive. Although religious toleration can be observed in the most varied regimes—the enlightened absolutism of Frederick the Great in Prussia, for example, or colonial Maryland under Catholic leadership—utilitarian calculations usually formed the basis for policies of toleration. Jellinek, however, was interested in the religious roots of the struggle for religious freedom—meaning religious freedom not just for one's own confession but for all believers. Accordingly, the hero of Jellinek's story is the Puritan preacher Roger Williams, who left Massachusetts in 1636 for Rhode Island, where he guaranteed religious freedom not only for Christians of all sorts but also "for Jews, heathens, and Turks." Jellinek's central thesis is that "the idea of legally establishing inalienable, inherent and sacred rights of the individual is not of political but religious origin. What has been held to be a work of the [French] Revolution was in reality a fruit of the Reformation and its struggles. Its first apostle was not Lafayette but Roger Williams, who, driven by powerful and deep religious enthusiasm, went into the wilderness in order to found a government of religious liberty, and his name is uttered by Americans even today with the deepest respect."[33] According to Jellinek, this is the source of all other individual rights, such as freedom of opinion, of the press, and of assembly. The whole idea that individuals not only have rights within a state, but also rights against the state, and that these are not simply conferred by the state, points to a religious origin, at least if we are looking for a historical explanation.

Our current state of knowledge necessitates three corrections to Jellinek's fourth thesis. The first comes from none other than Ernst Troeltsch. In contrast to Jellinek, for him it was not the Calvinists but the Baptists, Quakers, and certain types of free spirituality—the "stepchildren of the Reformation" as he famously called them—who helped win acceptance for a religiously founded idea of religious freedom, as he argued in his great work, *The Social Teachings of the Christian Churches* (*Die Soziallehren der christlichen Kirchen und Gruppen*). "The only real source of toleration is that individualistic form of spirituality which considers that all external religious forms are merely relative; the only Calvinistic element in this point of view is the feeling that the state has no right to interfere with religion."[34]

Jellinek himself accepted this correction in the third edition of his book, albeit a little reluctantly.

The second correction relates to the claim—historicist in the negative sense—to have found the seedbed of all human rights in religious freedom. This view cannot be defended. It certainly does not apply to France. Nor did religious freedom exist in most of the North American colonies or states. Indeed, it was not until the twentieth century that the separation of church and state at the national level was legally secured in the various states of the union. The historical codification of human rights was, of course, generally affected by the opportunistic and strategic considerations of social actors, by constellations of power, and by structures of opportunity. While it is true that the legal recognition of freedom of religion and conscience represents the first form of universal human rights, and represents in a sense the logical structure of all such rights, we should by no means ascribe to this legal recognition of one specific human right an autonomous causal power or overestimate its significance in the late eighteenth century. To do so would be an injustice to the actual dynamics of institutionalization.

At the same time, however—and this is the third correction—we should not underestimate the role of religious interpretations and motives at this time either. What we need to do is abandon this undialectical opposition of two explanatory hypotheses, one that identifies the source of human rights as American Protestantism, the other the French Enlightenment. Troeltsch, much more than Jellinek, recognized the transformative effects that Enlightenment thought exerted on Protestant Christianity in North America. In a well-known phrase, Americans in the eighteenth century learned their Enlightenment from the pulpit.[35] Conversely, there were also affinities between certain forms of Christian spirituality and Enlightenment rationalism. For Troeltsch, admixtures of this sort were nothing new. In his opinion, the entire history of Western culture was characterized by an interplay between the Christian idea of love and conceptions of natural law. Current work on the historical genesis of the American Declaration of Independence shows vividly just how impossible it is to draw any clear boundaries in America's Puritan-Enlightenment synthesis.

The statements with which the American Declaration of Independence begins have taken on an almost sacred character in the

American political and legal tradition, but also in the history of human rights: "We hold these truths to be self-evident, that all men are created equal, that they are endowed by their Creator with certain unalienable Rights, that among these are Life, Liberty, and the pursuit of Happiness.—That to secure these rights, Governments are instituted among Men, deriving their just powers from the consent of the governed . . ."[36] Yet despite the aura that has come to surround it, this text should not be read as though Thomas Jefferson received it from the hand of God like a latter-day Moses.[37] It is in fact the outcome of a collective process and came into being in difficult circumstances that did not allow leisurely composition. The second Continental Congress, held in Philadelphia, tasked not Jefferson but a committee of five members with composition of a declaration on the topic of independence (*on* rather than *of* independence). These five then asked Jefferson to produce a first draft; neither the instructions that the Congress gave its committee nor those the committee gave Jefferson have survived. In his haste, Jefferson drew on a number of documents, some of which he himself had written, some of which were composed by others. Initially, in view of the subject matter of the declaration as a whole, the preamble, which was to prove so crucial to the document's effective history, was most likely of secondary importance. The aim of the document was to establish a consensus within the colonies on the legitimacy of efforts to achieve independence and to garner greater sympathy for these efforts abroad, especially in France. When the draft, mainly composed by Jefferson, was presented to the plenum of the Continental Congress, to Jefferson's disappointment the members set about revising it substantially. The text was shortened by a quarter; several references to God as the supreme judge and the protection of divine providence were added to the text. So the final text cannot simply be put down to Jefferson's worldview.

Why are these details important to answering our key question as to the religious or secular origins of human rights declarations? Simply because they demonstrate to us that we cannot answer this question merely by referring to Jefferson's personal convictions. There is no doubt that Jefferson himself was a deist and that, like the contemporary Freemasons, he was a Christian only in the very limited sense that he accepted Jesus's teachings in a moral sense without viewing him as divine. In this, however, he was not representative of others—not even all the leaders of the American Revolution, let alone rank-and-file revolutionaries or the majority of the population. For them, the religious revivalist movements that preceded the Revolution were central. These established an overarching intellectual and spiritual framework that encompassed the various colonies, without which the revolutionary uprising seems almost unthinkable.[38] So it is more appropriate to refer to an alliance between a quasi-Pietist mass movement and an Enlightenment-rationalist elite—featuring a wealth of intersecting and transitional phenomena as well as a willingness to forge alliances on all sides. There were also simple pragmatic motives, particularly in the religio-political field; so there was a restrained approach to spreading one's faith beyond the borders of one's colony in order to encourage similar restraint from others. Jefferson in particular was willing to make alliances and accepted amendments to his text even if these deviated from his personal beliefs. As the struggle for independence entered this dramatic phase, when it was still unclear how the military conflict would turn out and whether all those responsible for the Declaration of Independence would end up being condemned for high treason, what mattered above all else was to secure the consent of the American people. Jefferson was aware that they would give their consent only if they had the sense of acting justly in the eyes of God. So the Declaration of Independence cannot be clearly classified either as deist or Christian. Neither group wished to exclude the other. What was needed was a language that was understandable to both sides and could inspire their allegiance. So all those who discern traces of both Enlightenment rationalism and biblically grounded Christian faith in this text are correct; but all those who see just one or the other are wrong.[39] Jellinek requires correction in the sense that the American declarations have religious roots, but not exclusively so. Though other human rights do not emerge organically from religious freedom, it is true that in the America of the late eighteenth century this was "viewed as the 'first freedom', as the most significant of liberties, which forms the foundation for the rest of the constitution."[40]

If true, this thesis has important implications for our understanding of modernity, of which human rights are incontestably a part. It destabilizes the view that the development of human rights is part of a larger process that has been called the sacralization or charismatization of reason. For some authors who build on Max Weber, human rights emerged exclusively in the context of a belief in rationality whose quintessential expression is Robespierre's quasi-religious "cult of reason," but which persisted in Marxism's pretensions to "scientific socialism."[41]

HUMAN RIGHTS AND "OCCIDENTAL RATIONALISM"

Let us, therefore, consult Max Weber himself at this point. However strongly he may have been influenced by Jellinek (and Troeltsch) in these matters, he gave their arguments a particular twist by integrating them into his theory of occidental rationalism and its future. At first glance, Jellinek's thesis seems to fit perfectly into this framework; this is no coincidence, given that Weber's own studies on Puritanism were strongly inspired by Jellinek's book. The way in which the subject of human rights surfaces in Weber's *Basic Concepts in Sociology* (*Soziologische Grundbegriffe*) is nonetheless a bit jarring. Though few have noticed it, Weber refers to human rights in this context as "extreme rationalist fanaticism" and as the epitome of those ultimate ends or values that, like "unusual acts of religious and charitable zeal" for those "not susceptible" to them, are almost if not entirely incomprehensible to anyone who does not share them or who "abhor[s]" them.[42] Here, Weber was surely thinking of the French-Enlightenment version of human rights. But for him there was no contradiction between this emphasis on the rationalistic character of human rights and their religious roots, since he was greatly interested in the religious roots of such "extreme rationalist fanaticism." For Weber, as a mere negation of tradition the Enlightenment would have been too weak to effect such an intensification of belief. In this sense, Jellinek's thesis anticipates Weber's views regarding the religious roots of the rational, capitalist spirit.

In other contexts Weber relates human rights to the expansion of capitalism and the progress of bureaucratization. For him it is clear that "these postulates of formal legal equality and economic mobility paved the way for the destruction of all patrimonial and feudal law in favour of abstract norms and hence indirectly of bureaucratization. It is also clear that they facilitated the expansion of capitalism." He draws a direct parallel between his own thesis that the "innerwordly asceticism" of the sects engendered the capitalist mind-set and the rationally acting *Berufsmensch*, and the claim that "the basic rights of man made it possible for the capitalist to use things and men freely." It is in this context that we encounter his remark concerning the charismatic transfiguration of reason as the core of the Enlightenment idea that individual freedom must result in the "relatively best of all worlds." This charisma of reason is the "last form that charisma has adopted in its fateful historical course."[43] This sentence is ambiguous since we do not know whether Weber meant the last form that has appeared up until now or the last form that will ever appear.

At this point it may appear that Weber has an almost functionalist and materialist understanding of the history of human rights. But the opposite is true, as particularly evident in his writings on Russia.[44] Here Weber is confronted with Jellinek's direct influence on leading liberal Russian politicians of the time, such as Peter Struve, during a short phase around 1905 when it appeared that the idea of human rights could unite the various wings of a rebellious Russian intelligentsia. The Russian political situation inspired Weber's passionate interest as it shed direct light on the question of whether civic freedoms and constitutionally certified rights could in fact be established afresh under modern conditions; that is, in a world of advanced capitalism and a (more or less) modern bureaucracy. Unlike some optimistic Western liberals and (later) modernization theorists, he did not believe that these modern conditions bore any particular affinity to democracy and freedom. But he analyzed the political and social forces of Russia in order to determine which side might successfully lead the fight against bureaucratic and Jacobin centralism, against authoritarianism within the worker's movement, and advance the expansion of modern individualism. The Russian situation seemed to him a tragic one: even if the liberal forces were successful in their struggle for the right to vote, by strengthening the peasantry this would be more likely to hinder than advance the rise of Western individualism.

His pessimism did not apply only to Russia, however. According to Weber, both the ideal and material preconditions for a belief in human rights have essentially vanished throughout the world. Because of the Enlightenment, Weber believed, the religious convictions that Jellinek saw as the source of the political individualism inherent in human rights can no longer arise as a mass phenomenon, at least not in their current form, while an "optimistic belief in the natural harmony of interests of free individuals" has been "finally destroyed by capitalism." This "specifically bourgeois individualism" "has already been superseded even within the classes of 'education and property' and will certainly not be embraced by the 'petty bourgeoisie.'"[45]

Today, in the context of global capitalism, when the future of human rights is itself at issue, the question of their origins is posed more sharply still. If Weber could imagine a capitalism of the future absent a belief in human rights, then how exactly should we understand the relationship between capitalist development in the past and the origins of human rights? How did Weber himself understand this relationship, given that he agrees not only with Jellinek's thesis regarding the Protestant origins of human rights but also with the view that freedom of contract was a functional prerequisite of capitalist economies? If one consults Weber's sociology of law in search of an answer, especially the long third section, "Forms of Creation of Rights," one finds astonishingly little about Jellinek, human rights, and rights to freedom, but rather extensive discussions of the freedom of contract, whose history, Weber claims, is much longer than the history of human rights à la Jellinek.[46] Weber emphasizes not only how common contracts were in premodern societies, which allows him to dispense with any simple model of social evolution based on the formula "from status to contract"; he also argues that the degree of freedom of contract is "naturally first of all a function of the expansion of markets."[47] The apparent contradiction in Weber's thought can probably only be resolved as suggested in an excellent essay by the French Weber expert Catherine Colliot-Thélène.[48] According to her interpretation, Weber saw the moral individualism of Protestantism as a historical opportunity for the systematization of all subjective rights; however, the willingness to incorporate the idea of freedom of contract into this system required certain preconditions that were by no means the result of this moral individualism itself. The history of freedom of contract therefore antedates the origin of human rights and would continue even if the epoch of human rights was drawing to an irreversible close. As Wolfgang Schluchter points out in his essay "The Sociology of Law as an Empirical Theory of Validity," the law would not be unaffected by this kind of uncoupling from moral universalism; it would certainly change its character, but by no means in the sense of a complete disappearance of those aspects that were necessary for a market-oriented economy.

But must we really see the future in such a bleak light? As salutary as it may be to abandon any simple trust in the stability of Western cultural traditions, we need not unquestioningly accept the scattered and fragmentary arguments that Weber uses to justify his gloomy perspective.

New forms of religious conviction have emerged during the twentieth century. The inherent tendencies of moral judgment promote universalistic moral orientations. The history of violence and of human degradation has led in some places to a clearer awareness that the dignity of the person must be inviolable. Capitalism has experienced long phases of prosperity, and the construction of welfare states has demonstrated that divergent interests can be reconciled in a peaceful and just manner, even if it has not revived the belief in a natural harmony of interests. The expansion of education has led to the emergence of new milieus in which a belief in human rights is widespread. And Weber surely exaggerated the degree to which the lower middle class and the entrepreneurial spirit were in retreat. Weber fuses his thesis of the religious roots of modern individualism and his diagnosis of the present to produce a tragedy. In this construction, religious forces bring about a regime that robs these very forces of their vitality.

If, however, Weber's historical prognoses—or, better, his sociological assumptions regarding the future—have not proven correct after the close of the twentieth century, then perhaps the relationship between our time and the emergence of the belief in human rights and human dignity need not be a tragic one. Treating this relationship as contingent opens up more space for historical complexity and allows for more hope. Indeed, insofar as it has been confirmed, I believe that we should remove Jellinek's thesis from Weber's framework. Weber assumed that the only alternative to cultural Protestantism, with its sometimes superficial and evolutionistic optimism about the future, was a heroic pessimism that defends liberal individualism against the tendencies threatening its existence together with a stark Kierkegaardian "Either-Or" approach to the choice between values. Troeltsch, by contrast, teaches us that another view of Christianity's potential role in the modern period is possible. What I have in mind here are productive reinterpretations and creative continuations of the Judeo-Christian tradition, new experiential foundations for a belief in individualistic values, and new religious organizational structures in which the characteristics of church, sect, and individual spirituality are bound together. This would result in a strengthening of Christianity as a support for the sacredness of each person over against the depersonalizing forces of modernity. This would enable us to move beyond an all too easy compromise between religion and modernity, of the sort found in cultural Protestantism, as well as the kind of antithetical opposition found in Weber and, in inverted form, much of Catholicism.

Liberating Jellinek's thesis from Weber's framework also permits us to conceive of the belief in human rights as something other than a sacralization or charismatization of reason. As I have tried to show, this interpretation has proved problematic as an empirically sustainable account of the motives leading to the first codifications of human rights. It is also problematic because it privileges a particular view of the human being that can by no means claim unquestioned validity. In the rationalism of the Enlightenment—both in the case of Thomas Jefferson and, in infinitely more nuanced form, that of Immanuel Kant—human rights are founded on the capacity for reason in human beings and this reason is believed to be at work in the autonomous understanding of moral obligations. But as by no means everyone is (already or still) endowed with reason in this sense, an ambiguity creeps into this explanation. In contemporary bioethical debates, reference is made to Kant both by those for whom human beings are simply entitled to dignity regardless of whether or not the individual empirically existent human being has the capacity for autonomous moral reflection, and those who quite explicitly attribute personal dignity not to all members of the human race but only to those who possess this capacity for reason.[49] Those guided by the moral intuition that all of us are equally entitled to universal human dignity and human rights may well be unconvinced by a concept of the human being that can articulate this universality only by making the capacity for reason supraempirical. Those who acknowledge the right to human dignity of newborn children, the mentally disabled, and dementia sufferers will look for ways of expressing this moral intuition different from those offered by an anthropology of the rational human being. So the notion of the charismatization of reason applies to certain thinkers and politicians, but not to the overall process through which codified human rights emerged and not to the moral intuition underlying this process. Rather than a charismatic transfiguration of reason, it would be better to refer to a charismatization of human personhood. The historical process of the depersonalization of charisma, as we might put it in Weberian terms, may lead to the charismatization of the person. The following chapter is devoted to this idea, to an interpretation of human rights as the charismatization or sacralization of the person.

NOTES

1. For a very clear example of this, see Lauren, *Evolution of International Human Rights*, esp. chap. 1.

2. Troeltsch, *Christian Thought*, 135 (for the German original, see Troeltsch, "Politik, Patriotismus, Religion," 85).

3. This chapter does not go into issues relating to Kant's philosophy, which are taken up in chapter 4.

4. Gay, *Enlightenment*.

5. Reinhard, *Paris pendant la Révolution*, 1:196 (quoted in McLeod, *Religion and the People of Western Europe*, 1).

6. Tackett, "French Revolution," 550 (which includes a reference to church attendance figures).

7. Ibid., 536.

8. Tocqueville, *Ancien Régime*, 22.

9. For a particularly vivid account, see Van Kley, "Christianity as Casualty," esp. 1098.

10. Hunt, "Introduction," 23.

11. Ozouf, "De-christianization," 20. On "revolutionary religion," see Ozouf's essay of that title.

12. Tackett, "French Revolution," 552.

13. Tocqueville, *Ancien Régime*, 27. I forgo examination of the validity of parallels with Islam at this point.

14. Of the extensive literature, I mention two titles that I have found particularly valuable: Sheehan, "Enlightenment"; Sorkin, *Religious Enlightenment*

15. Van Kley, "Christianity as Casualty," 1090.

16. Cassirer, *Philosophy of the Enlightenment*, 248.

17. I quote here from the English translation in Anderson, *Constitution and Other Select Documents*, 59–61; for the French original, see Gauchet, *Révolution*, i–ii.

18. The key example here is Gauchet, *Révolution*. A synopsis of his arguments can be found in Gauchet, "Rights of Man." Also of use are Sandweg, *Rationales Naturrecht*; Samwer, *Französische Erklärung*.

19. For an excellent account, see Gauchet, "Rights of Man," 822.

20. This clearly applies to Gauchet, but also, for instance, to Alain Touraine. See his interpretation of the declaration in Touraine, *Critique of Modernity*, 52–56.

21. This listing follows Hunt, "Introduction"; in light of it, Hunt develops the history of the Revolution as one of increasing inclusivity. However skeptical we may be about this idea if it implies a momentum of ideas, it is certainly true that the Declaration of the Rights of Man imposed increased pressure to justify exclusions from the category of human being.

22. See Gauchet, "Rights of Man," 819–20.

23. Schmale, *Archäologie*, 30. The following remarks are based in part on Joas, "Max Weber and the Origins of Human Rights."

24. Compare also the foreword by Jellinek's son Walter in the German edition; Jellinek, *Erklärung*, vi–vii.

25. As Max Weber put it in a commemorative address for his deceased friend at the wedding of one of Jellinek's daughters. See Marianne Weber, *Max Weber*, 473. Günther Roth has repeatedly pointed to the importance of Jellinek for Weber. See Bendix and Roth, *Scholarship and Partisanship*, 308–10. Astonishingly, for a long time the literature on the relationship between Jellinek and Weber often failed even to touch on the question at issue here. See Breuer, *Georg Jellinek und Max Weber*; Hübinger, "Staatstheorie und Politik." Despite its promising title, this also holds for Nelson, "Max Weber, Ernst Troeltsch, Georg Jellinek as Comparative Historical Sociologists." This has recently changed. See Ghosh, "Max Weber and Georg Jellinek"; Kelly, "Revisiting the Rights of Man"; Brugger, "Historismus und Pragmatismus."

26. Best known is the critique by Émile Boutmy, to which Jellinek responded at length. Compare both contributions in the collection by Schnur, *Zur Geschichte der Erklärung der Menschenrechte*: Boutmy, "Erklärung," and Jellinek, "Antwort an Boutmy." The debate originally took place in French: Boutmy, "Déclaration"; Jellinek, "Réponse à M. Boutmy."

27. Gauchet, *Révolution*, 14. Further examples can be found in Stolleis, "Georg Jellineks Beitrag," esp. 109–10. Jellinek is even accused of pan-Germanism by the authors cited here; his thesis is distorted in light of Lutheran claims to authorship of human rights.

28. In this I follow Ernst Troeltsch's suggestion. See his review of Jellinek's *Ausgewählte Schriften und Reden* in Troeltsch, "Rezension." For a similar view, see also Graf, "Puritanische Sektenfreiheit." For an interesting take on Troeltsch's own position on this subject, see Tétaz, "Identité culturelle."

29. For a particularly in-depth examination of these tensions in Jellinek's thought, see Kersten, *Georg Jellinek und die klassische Staatslehre*. He too sees Jellinek's theory of the state as an attempt at "mediation between facticity and normativity" on a historical and statist foundation (5; all translations are Skinner's unless otherwise credited). See also 410: "The theory of self-commitment aims to answer the question, pertaining specifically to German constitutionalism, of how a factual national will, conceived as formally free of any legal commitment, can include normativity." He criticizes Jellinek for privileging the state over citizens,

clearly placing him within the German tradition of the predemocratic power state, and for failing to understand basic rights in the sense of a charter agreed by a commonwealth of citizens (compare 427). Kersten's proximity to contract-theoretical ideas and the French tradition is clearly apparent here. He does not deal with their inherent problems, making his evaluation of Jellinek rather one-sided.

30. This is also the focus in Joas, *Genesis of Values*.

31. Hofmann, "Zur Herkunft," 844.

32. This persuasive account is from Stein, *Himmlische Quellen und irdisches Recht*, 195 n. 120. She thus rejects Rainer Forst's interpretation of Rousseau in his impressive book *Toleranz im Konflikt*, 363–79. On Stein's book, see also my review: Joas, "Mit prophetischem Schwung."

33. Jellinek, *Declaration*, 77 (57 in the German edition, *Erklärung*).

34. Troeltsch, *Social Teachings*, 673.

35. See Grimm, "Europäisches Naturrecht."

36. "The Declaration of Independence: A Transcription," National Archives, accessed November 15, 2012, www.archives.gov/exhibits/charters/declaration_transcript.html.

37. See Maier, *American Scripture*, 98. This is the most detailed examination of the genesis and effective history of this document.

38. See Marty, "American Revolution and Religion." For a more detailed account of the revivalist movements, see McLoughlin, *Revival, Awakenings, and Reform*. Also of value is Hoye, *Demokratie und Christentum*, 127–86.

39. For a compelling account, see Derek H. Davis, "Religious Dimensions."

40. Vögele, *Menschenwürde*, 103. For an account that refers to a "Liberal-Puritan synthesis" and its institutionalization, one that generally corroborates Jellinek and—exceptionally in the American literature—also makes explicit mention of him, see Stackhouse, *Creeds, Society, and Human Rights*, esp. 70–76. An excellent recent study of Roger Williams is provided by Hall, *Separating Church and State*.

The interpretation of the religious and other motives of Roger Williams, the extent of his influence on later developments and the role of Rhode Island as a role model or "outhouse" are contested in the research literature. In her history of freedom of conscience, Martha Nussbaum for example sees theological motives playing a fairly minor role in the case of Williams. A different picture emerges from the specialist literature, as reflected in critical responses to her interpretation. Nussbaum, *Liberty of Conscience*. For a contrasting account, see Zagorin, *How the Idea*, 196–208. See also Zagorin's trenchant response to Nussbaum ("Christianity and Freedom," 97), in which he disputes that stoic and natural law arguments played a major role in Williams's thinking: "Its animating conviction is that freedom of conscience and religion and the separation of church and state are absolutely essential to the spiritual welfare of Christianity." While Hall (in *Separating Church and State*) suggests that Williams's influence was quite limited in the eighteenth century, evidence suggesting the opposite is provided by

Hamburger, *Separation of Church and State*, esp. 38–53. In Forst, *Toleranz im Konflikt*, 242, Williams appears as the purveyor of a mere "transitional theory" for the simple reason that his arguments stand "on firmly Christian ground"!

41. Roth, *Politische Herrschaft*, 147; Breuer, "Charisma der Vernunft." In his extensive study on Weber's sociology of law, our topic is touched on by Gephart, *Gesellschaftstheorie und Recht*, 565–87. Also worth mentioning: Ouédraogo, "Sociologie religieuse." Winfried Brugger has provided a particularly in-depth treatment of Max Weber in his discussion of human rights in *Menschenrechtsethos und Verantwortungspolitik* and in "Sozialwissenschaftliche Analyse." Brugger's emphasis on the constitutive role of experiences of injustice is particularly interesting. See here also König, *Menschenrechte*, 78–138.

42. Weber, *Economy and Society*, 1:6.

43. Ibid., 3:1209.

44. These writings from the 1921 German edition are reprinted in Wells and Baehr, *Russian Revolutions*, 41–240. On Weber's Russian writings, see Pipes, "Max Weber und Russland"; Wells and Baehr, "Editors' Introduction"; Mommsen, "Einleitung." On Struve and Jellinek, see Pipes, *Struve*, esp. 302–7.

45. Wells and Baehr, *Russian Revolutions*, 66–67.

46. Weber, *Economy and Society*, 2:666–731.

47. Ibid., 668.

48. Colliot-Thélène, "Modes de justification des droits subjectifs." Here she draws on the thorough dissertation by Melot, "Notion de droit subjectif."

49. See the evidence-rich account by Stein, *Himmlische Quellen und irdisches Recht*, 225.

2

PUNISHMENT AND RESPECT

The Sacralization of the Person and the Forces Threatening It

The first step in developing my argument was to examine in detail the emergence of the first human rights declarations in the late eighteenth century. I suggested that while we must understand these declarations as concretely as possible in light of their highly contingent contexts of emergence, we will do justice to them only if we also grasp them as expressions of deeper processes of cultural transformation. But how can we adequately conceptualize these processes? It is by no means self-evident that the answer is to refer to the "sacralization of the person" as I propose.[1]

In this chapter I distinguish this proposal more precisely from alternative interpretive options and explain it in more detail. The gradual disappearance of torture as a legitimate tool of criminal justice in Europe may serve as an example of the process of cultural transformation I have in mind.

It is a well-known and uncontroversial fact that in the eighteenth century the European culture of punishment changed fundamentally, or rapidly began to do so. The most dramatic change was the turn away from torture as a means of ascertaining the truth or extracting confessions, and from ordeal as a public spectacle of punishment. What is also important, however, is that the death penalty was called into question, and partially abolished, at a time when many were challenging the state's right to dispose over its citizens' lives; significant too was the "birth of the prison" as the main locus of the penal system. On the basis of the large number of existing studies, which are often of excellent quality, it would be easy to write a vivid account of the stages of this process and to extend this history beyond the eighteenth century and into the present. We would have to consider various heroic efforts to extend these developments in eighteenth-century Europe to other parts of the world, such as the fight against "lynching," which was common in the southern United States until the twentieth century, torture and the death penalty in contemporary China, and the stoning of alleged adulteresses in places where this is still (or is again) a common practice. Despite unity among Europeans and North Americans on the defense of human rights and the condemnation of cruel and humiliating forms of punishment, we would be confronted with differences on whether the death penalty as such should be repudiated or only specific forms of its enforcement. We would also have to explore the prospects and limitations of the humanization of the penal system here and now, as well as the threat of retreat from what we are accustomed to regarding as the achievements of the Enlightenment era, such as the questioning of the categorical prohibition of torture in the theory and practice of the fight against crime and against real and putative terrorists.

In this book I take a different approach. As straightforward as it may be to describe these historical processes, understanding just what they involved is much more difficult. To shed light on the present-day prospects of defending or maintaining the modern European culture of punishment, however, it is crucial to examine, with as much conceptual precision as possible, just what happened in the eighteenth century. Metaphorically speaking, we undoubtedly stand on the shoulders of eighteenth-century reformers. I therefore begin by commenting on the two major and enormously influential interpretations of these developments. Both interpretations require a degree of simplification to bring out their main features, though this does mean presenting them in slightly overstated form and robbing them of some of their caveats. My real objective, however, is to go beyond analysis of the merits and weaknesses of these two predominant interpretations by at least adumbrating an alternative approach that does justice both to the epochal events of the time and to contemporary tendencies. Hence this chapter analyzes an exemplary case of value shift and proposes a theory that might inform the analysis of other cases. In light of this aspiration, I have much more to say about the theoretical underpinnings of this alternative than those of the interpretations I criticize.

THE MYTH OF THE ENLIGHTENMENT

The first story to be told to this end might be titled "The Myth of the Enlightenment." Its literary form is the heroic epic. The hero is a young and painfully shy Milanese intellectual. At the age of twenty-five and after intense discussions within his circle of friends, he sits down to write a manuscript in less than a year. This he publishes anonymously not in (Austrian) Milan—due to the strict censorship—but in the Grand Duchy of Tuscany in the year 1764. I am referring to Cesare Beccaria and his treatise *On Crimes and Punishments* (*Dei delitti e delle pene*).[2] This book, which was quickly placed on the index of banned books, soon ran to several editions and was translated into other languages, including German and English. In terms of its effective history the French edition is the most important as it brought the book to the attention of leading French Enlightenment figures such as Voltaire, Diderot, and d'Alembert. One of Beccaria's friends, Pietro Verri, summarized the historical impact of the book as follows: "Abuse and torture, these dreadful practices, were either eliminated or at least moderated in the trials of all States; *and this is the achievement of only one book*."[3]

Here, in a pure form, we have the ingredients of the kind of story adored by Enlightenment intellectuals. In stylized terms we might summarize it as follows. For a long time, but for reasons that remain incomprehensible, conventions, customs, and prejudices have held sway over people's lives. These have now lost their meaning, if they had any in the first place. So contemporary practices are viewed as mere relics to which the present continues to cling either due to inertia or because they reflect certain interests. Beccaria calls the rules inherent in the penal system "the residue of the most barbarous centuries . . . a few odd remnants of the laws of an ancient conquering race codified twelve hundred years ago by a prince ruling at Constantinople, and since jumbled together with the customs of the Lombards and bundled up in the rambling volumes of obscure academic interpreters—this is what makes up the tradition of opinions that passes for law across a large portion of Europe" (3).

Only brave and solitary initiative can counter these barbaric practices: "That philosopher who had the courage to scatter out among the multitudes from his humble, despised study the first seeds of those beneficial truths that would be so long in bearing fruit, deserves the gratitude of all humanity" (8). With his insights he seeks to address "the hearts of the few wise men" (71) scattered around the world. At the same time, however, he hopes that "the great monarchs, the human benefactors who rule us, love the truths which are expounded by humble philosophers with an unfanatical zeal"; he underlines the importance of identifying the "confusions" of these laws "in a style designed to ward off the unenlightened and impatient run of men" (3). Isolated but determined to make a difference, our intellectual puts forward a clear alternative to these age-old prejudices and barbaric practices. This conception, however, is presented not as the newly created work of this particular thinker, but as a return to the simplest of principles, whose validity, evident prior to all history, has been concealed by history. "It is, therefore, only after they have experienced thousands of miscarriages in matters essential to life and liberty, and have grown weary of suffering the most extreme ills, that men set themselves to right the evils that beset them and to grasp the most palpable truths which, by virtue of their simplicity, escape the minds of the common run of men who are not used to analysing things, but instead passively take on a whole set of second-hand impressions of them derived more from tradition than from enquiry." And these "most palpable truths" and simplest principles involve understanding laws as "contracts amongst free men" and developing them systematically from one single point of view; that is, with the aim of bringing about "the greatest happiness shared among the greater number" (7).

On this basis, through strictly logical deduction, we can obtain all the principles necessary to the proper organization of laws and criminal justice. The origin of punishments, then, can only lie in violation of the social contract to which individuals once committed themselves in order to do away with the permanently bellicose state of nature. This violation occurs when individuals seek to regain their natural, presocietal liberty. "What were wanted here were sufficiently tangible motives to prevent the despotic spirit of every man from resubmerging society's laws into the ancient chaos. These tangible motives are the punishments enacted against law-breakers" (9).

The limits of the legitimacy of all state punishment are derived directly from this origin of punishment: "Any punishment which goes beyond the need to preserve this bond [i.e., of this social contract] is unjust by its very nature" (11). Yet the power of this idea goes far beyond the establishment of general principles; it allows us to calculate with near-mathematical precision which punishment fits which crime. This calculability arises from the fundamental principle that crimes should become less and less frequent, "in proportion to the harm they do to society. Hence the obstacles which repel men from committing crimes ought to be made stronger the more these crimes are against the public good and the more inducements there are for committing them. Hence, there must be a proportion between crimes and punishments" (19). Any attempt to measure the seriousness of a crime in terms of the wickedness of the intention behind it is explicitly rejected.

The enthusiasm with which our author states his case here is certainly due in part to the assumption that both the harm that a crime does to society and the effect that a punishment has on the criminal can be quantified precisely. This enthusiasm leads Beccaria, the Enlightenment intellectual, to some genuinely perceptive observations. He notes that it is not so much the cruelty of threatened punishments that has a deterrent effect but the certainty that they will be carried out; that it is not the magnitude of a punishment but its relative position in the hierarchy of punishments that deters, and that the intensification of punishment is subject to a sort of law of decreasing marginal utility. In other words, as he puts it, as punishments become crueler, "human souls which, like fluids, find their level from their surroundings, become hardened and the ever lively power of the emotions brings it about that, after a hundred years of cruel tortures, the wheel only causes as much fear as prison previously did" (63–64).

Most fascinating are his passages on torture and the death penalty. From his perspective, torture can only appear as an inconceivably illogical means of determining the truth. How can anyone possibly deny that, rather than a way of ascertaining the truth, torture is merely a test of the suspect's resilience? It is "a sure route for the acquittal of robust ruffians and the conviction of weak innocents" (39). "The result, therefore, of torture depends on a man's predisposition and on calculation, which vary from man to man according to their hardihood and sensibility, so that, with this method, a mathematician would settle problems better than a judge. Given the strength of an innocent man's muscles and the sensitivity of his sinews, one need only find the right level of pain to make him admit his guilt of a given crime" (42).

The problem of the death penalty can be easily resolved on these premises. If punishments must be justified on the basis of the social contract model, it is from the outset implausible to assume that in concluding this contract any individual—who would have sacrificed only the smallest part of his "own freedom"—could have granted others permission to kill him. Beccaria also asks how it is possible that a society that makes use of the death penalty can prohibit and punish attempted suicide (as was common in his time). If individuals can yield to others the right to kill them, they must first have had the right to kill themselves. Following this logic, the death penalty can never be right. It is in fact "an act of war on the part of society against the citizen that comes about when it is deemed necessary or useful to destroy his existence." Beccaria sets about delivering a comprehensive argument to demonstrate that "death is neither necessary nor useful." He concedes just two exceptions: first, the killing of a citizen who "even if deprived of his freedom . . . retains such connections and such power as to endanger the security of the nation"; and, second, the killing of a citizen whose death "is the true and only brake to prevent others from committing crimes" (66–67). In sum, this amounts to a philosophy of punishment that demands that it be "public, speedy, necessary, the minimum possible in the given circumstances, proportionate to the crime, and determined by the law" (113).

The story so far is certainly a pleasant and in many respects heartwarming one. But is it too good to be true? I shall mention just three of the many possible objections. First: Is the assertion that this one book had a revolutionary impact historically verifiable? Doubts about this can draw on the text of the book itself, as it refers to the abolition of torture in Sweden in 1734 and in Prussia by Frederick II immediately after his accession to the throne in 1740, decades before Beccaria's book was first published in 1764. In France the so-called *parlements* (courts of appeal) had progressively restricted torture since the middle of the eighteenth century.[4] This is not to dismiss out of hand the important role of Beccaria's book, yet the sequence of events needs to be corrected. This correction highlights the fact that, rather than a sudden flash of enlightenment, Beccaria's text may have been the expression of a much more profound transformational process. Beccaria himself speculates about the circumstances under which the changes he demands might become possible. He believes that a long life spent in society has a generally mellowing effect on morals. Immediately after the conclusion of the social contract, we could therefore expect to find some rough and savage characters. But, "as souls become softened by society, [sensibility] grows. And as it does so, the severity of punishments ought to diminish, if the relation between the object and the sensation is to remain constant" (113; translation modified).

Beccaria does not characterize this process as the humanization of punishment but refers instead to increasing "sensibility" (*sensibilità*). He mentions two reasons why this sensibility has increased so strongly in, and even shortly before, the eighteenth century. One reason is growing prosperity; "luxury and ease of life," he claims, give rise to "the most precious virtues, humanity, charity, and toleration of human error" (18). He polemicizes against the idea that his own time is an age of decline in comparison to the past, which he believes was characterized by superstition, greed, and oppression. The other cause of improving morals and decreasing crime is the rise of printing. For Beccaria, knowledge of the law provides an important motive not to commit crimes.

A second objection to Beccaria's Enlightenment-based self-understanding highlights the striking contrast between the strictly logical elaboration of his own philosophy of punishment and his total inability to conceive of the practices and mentalities he is fighting as anything other than confused, illogical, or superstitious relics of a barbaric past. One encounters this lack of comprehension in his book at every turn. The idea that homicide must be considered the worst possible crime, for instance, for him "has its foundation in human nature" (77)—regardless of the fact that the history of law runs counter to this view: sacrilege, heresy, and blasphemy were often judged more harshly than the killing of a "profane" human being. He has absolutely no concept of "dignity" and "honor" with respect to criminal law. To his mind, the prohibition of suicide is an absurdity; he devotes more space in the relevant passage to the question of whether emigration should be punished. This is only consistent within his frame of reference, as he assumes that "one who kills himself does less harm to society than one who leaves its borders forever, for the former leaves all his belongings, whilst the latter takes with him some part of what he owns" (83). Beccaria, in sum, was quite incapable of comprehending the specific logic of the penal system he sought to overcome.

Finally: How satisfactory are arguments against the death penalty based on its lack of utility? What if in a given case we could prove the utility of a killing? Would the death penalty or the taking of a "useless" life or one "not worth living"—to quote the dreadful jargon of the Third Reich—be acceptable then? Here we touch upon present-day problems. We come up against the fact that a "utilitarian" philosophy of punishment cannot give voice to the moral intuition that some things—such as human life—must be categorically protected. But if this philosophy cannot articulate this intuition, either it must assert itself against it or we must conclude that the intuition represents a more adequate view of things.

In addition to the heroic narrative about an Enlightenment intellectual there is the one about the Enlightenment ruler credited with abolishing torture throughout Europe in the eighteenth century. The ruler generally mentioned in this context is Prussian king Frederick II; this is because, immediately after assuming the throne, as one of his first official acts, he issued a cabinet order on June 3, 1740, decreeing the "total abolition of torture in the inquisitions."[5] Both types of heroic narrative would coincide if it proved possible to demonstrate the decisive influence of an intellectual on this ruler or if the ruler himself might be viewed as a kind of intellectual on the throne.

Again, though, the facts are a serious obstacle to the heroic Enlightenment narrative. The very next passage of the cabinet order identifies exceptional cases in which torture may still be used: in cases of lèse-majesté and treason, or acts of murder involving several victims or the complicity of a number of offenders. It is not just that we must refer to the mere limitation of torture rather than its abolition. Frederick also wanted the decree to remain secret. He believed this would safeguard the deterrent effect. But who then was informed about the decree? The direct addressee was the lord high chancellor, who reacted with skepticism and immediately suggested further exceptions such as child murder, sodomy, and even theft, should the thief fail to hand over the stolen goods.[6] Finally, the courts to which the lord high chancellor passed on the order requested further exceptions. There are in fact further decrees issued by the king in subsequent years in which Frederick, while retaining his fundamental opposition to torture, de facto permitted it in certain cases. All of this is quite apart from the practices of criminal justice, which proved resistant to such reformist tendencies in Prussia and elsewhere.

So the abolition of torture did not come about as a result of one isolated act in Prussia, but gained ground in a wide variety of European countries in the eighteenth century in such a way that by around 1830 there was nowhere left where it was regarded as fundamentally permissible. Each of the intellectual objections to torture put forward by Beccaria has a lengthy history behind it.[7] This enables us to trace histories of influence, to determine the relative significance of Christian or secular motives, in the case of every individual Enlightenment thinker and every ruler who opposed torture. Both types of motive existed; both entail an intellectual history of torture criticism. But this also means that it was not simply the Enlightenment that identified these arguments and helped them gain acceptance. A number of historians go so far as to describe Enlightenment intellectuals provocatively as "epigones" of the torture discourse.[8] On this view, the success of their writings is due to the fact that their readers were already convinced when they were published. In fact, it appears that the demand for the abolition of torture united the Enlightenment intellectuals and, as this step was in the air, they felt there was a realistic prospect of success.[9] So the reasons why abolition was achieved so easily must lie elsewhere.

THE TRANSFORMATION OF POWER?

We must now tell the second story, one that could hardly contrast more sharply with the "myth of the Enlightenment." It is to be found in a book that, more than any other, has shaped debates on punishment over the last thirty years. Michel Foucault's *Discipline and Punish: The Birth of the Prison*, first published in 1975, describes changes in the criminal justice system in light of what we might call the "reconstruction of techniques of power."[10] This is a well-known book, so there is no need to provide a detailed account of it here. It begins with a disturbing—not to say disgusting—description of the brutal public torture and execution of Damiens, who had attempted to murder the king, in Paris in 1757. This description is the foil for an analysis that seeks to show that over time the body diminished in importance as the target of punishment. The focus shifted instead to the "behavior" and "mind" of the convicted, while public execution became rarer, ultimately ceasing altogether. The flip side of this was allegedly the attempt to discipline prisoners, to condition them, to drill mind and body. According to Foucault, the symbol of this new conception of punishment was the birth of the modern prison. Dungeons had long existed, but the new prisons were constructed, architecturally and organizationally, in such a way as to enable the complete surveillance of prisoners, or at least to give the prisoners this impression. Foucault has portrayed this to compelling literary effect. He declared the so-called panopticon—a plan, dating from 1836, for a prison in which cells are arranged in a circular manner such that all of them can be overseen from the warden's central post—the epitome of the modern penal system. This must have seemed obvious to him given that, as philosopher and penal reformer, Jeremy Bentham, the inventor of the panopticon, took his "utilitarianism" much further even than Beccaria. The new penal system, Foucault claims, is no longer concerned with the destruction of the body but with exercising greater and more effective control and power over body and mind. Furthermore, for Foucault (and many of his readers), the rise of the modern prison is only one element within a comprehensive system of modern techniques of power and discipline. The drilling of soldiers and industrial workers is part of this ensemble as well. So Foucault does not interpret the fundamental reforms of the criminal justice system as a sign of any kind of humanization. Rather, in Nietzschean style, he regards them merely as a transformation of power, which loses any identifiable social locus as a result, becoming ever more tacit and inconspicuous—yet omnipresent.

For many readers, Foucault's story was, and still is, a credible guide to positive knowledge about the development of criminal justice. This is astonishing given that Foucault never made any secret of his distance from professional historiography, indeed of his contempt for the field and its methods. It is also dangerous, as historians were withering in their assessment of many of the details of his account.[11] I shall leave these details to one side here. As with the "myth of the Enlightenment," the crucial thing is to examine the major objections to Foucault's construction.

The first two objections to the myth of the Enlightenment certainly do not apply to Foucault. He cannot be accused of overestimating the impact of specific intellectuals, or of ignoring the inner logic of the pre-Enlightenment penal system. With regard to the first objection, Foucault tends to go to the other extreme. He embeds all his individual analyses within a supposed process of social disciplining, while failing to identify the actors who advance, justify, or resist this process. This leads to a profound overestimation of the efficacy of power and control. Neither industrial organization nor the armed forces nor the prison are truly consonant with the picture painted by Foucault. He does, however, reconstruct the inner logic of torture and ordeal in detail and with great sensitivity. For him, torture is a duel with strict rules; ordeal, on the other hand, is symbolically related to the confessed crime. In the era of absolutism, moreover, the sovereign's power manifests itself in the "festival of ordeals": "It is a ceremonial by which a momentarily injured sovereignty is reconstituted. It restores that sovereignty by manifesting it at its most spectacular. . . . Its aim is not so much to re-establish a balance as to bring into play, as its extreme point, the dissymmetry between the subject who has dared to violate the law and the all-powerful sovereign who displays his strength" (48–49).

For Foucault, then, ordeal in the eighteenth century is by no means, as for Beccaria, a mere relic of barbaric times, but a logical component of a penal system "in which the sovereign, directly or indirectly, demanded, decided and carried out punishments" (53); that is, of a penal system in which every offense entails a *crimen majestatis*. Foucault reconstructs the new penal system as well as inherently logical. In contrast to the Enlightenment view of history, he also distinguishes the reform period from the normalization of the prison sentence that soon followed. He traces this rapid normalization back to a process, long characteristic of many other areas of society, which had already put in place the preconditions for perfecting the system of control.

I would like to disregard all the methodological objections to Foucault's account and address just two problems of significance to the present context.[12] First, we might ask whether his idea of an advancing disciplining process is not only greatly overstated (as mentioned above) but altogether ill suited to comprehending key aspects of the penal reforms carried out in the eighteenth and nineteenth centuries. Against Foucault's studies of the history of "madness," some—such as Marcel Gauchet—have proposed a radical change of perspective.[13] According to Foucault, in medieval times the lunatic was tolerated as a normal part of creation; only in the "age of reason" was he excluded from life and imprisoned in "total institutions." This interpretation, however, is based on a profound misconception. The supposed tolerance of the lunatic rested upon the establishment of a radical distance from him. The lunatic was regarded as a fundamentally different creature occupying its own particular place in a richly differentiated cosmos, but not as fully human. According to this worldview, the lunatic is not a human being like you and me, but virtually a member of a different species. From this perspective, which diverges from that of Foucault, under absolutism a leveling process gradually renders all citizens the subjects of the one sovereign, although never with complete consistency. As paradoxical as it sounds, confinement in asylums may be regarded as a first, albeit inconsistent step toward the integration of the lunatic into the human species. Thus it is not disciplining but inclusion that is crucial; disciplining is only an inadequate attempt to facilitate inclusion. This insight can also be applied to the field of criminal justice. The penal reformers inspired by the utilitarian version of the Enlightenment are thus a specific, in many ways one-sided expression of a process of inclusion rather than disciplining. Beccaria declares the criminal a human being both before and after the crime; for him the criminal is not an inherently different being, and it is impossible to simply cease feeling compassion for him in view of his punishment.

The second objection arises from one of Foucault's undoubtedly correct insights into the myth of the Enlightenment. He writes in full awareness of the fact that the Enlightenment thinkers' hopes for the reeducation of offenders (and later their therapeutic treatment) were never realized—or at least to nowhere near the extent envisaged. The reformed penal system did not quite have the effect it was expected to. As a result, subsequent discourse on punishment has waxed and waned: the failure of attempts at reeducation may lead to its intensification, or to resignation and, consequently, to a renewed emphasis on repression. And the treatability of certain categories of sex offenders—at least given current therapeutic tools—has in fact been overestimated in the recent past, so that a backlash from a disgruntled public can come as little surprise. Such cases entail tragic trade-offs, an irresolvable tension between repression and prevention, and various forms of compromise between the two. Each objective may discredit the other. We may read Foucault's book as an expression of this dilemma. As French sociologist Jacques Donzelot writes: "At the moment when repression began to see itself as harmful and prevention seemed no more than an advanced form of repression, Foucault said that the king was naked, that the reformism of the modern philosophy of criminal law was merely a fraudulent cover for a new art of social control; its supposed aspiration to prevent rather than repress actually involved nothing more than extending surveillance to the entire population."[14]

Foucault himself by no means resolves this dilemma. Though he attacks his subject with radical gusto his ideas are opaque. There is no prospect here of an eventual humanization of the penal system. Instead, to aporetic effect, he questions the right of state or society to impose punishment.[15]

THE SACRALIZATION OF THE PERSON

These questions and objections directed toward Foucault, and Enlightenment thinkers' self-conception, at least point to the key desiderata of an alternative interpretation to both these narratives. Let us suppose that it is inclusion rather than disciplining that provides the key to understanding the changes that occurred in the eighteenth century. Inclusion here means integration into the category of human being, integration of those—such as criminals or slaves—who had not been self-evidently included within this concept. Let us also suggest that—contrary to the ideas of the Enlightenment—it is not at all natural to conceive of murder as the worst possible crime. In the history of criminal law, the worst crime has generally been that which violates the sacred core of the community. So it seems reasonable to trace changes in the penal system back to changes in the understanding of the sacred. This is why I refer to the alternative interpretation proposed here as the "sacralization of the person." From this perspective, the reforms of penal law and penal practice, and the rise of human rights in the late eighteenth century, are the expression of a profound cultural shift in which the human person became a sacred object. The great French sociologist Émile Durkheim was the first to think in these terms.[16] In 1898, amid the turmoil of the Dreyfus scandal, he gave dramatic expression to the basic idea that we should regard the belief in human rights and universal human dignity as the "religion of modernity":[17]

> The human person, whose definition serves as the touchstone according to which good must be distinguished from evil, is considered as sacred, in what one might call the ritual sense of the word. It has something of that transcendental majesty which the churches of all times have given to their gods. It is conceived as being invested with that mysterious property which creates an empty space around holy objects, which keeps them away from profane contacts and which draws them away from ordinary life. And it is exactly this feature which induces the respect of which it is the object. Whoever makes an attempt on a man's life, on a man's liberty, on a man's honour inspires us with a feeling of horror, in every way analogous to that which the believer experiences when he sees his idol profaned.[18]

Durkheim begins his argument, which aims to demonstrate the "sacredness" of the individual in modernity, by stating that the concept of "individualism" is deeply ambiguous. He believes this to be necessary because the "anti-Dreyfusards" accuse of individualism all those who are willing to accept a weakening of the army's authority because of the rights of an individual and "obstinately refuse to bend their logic at the word of an army general"; they also declare this individualism the dissolution of all social order and solidarity, and thus the "great sickness of the present time."[19] For Durkheim there is certainly a destructive, anarchical form of individualism. This he sees in cases where individuals are guided by no higher goal than their egoistic pleasure or economic utility. He yields to no one in his criticism of this kind of individualism. But he sees it as completely unacceptable to equate this individualism in any way with the moral philosophy of Kant or Rousseau or the individualism "which the Declaration of the Rights of Man sought, more or less successfully, to translate into formulae." For him, this second individualism is in many ways the exact opposite of the first, in that it views merely personal interests with great skepticism and—as in the work of Kant—mostly as a source of evil. This well-understood individualism has nothing in common with an "egoistic cult of the self," the "apotheosis of comfort and private interest" (61). Rather than abandoning themselves to whatever natural impulses they may have, individualists in this second sense are geared toward an exacting ideal—to act in such a way that everyone might approve of their action or to ensure that the precept underlying their action is universalizable.

Durkheim refers to the holiness, the sacredness of the person. In justifying this use of language he does not refer to Kant, though he could have done so as Kant also refers to "holiness" in the *Groundwork of the Metaphysics of Morals* as he develops the concept of "dignity." "Dignity" for Kant is everything that has and can have no price, but is "raised above all price and therefore admits of no equivalent."[20] On this view, the notion of dignity "cannot be brought into comparison or competition at all [with a price] without, as it were, assaulting its holiness."[21] But what was perhaps no more than a momentary flash of insight for Kant, an insight in any case for which he provided no explicit justification, is for Durkheim the jumping-off point for his theory of religion, which he never ceased to develop, and for the idea of viewing the person as such as a sacred object in modern societies. We shall return later to the question of exactly what this means.

We must immediately clarify two further conceptual issues. Durkheim himself switches between references to the sacredness of the individual and of the person, as if the two concepts were interchangeable.[22] If the concept of the individual is genuinely safeguarded against any utilitarian-egoistical misconceptions, then this is unproblematic. Durkheim can then interpret the cult of the individual for the individual's sake as a superstitious, degenerate form of genuine individualism. I myself refer to the sacredness of the person rather than the individual, in order to ensure that the intended belief in the irreducible dignity of every human being is not immediately mistaken for the unscrupulous, egocentric self-sacralization of the individual and thus the narcissistic inability to break away from self-referentiality.[23] The concept of the person has the additional advantage that unlike that of the individual it cannot be understood as contrasting with society (or community). Instead it implies the inevitable sociality of the individual and a specific type of social life of which the personhood of every individual is constitutive.[24]

So Durkheim articulates the belief in human rights and human dignity as an expression of the sacralization of the person. In this sense it is understandable and appropriate that he attributes to the person the same aura peculiar to sacred things. Characteristically, though, he goes too far when he calls the morality of human rights a religion in which "man is, at the same time, both believer and God" (62). By demonstrating how fruitful the idea of the sacredness of the person is, he has by no means shown that the human being is also the source of his own holiness. Durkheim, the rabbi's son, allows his programmatic atheism to engulf his argument. If we regard this lacuna as indicative, his atheism is dogmatic. Rather than allowing for the possibility that the belief in the sacredness of the person may have competing origins, Durkheim closes his mind to the idea that religion may continue to be a source of support for human rights into the future.

Next, Durkheim attempts to show that this belief that, building on Auguste Comte, he calls the "religion de l'humanité"—that is, the religion of humanity and/or humaneness—is absolutely capable of integrating whole societies. In an earlier book he himself had still assumed that the "cult of the individual" is an anomaly among beliefs and ideals, as it directs the will toward a common goal but this goal is not a social one and could not give rise to any genuine social bond.[25] But now Durkheim has lost his skepticism as he has come to realize that this well-understood individualism is not a matter of the egocentric glorification of one's self, but relates to human personhood as such. The mainspring of this belief is thus not egoism but sympathy "for all that is human, a wider pity for all sufferings, for all human miseries, a more ardent desire to combat and alleviate them, a greater thirst for justice" (64). Having briefly dispatched the notion that freedom of opinion could only result in anarchy by pointing out that in the case of the sciences consensus and rational authority are entirely compatible with absolute freedom of thought, Durkheim goes considerably further. For him, the sacredness of the person is not just one possible system of belief with socially integrative effects, but the only system of belief that can now "ensure the moral unity of the country" (66). With this far more extensive proposition, Durkheim is taking on a double burden of proof. First, he must show that modern societies have structural characteristics that suggest that it is functionally imperative to achieve social integration through moral individualism. Second, he must set out how this moral individualism relates to the traditional religions. Naturally, his essay on the Dreyfus debate merely hints at his views on these two issues.

But we can easily make out the basic thrust of the argument. Immediately palpable is Durkheim's aversion to all those who call for the strengthening of religion solely in terms of the need for social harmony. And indeed no one can believe in a religious sense solely because it would be socially useful to do so.[26] It is a sociological truism that "a society cannot hold together unless there exists among its members a certain intellectual and moral community" (66), but simply calling for such community does little to help develop it. It is also possible that under new circumstances old commonalities no longer have the desired effects, such that the call for a return to a former state of cohesion is usually no more than the articulation of a problem rather than its solution. For Durkheim the solution must lie in the sacralization of the person, as this is the only process in which the means of constituting social cohesion does not contradict the sociostructural tendencies that made the former cohesion impossible. Two such sociostructural tendencies are mentioned: the increased territorial extent of societies and an advancing division of labor. The larger a society is in spatial terms, the harder it is for it to achieve a homogeneity of traditions and practices. This is insignificant, we might add, if there is very little association between the inhabitants of different parts of the country. But if association and exchange increase, then differences must be systematically repressed if they are not to be permitted. If they are permissible, then there are numerous variations rather than a single unified culture. The advancing division of labor reinforces this tendency even in small areas. Professional specialization, for example, generates different knowledge, attitudes, and perspectives on the world. Division of labor and territorial expansion thus give rise to conditions in which people can identify ever less with one another through a set of unique commonalities. So increasingly the only resource that can underpin community is the "idea of the human person" itself, an idea that "survives, immutable and impersonal, above the changing tides of particular opinions" (67).

And how does this idea relate to Christianity? Durkheim thinks that we are dealing here with a modern articulation of impulses originally generated by Christianity. Compared with the religions of the ancient city-states, "Christianity expressed in an inward faith, in the personal conviction of the individual, the essential condition of godliness. . . . The very centre of the moral life was thus transferred from outside to within and the individual was set up as the sovereign judge of his own conduct having no other accounts to render than those to himself and to his God" (68).

So we cannot overstate the significance of Christianity as a cultural prerequisite for the emergence of modern individualism. In his writings, Durkheim took an interest in various aspects of these cultural processes, with respect, for example, to the concept of the soul in Christianity and the question of its continuity with this idea as found in "primitive" religions, the role of Christianity in the history of Western educational institutions, and with respect to the history of law.[27] In his politically and morally trenchant credo of 1898 he therefore rejects any notion that he is breaking with the Christian tradition. On the contrary, he presents his call for human rights as a continuation of the Christian tradition. But here continuation also means overcoming. On this view, Christianity is a form of "restricted individualism" that must now be replaced by a "more developed individualism" (68). This is not a matter of embedding the belief in human rights in Christianity; instead, this belief is to replace Christianity, which is merely acknowledged to have paved the way for this belief.

At this point, however, we are inevitably faced with the question of whether the idea of human rights can ever be considered a religion in the true sense of the term. How we answer this question obviously depends on what we mean by religion. Defining "religion," however, is an unedifying task. The diverse range of phenomena encompassed by this term consistently defies any neat conceptual schema. Even Max Weber, a man trained in law who provided a host of perceptive conceptual definitions in his work, demurred in this case.[28] Émile Durkheim, however, did put forward a definition in various of his works, most importantly in his magnum opus *The Elementary Forms of Religious Life*, though his intention was to open up and orient debate rather than provide a conclusive definition.[29] As he famously stated: "A religion is a unified system of beliefs and practices relative to sacred things, that is to say, things set apart and surrounded by prohibitions—beliefs and practices that unite its adherents in a single moral community called a church."[30] This definition has a number of notable aspects. All I want to underline at this point is that it goes against the tendency to define religions via a belief in God and a distinction between natural and supernatural. Neither type of definition is well suited to the phenomena of particular interest to Durkheim; namely, totemism and, as they were called at the time, "primitive" religions. Instead, reference to a sphere of the sacred now moves center stage. The risk here is that the definitional problem is merely deferred. Where formerly we needed to determine what religion is, we now need to clarify the nature of this "sacred" element supposedly inherent in every religion. In an article written shortly before his death, he expressed his conception of the sacred in a particularly concentrated form.[31] Here the sacred is initially introduced as part of a conceptual pairing in which its counterpart is the profane. Neither can be understood without reference to its opposite. But Durkheim was no structuralist for whom difference alone is constitutive of meaning. So when we scrutinize the unique character of the sacred, in the first instance there is no room for the notion of superior value. Though such superior value may be found in the higher forms of religion, for Durkheim amulets and fetishes show that this is not fundamental. In most cases sacred things are characterized by the fact that they are protected and defended by prohibitions, while profane things are subject to these very prohibitions and may come into contact with holy things only within the framework of established rituals. But sometimes prohibitions also apply to the sacred in order to prevent it from coming into contact with the profane. So the crucial point is a different one; namely, the fact that the sacred is experienced as the location of a "force," an "energy" that impacts on the profane, while the profane can do no more than bring about the discharging of this energy and transform its character, from purity to impurity, from salvation to damnation.

The physical metaphors that mark Durkheim's language here ("force," "energy") may result in the misunderstanding that the encounter with the sacred is independent of the interpretive schemas already present in people's minds and that this encounter is characterized not by subjective experience but a kind of physiological reaction.[32] While it is true that Durkheim fails to provide an entirely persuasive account of the role of interpretation and experience, such a reading would be a misunderstanding. Durkheim's thinking is informed by William James's idea that in the first instance religious faith must be understood not as a cognitive event in which we believe something to be true, but as a sure sense of the presence of a greater force, a force on which our own vital force in turn relies.[33] We spontaneously ascribe the quality "sacredness" to objects when we have an experience so intense that it constitutes or transforms our entire worldview and self-understanding. The components of the experiential situation are associated with the cause of this intensity. Sacred objects "infect" other objects, thus spreading sacredness; through acts of consecration, sacredness may also be intentionally conferred.

Durkheim was not the first to emphasize sacredness as the basic phenomenon characteristic of all religions; we can only describe him as the most systematic exponent of this conception in the social sciences.[34] And this conception is not uncontested. The notion that the clear-cut conceptual dichotomy sacred/profane is found unambiguously and universally in cultural worldviews and in individuals' emotional world has often been disputed.[35] But claims of empirically demonstrable transitions between the sacred and profane, individual variants, and context-dependent blurring do not, in my view, really call into question the utility of this conceptual distinction or the idea that it is of constitutive importance.

All of this must be left to one side in the present context. Only two points are of significance here. First, it is clear that Durkheim does not derive the concept of the sacred from that of religion, but regards it as constitutive of religion. From this perspective, it is not just religious believers who have something that is holy to them. The sacredness found in all individuals and cultures may, conversely, generate religion if the beliefs and practices associated with this sacredness, to which the definition of religion referred, are systematized and organized socially. The secular/religious distinction must not be confused with the profane/sacred distinction.[36] There is a charge of sacredness in the objects and content of worldviews that consider themselves secular, in both secular nationalism and Marxism, but also in secular liberalism. For Durkheim, the belief in the autonomy of the individual's rationality is the dogma of the system of sacredness characteristic of this individualism. His own views are not so far from this dogma, but he wishes to help it achieve a more adequate self-understanding through his theory of religion.

We must be particularly careful not to misunderstand a second aspect of this conception of sacredness. The emphasis on sacredness could be seen as contrasting with the idea and praxis of rational argument and debate. Jürgen Habermas has gone further than anyone else in fleshing out this concern, directing his remarks specifically at Durkheim.[37] As Habermas sees it, increasingly throughout human history and definitively in modernity, language has replaced and must replace religion, while rational discourse has replaced and must replace the experience and symbolization of sacredness. He has coined the expression "linguistification of the sacred" for this process, which entails one of the most radical conceptions of secularization ever put forward. What he means is that sacralization and the ritual practices associated with it are increasingly losing, and will ultimately completely lose, their meaning and are being replaced by rational discourse. But we might also understand the linguistification of the sacred in a very different way than intended by Habermas, not as the replacement of the sacred by language, but as the linguistic articulation of the sacred. On this view, language and especially the culture of rational argument would have given rise to something new, something that pervades and transforms the experiential basis of our ideal formation, but does not replace it.[38] The institutionalization of rational argument itself—in parliament, in public political debate, in the scientific seminar or conference—also remains dependent on an emotional commitment to values and practices.

Durkheim himself mentioned the idea of the sacredness of the person in many of his writings and applied it to a range of different subjects: to the ethos of scientific debate in which, regardless of a person's status, every argument must count, and to understanding the process of sensitization to sexual approaches not approved by the subject.[39] Durkheim thus revised his own earlier ideas about the development of law, which suggested that it was subject to an inexorable process of desacralization. "A number of developmental strands [intersect] in his analysis of modern law . . .: *desacralization* and *resacralization*, *juridification* in the sense of the *de-moralization* of diffuse solidarity-based relations and finally the call for the *re-sacralization* of civil law."[40] Other commentators have attempted to examine a wealth of other phenomena from this perspective, ranging from everyday courtesies, such as greetings and reciprocal face-saving in conflicts, to interactions between doctors and patients, for example, patients' right to information and to help shape the course of therapy. All these attempts demonstrate how false it would be to characterize our contemporary moral situation through terms such as "liberalization" or "value loss." The relaxation of norms in certain areas often contrasts with greatly increased sensitivity in others. The growing public awareness of sexual molestation in general and child sex abuse in particular, for example, is surely due to an enhanced appreciation of their harmfulness rather than a mere increase in the number of cases.

In relation to our topic of criminal justice, Durkheim alluded to a double effect of this sensitization in an attempt to comprehend the laws governing the development of criminal justice.[41] The same process that teaches us to reject cruel forms of punishment—because we see the human being in the criminal, whom we therefore respect—makes us more sensitive to the cruelty of crimes. This both stimulates and inhibits the drive to punish. It ties in with the fact that—as described by Foucault—not only has corporal punishment declined, but it is only over the last two centuries that the validity and distinctiveness of the right to physical integrity have, increasingly, been acknowledged. This valorization of the body cannot be understood through the prism of disciplining.[42] If, however, we assume the sacralization of the person, we can see the irresolvable contradiction between the need to punish every violation of the person's sacrality and the violation of this sacrality inherent in the act of punishment itself. Given its irresolvable nature, this contradiction can only be mitigated. Durkheim thought this explained why prison sentences have come to replace corporal punishment—at least when and where the sacralization of the person endures. Prison sentences offer a way out of the dilemma. Durkheim can thus attribute a milder penal system to more developed societies, although he has one major reservation: the more absolute the power of a regime is, the greater the likelihood that severe punishments will be enforced. This caveat does justice to the fact, overlooked by Beccaria but established by Foucault, that the draconian punishments of absolutism are not a relic but a radicalization of medieval penal practices. Durkheim did not provide a proper theory of sacralization. He merely related the particularities of modern society to the fact that we are "becoming more alive to what touches on the human personality."[43] But he does not provide a truly causal or processual explanation. Had he done so, he would naturally have had to take the role of power into account. It is not power as such that would have played a constitutive role here—as in Foucault's approach—but only specific types of power and their various forms, along with their legitimation and intention.

Over the last few years, influenced by Durkheim's observations, leading American historian Lynn Hunt has analyzed the history of the abolition of torture, and the history of human rights in general.[44] She shows persuasively the development over the course of the eighteenth century of both a discourse on fundamental rights and an emotional repugnance at torture, but also how little synchrony there ever was between the two. Even the intellectual elites did not immediately make the connection; so the renunciation of torture cannot simply have been the consequence of the discourse on fundamental rights. Voltaire made a vehement public intervention in one of the great legal scandals of the ancien régime—the Calas case—without immediately emphasizing the unacceptability of torture. Hunt shows that even for Cesare Beccaria the notion of rights was marginal; it was his French translator who interfered with his text, moving a passage from another chapter into the introduction that was not there in the original.[45] But the French edition formed the basis for subsequent translations and even new Italian editions. Hunt's point is that through a virtually imperceptible process, certain perceptual blinkers were removed by enhanced empathy and increased sensitivity to the capacity for suffering of the other's body, including the body of the criminal. It is only consistent that she refers to a shift in self-evidence. The human rights declarations declare something, while at the same time claiming that it is self-evident. In Hunt's view such a shift in self-evidence is not the result of intellectual or legal influences. Its roots lie in a deeper cultural transformation.

As she views the expansion in empathy for others as the key transformation, she believes that the development of art played a significant role, particularly the epistolary novel in the age of sentimentalism, but also portraiture. From this perspective, empathy for the suffering of imaginary others releases a potential that is articulated legally in human rights universalism. This is an original and fruitful approach. But does this approach really follow from Durkheim's thesis, which Hunt convincingly applies to public executions in the ancien régime and to the execution of King Louis XVI in the Revolution?[46] How does the hypothesis of the expansion of empathy differ from that of the progressive sacralization of the person? The dimension of sacralization seems to me more fundamental than that of empathy, as the latter is not simply a capacity—if it has in fact been developed—that is brought to bear independent of its motivation and object. Those unwilling to empathize do not allow their capacity for empathy, which they may well possess, to come into operation. In thrall to ideologies, people capable of empathy often dehumanize whole categories of their fellow human beings, thus excluding them categorically as objects of their sensitivity. Only the motivation for empathy, or at the very least an open-minded attitude, can prompt us to make the effort to understand, but we must always make this effort anew. So the de facto efficacy of empathy requires a personal motivation fueled by substantive values. The sacralization of the person motivates us to show empathy; empathy alone does not engender the sacralization of the person, of all persons.[47]

THREATS

However, the reader should not come away with the impression that the sacralization of the person is the only form of sacralization occurring in modernity, or that it refers to a sort of linear advance, an ever-deeper and more universal understanding and protection of human dignity. Such uninterrupted advance is obstructed by countervailing forces, and the sacralization of the person constantly competes with other forms of sacralization, such as that of the nation or classless society. The most unambiguous countervailing forces in the twentieth century are of course fascism and National Socialism. In the context of the Dreyfus affair, which divided France, we find not only Émile Durkheim's ideas on human rights as the sacralization of the person, but also the French protofascist Charles Maurras, who declared that the cause of the nation was so important that individuals and their rights would simply have to be sacrificed. Italian Fascism and German National Socialism took this idea even further, inspiring slogans such as "You are nothing, your *Volk* is everything." Beyond radical anti-individualism and the mobilization of the nation in fascist ideology, the strategic meaning of racist ideology consisted precisely in declaring whole categories of human beings worthless and their elimination permissible or even morally imperative.

But it is not just that opposition to the advancing sacralization of the person hinders progress; the internal difficulties of punishment itself also give rise to abuse. We cannot radically deemotionalize punishment and crime as envisaged by the utilitarians—as well as Foucault. Outrage remains the most reliable indicator of the violation of key values; if crime as conceived by criminal law constitutes such a violation, then passionate resistance is inevitable. The constitutional state translates this resistance into procedures, at least channeling the emotions involved. Because of this, however, crime and punishment also lend themselves to the construction of friend-foe schemas and thus to the integration of social formations through shared aggression toward the enemy within, which is what the criminal is declared to be. In his classic essay "The Psychology of Punitive Justice," published in 1917, the American philosopher and social psychologist George Herbert Mead observed that "while then the attitude of hostility, either against the transgressor of the laws or against the external enemy, gives to the group a sense of solidarity which most readily arouses like a burning flame and which consumes the differences of individual interests, the price paid for this solidarity of feelings is great and at times disastrous."[48] If it is to endure, this form of unity, the creation of a collective identity through the exclusion of enemies, requires a constant supply of new enemies, or an ongoing state of hostility.

This is exactly the point at which questions of criminal justice merge with the positing of relations of enmity. At the start of this chapter I highlighted the death penalty and torture as highly charged topics at present, the subject of particular dispute between Europe and the United States. Where should we locate them within this field of tension? They cannot always be derived from the contradictions inherent in the sacralization of the person. Attempts by American government lawyers to circumvent the ban on torture of terrorists or suspected terrorists, or to justify this circumvention, are not tragic trade-offs. A far better example of such trade-offs is the case of the Frankfurt police chief who threatened a kidnapper with torture in the belief that this was the only way to save the life of an abducted child. Winfried Brugger's comments on this case caused quite a stir; they too are rooted in the desire, for the sake of honesty, to take appropriate account in law of such moral dilemmas facing the police. Very different, however, are American memoranda that regard suspected terrorists as enemies of the state, denying them their rights under the Constitution and removing them from the ambit of international agreements protecting prisoners of war. This is the abuse of an emotionally charged situation, based on the collective sense of threat associated with alleged terrorism; the aim here is to empower the executive by relaxing or suspending legal safeguards and creating legal black holes. Germany too has recently been engaged in an analogous discussion on the need for a "criminal law for enemies" (*Feind-Strafrecht*). These developments can only be interpreted as running counter to the sacralization of the person, not as a sign of its internal contradictions.

To understand the persistence of the death penalty in the United States within this interpretive framework we must first grasp that—contrary to stereotypical ideas about the country—the struggle against the death penalty, as an expression of the sacralization of the person, has deep roots in American culture. Certain states, such as Michigan, were in fact among the first in the world to abolish the death penalty. The death penalty in the United States has a clear regional focus in the South. It is there that racist divisions, a tradition of violence, and a conception of Christianity as a nonuniversalistic, nationalistic civil religion have fused to the point where the death penalty is justified with quotes from the Bible. Just as Mead perceived, in the South and throughout the country terrible crimes may be used to whip up public sentiment, to down political opponents, and camouflage political objectives—as most famously seen in the senior George Bush's election campaign against Michael Dukakis. This is the collision of two different cultures within the United States itself: the sacralization of the person and the civil religion of the South.

Not even in the core regions of the West, then, has the sacralization of the person been firmly cemented. So we can in no way assume that the associated culture of punishment will be universalized through any kind of automatic process. It is not just because they take ancient legal texts literally that contemporary Islamic fundamentalists declare the imposition of cruel punishments central to their identity, a symbol of resistance to the secularist decadence apparently emanating from the West, but precisely because the West or modernizing forces take such umbrage at these punishments. Even multicultural and hypermodern Singapore not only privileges constructs such as "Asian values"—which can only be understood as an attempt to highlight a contrastive identity—but demonstratively imposes corporal punishment as a supposedly authentic expression of this otherness. The situation in China is different again. It is in fact the most appropriate target for the contemporary critique of arbitrary executions and the habitual use of torture. Here it is the continued existence of a "communist" political structure and culture of punishment—"rule by law" instead of "rule of law"—that results in these excesses, prevents those affected from defending themselves, and thwarts all opposition to them. The hopes of the Enlightenment philosophers, as well as those of Émile Durkheim, revolved around the civilizing consequences of economic modernization: increasing prosperity and education. Durkheim already knew that the democratic control of power was an additional prerequisite. Now that the twentieth century is over, it is clear to us that the sacralization of the person remains always and everywhere at risk. With unprecedented clarity, and no certainty about the outcome, the Chinese case illustrates the tension between economic modernization and its demands, such as legal certainty, and the value system of universal human dignity.

By interpreting the cultural changes of the eighteenth century as a manifestation of "inclusion" in the sense of the sacralization of the person we can account not only for the transformation in the culture of punishment but also many other aspects of moral change. The term "monster," which we are accustomed to using to describe particularly despicable criminals, was used for so-called freaks—seriously disabled infants—as late as the eighteenth century. Such forgotten aspects of history as the overcoming of the idea that these children were intermediate forms between human and animal, or the abolition of castration as a means of attaining a certain vocal pitch in the eighteenth century, now begin to make sense. The picture that emerges is not one of disciplining but neither is it a process of enlightenment in the utilitarian sense. The rise of human rights is part of this picture. One generation later, the idea of human rights became the demand for the abolition of slavery—another radical movement for inclusion. The conceptual frameworks of Enlightenment or social disciplining have been applied to the history of the antislavery movement, with as little success as in the case of the history of punishment. The crucial role in this movement was in fact played by the originally Christian impulse toward moral decentering. This means viewing the world not just from the perspective of those with whom we are linked by self-evident affective bonds, but from the perspective of the "least of my brothers." In addition, the expansion of trade relations enabled morally decentered actors to causally relate the sweeping moral repugnance felt toward wrongs done in other parts of the world to their own moral actions, making it seem realistic and morally imperative to take responsibility for righting these wrongs.

The sacralization of the person carried forward Judeo-Christian motifs, even if some Enlightenment philosophers emphasized the rupture with religious tradition, prompting the churches to oppose them. Durkheim was ambiguous here. On the one hand he stressed that in ancient times the laws of the Jews were much milder than those of their neighbors. He put this down to the quasi-democratic character of ancient Judaism. He also underlined that the medieval

Church always had a mitigating impact on penal practice. But for him this meant that religious tradition must now be both continued and overcome. For Durkheim, the sacralization of the person is rooted in religious traditions, but also renders them superfluous.

Again, the question that arises is whether this perspective can provide a foundation for the categorical protection of the person. The concept of "sacredness" asserts the dignity of the person as the core of the modern culture of punishment. The role of utilitarian considerations is rejected as the basis of law as it so rarely conforms with people's attitudes toward the law. At present the sacralization of the person has the potential to span the globe but faces a number of threats. In this context it would be disastrous if we in the West were to embrace interpretive models that distort and misconstrue the meaning of the progress made in the culture of punishment (models such as a simplified utilitarian version of the Enlightenment or the ideas of Foucault). Only a keen awareness of the historical underpinnings of the European culture of punishment can ensure that people remain committed to it despite the forces ranged against it.

NOTES

1. This chapter is based partly on Joas, "Punishment and Respect."

2. In the following discussion of Beccaria I make use of two different editions of Beccaria's work. My main source is *Über Verbrechen und Strafen* (a German translation of the 1776 edition with a foreword by Wilhelm Alff). Unless otherwise indicated quotations in the main text are from the 1995 English edition, *On Crimes and Punishments*; page references are given in the main text.

3. Verri, in Beccaria, *Über Verbrechen und Strafen*, 181; my italics.

4. An account of this process that fits very well with my argument can be found in Hunt, *Inventing Human Rights*, 70–112.

5. Quoted in Schmoeckel, *Humanität und Staatsraison*, 19. This book is a methodologically impressive attempt to provide a thorough analysis of this particular event in terms of its causes, effects, and parallels. It is not a heroic epic. Schmoeckel also provides an in-depth examination of the development of penal law and its internal problems, which I pass over here. He was preceded by a number of English-language authors, above all Langbein, *Torture and the Law of Proof.*

6. Schmoeckel, *Humanität und Staatsraison*, 19–49.

7. Ibid., 89–164.

8. Ibid., 178, and Langbein, *Torture and the Law of Proof*, 63. Langbein (11) goes so far as to ironize the hypothesis of Enlightenment influences as a "fairy tale."

9. Schmoeckel, *Humanität und Staatsraison*, 79. There is a wonderful reference here (480) to executioners in Paris in 1781 complaining about an epidemic of *sensibilité*.

10. Page references in the main text are taken from the 1977 London edition.

11. Representative of many is Léonard, "L'historien et le philosophe." I owe numerous bibliographical references to Foucault's reception in the humanities to Martin Saar. The most detailed overview of historical criticisms is provided by Garland, *Punishment and Modern Society*, esp. 157–76.

12. For an excellent discussion in social theory terms, see Honneth, *Critique of Power*, 176–202. I do not examine whether Foucault's later work represents a revision of his early writings. To my knowledge Foucault never provided a self-critical account of his history of criminal justice.

13. Gauchet, "À la recherche."

14. Donzelot, "Mißgeschicke der Theorie," 148.

15. Building on Durkheim by way of Jeffrey Alexander, Philip Smith has elaborated an alternative to Foucault of far greater breadth than I am able to set out here, with respect to both the history of criminal justice and that of military discipline: Smith, *Punishment and Culture* and "Meaning and Military Power."

16. Durkheim, "Individualism and the Intellectuals," 62. See Joas, "Human Dignity." I draw here on some of the ideas presented in this text. Of the secondary literature on this idea of Durkheim's, the following are particularly valuable: Bellah, "Introduction"; Marske, "Durkheim's 'Cult of the Individual'"; Tole, "Durkheim on Religion"; Thomas, *Implizite Religion*, esp. 168–83.

17. On the circumstances in which Durkheim's text was written, the most detailed account is chapter 11 in the thorough biography by Fournier, *Émile Durkheim*, 365–90. Pierre Birnbaum's writings demonstrate that however universalist Durkheim's arguments may have been, he also articulated a specifically Jewish dismay. To a Jew intent on assimilation, the Dreyfus affair came as a biographically significant shock. See Birnbaum, *Geography of Hope*, 83–122 (the chapter is strikingly titled: "Émile David Durkheim: The Memory of Massada"). From Durkheim himself, see "Anti-Semitism and Social Crisis."

18. Durkheim, "Individualism and the Intellectuals," 61.

19. Ibid., 59, 60. (Subsequent quotations from this essay are indicated by page numbers in the main text.)

20. Kant, *Groundwork of the Metaphysics of Morals*, 42.

21. Ibid., 43.

22. I have more to say about the concept of the person in chapter 5. On the terminology used by Durkheim and his philosophical teacher Charles Renouvier, who published a book titled *Le personnalisme* in 1903, see Filloux, "Personne et sacré chez Durkheim."

23. Where, apart from Durkheim, can we find the concept of the "sacredness of the person" in theology, sociology, or religious history? I have not carried out in-depth research in conceptual history, but the most explicit reference to the "sacredness of the person" I have found is in the work of American Congregationalist theologian Henry Churchill King (1858–1934). The notion of the moral personhood and above all the idea of Christ as a personal revelation of God (and not therefore in the sense of participating in a divine substance) were central to his thinking. But he also explicitly claimed that we may regard a growing understanding of the value and sacredness of the person as "the most notable moral characteristic of our time"; to illustrate, he referred above all to the growing insight into the rights of the child, which even parents may not violate. See King, *Theology and the Social Consciousness*, esp. 16–18 and 179–246. On King's theology and the influence of Hermann Lotze and Albrecht Ritschl on him, see Rohls, *Protestantische Theologie der Neuzeit*, 2:53. Marcel Mauss builds directly on Durkheim in his essay on the concept of the person in which he refers to the "sacred character of the human person" (Mauss, "Category of the Human Mind," 22). William James referred to the "well-known democratic respect for the sacredness of individuality" now and then and in connection with his idea of the inevitable perspectivity of knowledge (James, *Talks to Teachers on Psychology*, v). When English jurist Hersh Lauterpacht published a proposal for a human rights declaration in 1945 with the support of the American Jewish Congress, the preamble contained the phrase, "Whereas the *sanctity of human personality* and its right and duty to develop in Freedom to all attainable perfections must be protected by the *universal law of mankind* through international enactment, supervision and enforcement . . ."; Lauterpacht, *International Bill of the Rights of Man*, vii (quoted in Vögele, *Menschenwürde*, 218; italics in the original). The Anglican bishop of Chichester, George Bell, who played an important role in human rights debates, referred (1949) to the "sacredness of the human personality" (see Moyn, "Personalism," 103). Martin Luther King also talked of the sacredness of human personality (King, "Ethical Demands of Integration"). King's studies had brought him into contact with theological personalism through the writings of Edgar S. Brightman (see Branch, *Parting the Waters*, 90–91).

24. This is clearly acknowledged by Bruno Karsenti in his studies, building on Durkheim, as evident in the title of his book: *Société en personnes*; see also, e.g., 5.

25. Durkheim, *Division of Labour in Society*, 201–2.

26. For more detail on this, see the opening chapter of my book *Do We Need Religion?*

27. Durkheim, *Elementary Forms of Religious Life*, 240–69; *Evolution of Educational Thought*; *Professional Ethics and Civic Morals*.

28. "To define 'religion,' to say what it *is*, is not possible at the start of a presentation such as this. Definition can be attempted, if at all, only at the conclusion of the study." Weber, "Religious Groups," 399.

29. This is rightly emphasized by theologian Günter Thomas, whose excellent interpretation of Durkheim's theory of religion is yet to receive the attention it deserves: Thomas, *Implizite Religion*, 125–83, here 135.

30. Durkheim, *Elementary Forms of Religious Life*, 46.

31. Durkheim, "Sacré" (in Durkheim, *Textes*, 2:64).

32. For a brilliant discussion of the risk of such a false naturalistic-reductionist interpretation of Durkheim (that mainly considers the writings of Randall Collins), see Pettenkofer, "Protest als ritualgestützte Glückserfahrung."

33. See Durkheim, *Elementary Forms of Religious Life*, 209. On the links between James and Durkheim and the question of the interpretation of experience in Durkheim, see Pettenkofer, *Radikaler Protest*; Joas, "Sociology and the Sacred"; Joas, *Genesis of Values*, 54–68.

34. There are a number of very good accounts of the debate on the sacred that kicked off toward the end of the nineteenth century. There is disagreement over who exactly influenced whom and how and thus over who should be viewed as the prime mover. See Colpe, *Über das Heilige*; Colpe, *Diskussion um das "Heilige"*; Molendijk, "Notion of the Sacred." For an excellent, comprehensive account of the further development of the sacredness discourse in the Durkheim school and among scholars of religion in general, including the break with this discourse in the work of Lévi-Strauss and the antireligious motives of this break, see Tarot, *Le symbolique et le sacré*. This book is only available in French, but there is a concise summary of a number of aspects in English: Tarot, "Émile Durkheim and After."

35. A summary of criticisms can be found, for example, in Pickering, *Durkheim's Sociology of Religion*, 115–62. His thesis that Catholics and Jews find Durkheim's emphasis on the sacred plausible but Protestants do not is undermined by the major role played by Protestants (Nathan Söderblom, Rudolf Otto) in the discourse on the holy at the time. On Pickering, see Joas, "Review."

36. The two are constantly equated in the literature on human rights—whether affirmatively or critically. See, e.g., Perry, *Idea of Human Rights*, 13, and the related critique in Kohen, *In Defense of Human Rights*, 13–37. Conversely, for a helpful way out of the dead-end debates on abortion informed by a notion of the sacredness of human life that is shared by believers and nonbelievers, see Dworkin, *Life's Dominion*, esp. chap. 3 ("What Is Sacred?"), 68–101.

37. Habermas, *Theory of Communicative Action*, 2:77–112.

38. In their interpretations of Durkheim, Robert N. Bellah and Edward Tiryakian have always resisted the supposition of advancing rationality. See, e.g., Bellah, "Durkheim and Ritual"; Tiryakian, *For Durkheim*. (Tiryakian, on 89–114, also traces the interplay between Durkheim's sociology of religion and the historiography of the French Revolution, forming an interesting bridge between the first and second chapters of the present work.)

39. For a list of examples, see Thomas, *Implizite Religion*, 171–72, and Sellmann, *Religion und soziale Ordnung*, 307–22. Sellmann's remarks on my writings

(313–23) represent an astonishing extrapolation in the direction of the present book.

40. See Gephart, *Gesellschaftstheorie und Recht*, 413. Durkheim's self-revision, of course, tends to mitigate criticisms of his earlier ideas.

41. Durkheim, "Two Laws of Penal Evolution." A critical account of the state of research can be found in Reiner, "Crime, Law and Deviance," esp. 194–201; but above all Garland, *Punishment and Modern Society*, 23–82. On the comparison between Durkheim and Foucault, see also Ramp, "Durkheim and Foucault."

42. See Kalupner, "Vom Schutz der Ehre."

43. Durkheim, *Professional Ethics and Civic Morals*, 68. On Niklas Luhmann's attempts to link functional differentiation and the codification of subjective rights, an approach to building on Durkheim very different from my own, see Joas, *Do We Need Religion*? 140–41.

44. Hunt, *Inventing Human Rights* (on the abolition of torture, see esp. 70–112). See also the important essay by Hunt, "Paradoxical Origins of Human Rights."

45. Hunt, *Inventing Human Rights*, 102–3. For a similar approach, see also the early contribution by Laqueur, "Bodies, Details, and the Humanitarian Narrative."

46. Hunt, *Inventing Human Rights*, 92–112, and "Sacred and the French Revolution." Hunt, it seems to me, underestimates Durkheim when she imputes to him a lack of interest in the origins of sacredness (*Inventing Human Rights*, 27). Cf. my interpretation in Joas, *Genesis of Values*, esp. 57ff.

47. On the relationship between empathy and values, see Joas, "Morality in the Age of Contingency."

48. Mead, "Psychology of Punitive Justice," 592.

3
VIOLENCE AND HUMAN DIGNITY
How Experiences Become Rights

A commitment to values may stem from experiences that fill us with enthusiasm. When we have a sense of having clearly recognized what is good, we feel the urge to bestow this knowledge on others, to get them to rethink or change how they act; we also wish to translate our ardent belief into actions. But it is not just galvanizing experiences that give rise to value commitments. Experiences of powerlessness also shape us profoundly. When we come up against our limits and experience how little we can steer our fate or that of others, or when we become radically aware of the finitude of our existence through experiences of illness, disability, or the inevitability of death, this too transforms our relationship to ourselves, the world, and our values.[1]

In experiences of the holy—as Rudolf Otto has brought out with great lucidity—experiences of inspirational attraction are interwoven with those of distress and fear; in Otto's terms, the "fascinans" is entwined with the "tremendum."[2] The experience of violence may entail enthusiasm for the perpetrator while triggering feelings of powerlessness on the part of the victim. Here again, though, it is realistic to assume complex interleavings, with the perpetrator experiencing gnawing problems in integrating into his self-image the thrill of violence, and the victim struggling to avoid developing a bond with the perpetrator. We cannot bring order to the phenomenology of violence by applying purely moral categories. Accounts of enthusiastic value commitments paint a picture in which the opening of the symbolically drawn boundaries of the self seems voluntary and positive, and reintegration into everyday life via value commitments seems achievable. But broadening our perspective to include experiences of violence and powerlessness shows that the boundaries of the self may also be forced open "against our will"—as in rape; that there are destructive and self-destructive forms of personal boundary removal. If we experience this persistently it may alienate us from everyday life and make us "crazy." It is crucial to grasp that the experience of violence is a peculiar inversion of the value-constitutive enthusiastic experience. This helps us understand such important phenomena as our potential to develop a negative self-identity as we process our own acts of violence, and the potential of the innocent victim of violence, who ultimately escapes, to develop guilt feelings toward those who were not so fortunate ("survivor's guilt").

But I am concerned here not just with such parallels between very different types of experience, but with whether experiences of violence may themselves be transformed in such a way as to generate the energy needed for positive value commitments.[3] Applied to the history of human rights and the value of universal human dignity, we must pose this question in a dual sense. What role has the experience of violence played in the history of human rights? How is it ever possible to transform experiences of violence into value commitments, indeed, universalist ones?

In answering these questions, my approach is first to look for any signs that key human rights-related texts have managed to process the history of violence. In a second step, I then reverse perspective to examine how comprehensively the history of violence has entered into human rights discourse. The result of this second step is basically negative: human rights discourse has been undeniably selective. So the next question will be how we can do theoretical justice to those experiences of violence that have been far from adequately articulated and largely excluded from this discourse. Here, in a third step, we may draw fruitfully on the concept of trauma. I briefly introduce this concept and explain its potential before highlighting the problems associated with the common conception of "cultural trauma." In the fourth stage, with reference to an exemplary human rights movement, I systematize some of the preconditions for the successful transformation of experiences of violence into a universalist commitment to values. Finally, I set out the moral philosophical import of these reflections.

HUMAN RIGHTS AND THE HISTORY OF VIOLENCE

If we seek to determine the role of experiences of violence in the history of human rights in light of the existing codifying texts, the importance of the history of violence quickly emerges. Protestant theologian Wolfgang Vögele has provided a detailed account of the prehistory of the human dignity clause at the beginning of the German constitution.[4] The concept of human dignity appears both in the principles of the Kreisau circle (*Kreisauer Kreis*) for the reorganization of Germany and in early postwar texts of Social Democratic and Christian Democratic provenance, as a basic guide to a future constitution. Plainly apparent in these cases is opposition to the crimes of National Socialism; but there is no evidence of a direct impact on the constitution. In the German *Land* constitutions adopted before 1949, there are unmistakable references to the defeated Nazi tyranny. I mention two of them here. This from the preamble to the Bavarian constitution of 1946: "Mindful of the physical devastation which the survivors of the Second World War were led into by a godless state and social order lacking in all conscience or respect for human dignity . . ." The preamble to the Bremen constitution of 1947 is particularly striking: "Appalled by the annihilation caused in the ancient Free Hanseatic City of Bremen by the authoritarian regime of the National Socialists, with its contempt for personal liberty and human dignity, the citizens of this *Land* agree to create a system of social life in which social justice, humanity, and peace are nurtured, in which the economically weak are protected from exploitation and all those willing to work are assured a life of human dignity."[5]

These documents make direct reference to "barbarism" and "annihilation," though in words whose value judgment is clearer than their empirical object. Far more common in this period are indirect references, in the form, for example, of the sudden and brief renaissance of natural law conceptions, as these were perceived as the only alternative to a nihilistic relativism. Evidence of this can be found in the pastoral letters of Catholic bishops from this period, which had a substantial political impact.

This grounding in natural law was subject to dispute in the deliberations of the delegates sent by the minister-presidents in Herrenchiemsee, and even more so in the plenum and committees of the Parliamentary Council. But there was agreement that the protection of human dignity should have a prominent place in the constitution. All those involved were utterly determined to proclaim the status of such basic rights as antecedent to the state. They wanted to respond to the National Socialist experience, and to do so in such a way that consent was not dependent on consenting to a particular philosophical or religious conviction. In the subsequent history of West Germany, the philosophy of Kant came to play a central role in the understanding of the postulate of human dignity found in the constitution; but it played a vanishingly minor role in these deliberations. There is no dispute over the unifying reference to experiences of violence and injustice. What is contested is the extent to which these experiences impacted on the deliberations, directly or via the strengthening of natural law perspectives.

Of course, these deliberations were not a purely German affair. Work on the future constitution took place under the eyes of the victorious powers of the Second World War, in this case the Western Allies. While this is obvious, it is important to mention that a preliminary draft of the Universal Declaration of Human Rights also influenced the deliberations: following its publication in a German newspaper, copies were handed out among the participants by a delegate of the Social Democratic Party (SPD).[6]

In any case, what matters more here than German history are international developments. The most important document in the recent history of human rights is undoubtedly the Universal Declaration of Human Rights, proclaimed by the UN on December 10, 1948. The preamble to the Charter of the United Nations from 1945 explicitly related its founding to a determination to "save succeeding generations from the scourge of war." The Declaration of Human Rights itself explains the commitment to human dignity with reference to the fact that "disregard and contempt for human rights have resulted in barbarous acts."[7] This was an attempt to make a connection with the battle against National Socialism. A number of authors have examined the genesis of this declaration in great detail in recent years. Johannes Morsink has examined every article of the declaration, scrutinizing how the debates held in the committees that produced the declaration related to the experience of the Nazi dictatorship, the war, and the Holocaust.[8] He describes the experience of the war begun by Nazi Germany as the "epistemic foundation" of the declaration, which enabled agreement among participants whose religious and ideological views differed greatly, giving them the confidence and sense of certainty so vital to the declaration. Alongside National Socialism, fascism is also occasionally mentioned in the texts in this sense of a "negative" foundation for human rights. The paradoxical expression "epistemic foundation" is very well chosen: here the very lack of a shared foundation in the philosophical sense itself served as a foundation.

I would like to briefly present some of the detail of how the horror of Nazi crimes was processed in the wording of the declaration. The emphasis on the unity of the human race in Article 1 is consciously intended to counter the destruction of universalism in racial theories. The emphasis on the "right to life" in Article 3 was just as consciously inspired by the Nazi "euthanasia" of the disabled. Article 4 opposes slavery and "servitude" in part as a means of denouncing the forced labor among the citizens of conquered countries of the kind that occurred during the Second World War in Germany. Article 5 not only declares a ban on torture, but also "cruel, inhuman, or degrading treatment or punishment" in order to preclude crimes such as the medical experiments carried out by National Socialist doctors on death-camp inmates and disabled people. The declaration of the right to asylum in Article 14 ("Everyone has the right to seek and to enjoy in other countries asylum from persecution") can be traced back directly to the mass expatriations of the Third Reich. The wording was, however, weaker than initially planned. The original formulation, "the right to seek and be granted asylum," was toned down at the behest of the Arab states, which felt that an obligation to grant asylum to the half a million Palestinians displaced as a result of the founding of the state of Israel was supportive of Israeli policies of expulsion—a truly tragic link with National Socialism. Article 21 declares the right to political participation. This was aimed directly at the fascist doctrine that the true will of the people should be embodied in a leader with unchecked power. Again, though, this was toned down by deletion of a reference to secret elections, as this seemed infeasible to Great Britain in view of its colonies. Article 30 provides the beginnings of an "internationalist" interpretation of human rights that makes the international community collectively responsible for policies and envisages a legal system consonant with human rights in individual states. This is bound up with the fact that the struggle against National Socialism in Germany before the war was by no means regarded as the responsibility of other states.

THE SELECTIVITY OF THE HUMAN RIGHTS DISCOURSE

So if we look back over the history of violence in light of this Declaration of Human Rights and German constitutional texts, the picture seems unambiguous. But we cannot simply reverse perspective here. Even if it is true that positive values may be distilled from negative experiences, it would be quite false to suggest that wrong always gives rise to right, that violence always leads to progress. On the contrary, "according to the inescapable pragmatism of all action," as Max Weber wrote in the famous "Intermediate Reflections," ". . . force and the threat of force unavoidably breed more force."[9] Suffering alone does not give rise to values. If injustice, bondage, and violence are not to engender hopelessness and despair, or cyclical spirals of violence from which it seems impossible to escape, the other vital component is the energy to transform the experience of suffering into orientational values. While the crimes of National Socialism played an important role in the history of human rights, we should bear in mind that these crimes are not the only case of mass slaughter in the twentieth century. In recent years historian Mark Mazower has highlighted the fact that it is by no means self-evident that we should view the Nazi model, and thus the central role of state violence and modern mass violence, as paradigmatic of every case of collective violence in the twentieth century.[10] For obvious reasons, the crimes of Stalinism—the "Gulag," as the common abbreviated formula would have it—had not been properly processed when the UN Declaration of Human Rights was composed. Certain aspects of Stalinism may no doubt be viewed as analogous to the crimes of National Socialism, with the theory of totalitarianism, for example, providing a bridge here. But the question is whether this theory really helps explain the Stalinist regime's propensity for violence in all its facets.

Ethnic categories became increasingly important during the first few decades of Soviet history.[11] All the peoples that straddled the Soviet border were soon being eyed with suspicion. Sometimes severing links made no difference and attempts to destabilize neighboring countries failed; this inspired visions of resettlement, initially focused on activists and elites. In the context of the Second World War, entire ethnic groups suspected of tenuous loyalty to the Soviet system, such as Chechens and Crimean Tatars, as well as *Volksdeutsche*, or ethnic

Germans, were resettled in Central Asia; though Kurds and Iranians had in fact already suffered a similar fate before the war. There was clearly an ethnic component to the mass extermination of Cossacks and the planned starvation of millions of Ukrainians in the wake of the forced collectivization of agriculture, as well as the crushing of opposition to atheism campaigns in Islamic areas of the vast empire. In the case of the Poles and Balts, the Soviet approach was to exterminate the national elites. Analogous plans had already been made for Finland. We can no longer evade the question of how the text of the declaration would have looked had the crimes of Stalinism been fully considered by the delegates.

Dispensing with a Eurocentric perspective and including the history of colonialism and imperialism changes the picture again. Often it was not the state that was responsible for displacing people and annihilating tribes or peoples. "In areas such as Australia, Russia, Africa, and the Americas, violence against natives was perpetrated by mostly European colonists, sometimes backed from afar by the metropolitan power but often the result of local initiatives in these frontier societies, motivated by the colonists' desire to control land, water, and other resources."[12] And this—see Brazil and Israel/Palestine—is by no means just a phenomenon of the distant past. Hannah Arendt claimed there were connections between colonialism and the Nazi policies of settlement and extermination in Central and Eastern Europe. This is probably not true in any causal sense, but the parallels between the two cases are obvious.[13] Others, like Jörg Baberowski, have brought out the continuities between Stalinism and czarist policies of colonization and Russification in the Caucasus and Central Asia.[14] It is vital to get to grips with these connections, along with the violence perpetrated by the colonial powers themselves during the colonial period. Examples of such violence include the struggle to end colonial rule in Algeria and Indonesia, as well as the civil wars, expulsions, and brutal regimes that came after colonial rule. I mention all of this here because interpreting mass violence mainly in terms of state action is problematic, but above all because it is important to grasp that in many of these cases people have yet to come to terms with the past. In many respects, this process has only just begun.[15] We don't know how this process will change the discourse of human rights, but we must not attempt to insulate this discourse from such change.

CULTURAL TRAUMA?

This, however, compels us to turn to the consequences of the history of violence if such a process of coming to terms has not or not yet occurred; we might also ask whether, given the scale of these crimes and the suffering they have caused, the notion of "coming to terms" is really appropriate. Even if the experience of violence is transformed into universalist value commitments, as in the case of human rights, this certainly does not mean that those involved have found solace, or that violent events have been retrospectively endowed with meaning. This would be to relapse into teleological philosophies of history. To get to grips with these two issues—the long-term consequences of violent experiences and the tension between this experience and every attempt to articulate it—we require a new approach. One term has taken hold over the last few decades to the point where it has become a fashionable term in the contemporary human sciences. This is the term "trauma." My next step will be to present some thoughts on how this term and the associated concept may be of help in illuminating these issues—and where its limits lie.

What is a trauma? Since the term comes from medical psychiatry, it makes sense to look for a definition in the relevant textbooks. Patricia Resick's handbook on the foundations of psychotraumatology provides a definition according to which a person has been confronted with a traumatic event if two criteria apply: "1. The person experienced, witnessed, or was confronted with an event or events that involved actual or threatened death or serious injury, or a threat to the physical integrity of self or others. 2. The person's response involved intense fear, helplessness, or horror. Note: in children, this may be expressed instead by disorganized or agitated behavior."[16] The official definition provided by the American Psychiatric Association is very similar. Comprehensive attempts have now been made to trace the history of the concept.[17] It initially referred to physical injuries such as the intrusion of a foreign body, but Sigmund Freud and others applied it to psychological processes. In an approach that was central to the development of psychoanalytic theory, Freud vacillated between viewing psychological and physical injury as literally parallel processes and interpreting psychological injury, such as supposed sexual seduction during childhood, as the result of mere fantasy; this is a theme that has pervaded the psychoanalytic literature and critiques of psychoanalysis ever since. It was without doubt the twentieth-century history of violence that refocused attention, including Freud's, on the importance of real experiences of violence as traumatizing events. This refocusing occurred first during the debates on "war neurasthenia," "trench neurosis," and "shell shock" during the First World War and then with greater intensity in the wake of the Vietnam War, which led to the definition of "posttraumatic stress disorder." It is also evident in the literature on the consequences of the Holocaust for its victims and their descendants.[18]

Here, initially with reference to a literary example, I explain the potential of the trauma concept for understanding the dynamics of value genesis. The most impressive work in this respect is a novel by Alfred Döblin entitled *Tales of a Long Night*.[19] The story centers on a Second World War British soldier who has returned home from the front. During a kamikaze attack on his transport ship he is seriously injured, losing a leg. As a result of this experience, a traumatic one according to the above definition, he descends, as the title says, into the "long night" of utter alienation from his former life. Efforts to rehabilitate him in a clinic through psychotherapeutic means having failed, his mother decides to take care of him herself in an attempt to free him from his deathly torpor. It soon becomes apparent, however, that her son needs more than care and more than motherly love; as soon as he is in a fit state to engage in conversation, he is driven by a "passion for questioning." He must find out who is to blame not just for his mutilation, but also for all the other victims, who may themselves no longer be in a position to ask such questions. Who and what, he needs to know, is responsible for this war and the historical catastrophe that has dragged on since 1914? His mother cannot provide him with an answer, nor can his father. As a great and successful writer, he should have been predestined for this task, but his art has become a means of evading such questions of blame and meaning rather than shedding light on them. He is portrayed as a man who believes that "wars, seen in the light of world history, recur among human beings from time to time like the flu, typhus, scarlet fever, and that no cure had yet been found for them."[20] Nonetheless, his father has an idea that begins to change things; it sets in motion both his son's healing process, which is full of surprises, and the complex mechanics of the novel itself, which is rather like a series of novellas. His father knows that discussion is not the correct medium when we are dealing with questions of meaning. What we need are narratives. So he suggests that they "tell stories and let each listener draw his or her own conclusions from them."[21] Story evenings are organized at which family members and friends tell all kinds of stories, old and new, familiar and unfamiliar. Edward, the son, attends these evenings. He is initially silent and withdrawn, as he has generally been since his shocking experience. An oppressive, threatening presence for those around him, a "ticking time bomb," he begins to react to certain passages of the narrated stories; increasingly, he becomes a participant. The stories are entirely independent on a formal level, but Döblin skilfully structures them in such a way that they touch upon the son's experiences and his profound search for meaning. Yet the book is by no means a linear progression culminating in Edward's healing. The story evenings also provide the narrators with numerous opportunities to reinterpret their relationships with the other participants through the medium of their stories. This applies above all to the parents. As Edward begins to come alive again, cracks begin to show in his parents' marriage. The path toward truth that must be trodden for the sake of Edward's healing is a hazardous one for a marriage that had long since become a relationship of covert animosity and mutual concealment; Edward had earlier gone off to war to escape the loveless atmosphere. The original German title of the novel, *Hamlet; or, The Long Night Comes to an End*, alludes to the fact that here, as in Shakespeare's play, a son uncovers old guilt within the family, as well as something rotten in the state of Denmark; only in this way can the long night of lies with its many ghosts come to an end. This ending does not, however, bring healing, but a new process of breakdown. This relates first of all to the family. The father, infuriated by his wife's insinuations, becomes violent toward her and flees the house, as does she. Then comes Edward's breakdown as he begins to understand how destructive his clear-sightedness and insistence on truth is bound to be in a world that tries to immunize its meaning against the history of violence by rejecting any sense of responsibility.

I leave to one side the further progress of the parents, who now experience for real things with which they had merely toyed in their stories. Faced with death, they are ultimately reconciled. Edward is finally free to start a new life. But Döblin was of two minds about how Edward should use his freedom. Should he embrace life by pursuing social reforms or turn away from the world by entering a monastery?

It is unclear whether the deletion of the latter ending from the published version was a matter of adapting to the circumstances of the book's first publication in the German Democratic Republic or a case of balking at an ending that was bound to seem paradoxical to nonreligious readers.

This tremendously vivid novel contains all the elements that my reflections here try to convey in a more abstract scientific language: the shock of the experience of violence itself, which intrudes into the sacred sphere of the body; the trauma that results from this unsettling of fundamental certainties inherent in our relationship with the world; the impossibility of overcoming trauma by any means except narration; the necessary connection between narration and the constitution of new meaning and new values; the shattering impact of the constitution of new values and meaning on the prevailing social context; the inevitability of extending questions of political meaning into the existential and religious realm.

So there can be no doubt about the potential of the trauma concept to illuminate the questions of interest to us here. But when we examine the relevant literature it rapidly becomes clear that it may be used in an excessive, highly problematic way. Here questions are concealed rather than answered. Under the influence of poststructuralist literary theory, specific features of the experience of violence are equated with the "supposedly traumatic components of all human communication."[22]

Meanwhile, the concept of "cultural trauma," as expounded mainly by the cultural sociologists around Jeffrey Alexander at Yale University, applies the concept of trauma not only to collectivities, which is quite plausible, but also to whole cultures, thus "subjectivizing" it. Here the term is defined as follows: "Cultural trauma occurs when members of a collectivity feel they have been subjected to a horrendous event that leaves indelible marks upon their group consciousness, marking their memories forever and changing their future identity in fundamental and irrevocable ways."[23] How does this definition differ from the usual definitions of trauma in psychological-psychiatric textbooks? Certainly not in its reference to "horrendous events" or "indelible marks," to the molding of memory and identity irreversibly and for all time. All of this also forms part of the psychological definition of trauma. It does add a reference to collectivities, in contrast to the psychological definition, which is mostly geared toward individuals. But this should be unproblematic: it is often not just individuals but groups of people that suffer trauma as a result of terrible events. We would have to classify all of them as traumatized; their social cohesion may be so irreversibly damaged that the collective processing of these terrible events becomes essential. But it is not this reference to the collective dimension that is the key innovation, but the reference to cultures and the associated "subjectification" of the trauma concept, which may quite easily be overlooked: "when members of a collectivity *feel* they have been subjected to a horrendous event" (my emphasis). Is it possible to extend the trauma concept to cultures? Are there "cultural" traumas? Is the presence of a trauma dependent on those affected defining it as such?

It is no secret which specific historical realities have inspired the culturalist version of the trauma concept. The more time passes, the more (not less) the Holocaust is viewed as a massive trauma for Jews (as victims), but also for Germans and others (as perpetrators) and indeed for the whole of humanity. The more time passes, the more (not less) the enslavement of Africans transported to North America is defined as a trauma for African Americans and US society as a whole. In this respect, Alexander's definition is based on social facts. It is rooted in sympathy for the victims of slavery and the Holocaust and guided by an interest in the cultural preconditions for the expansion of moral universalism. But is this a viable approach in conceptual and theoretical terms? Or does it lead us astray, squandering the potential value to historical sociology of psychological trauma research?

The controversial point is not whether statements about traumatization are social constructions or not, but whether these constructions point toward something that has unique qualities of its own that may make themselves felt irrepressibly in the process of construction; in other words, whether the traumas themselves are "mere" constructs. The key question we need to answer is whether traumas are typified by a certain nonassimilability, making it extremely difficult for an individual to incorporate them into the interpretive framework available to her. If so, should we ascribe to this nonassimilability the status of objective reality?

One could express the controversy in the following slightly simplified terms: The question is whether we can ascribe to the nonassimilability of the traumatic experience the status of an objective fact that, as such, is independent of the dynamics of the cultural interpretive event.

To prevent misunderstandings, I shall clarify what I do *not* mean by trauma as an objective fact. First, I do not mean an ignorance of the psychological and cultural context of experience. Depending on their mental prehistory and disposition, different people may certainly experience the same event very differently, and different cultures undoubtedly provide differing means of interpreting events. But just as George Herbert Mead referred to the objective reality of subjective perspectives, I would refer to the objective fact of this individually specific subjective experience.[24] This experience is not itself a construct. But what we say about it certainly is, and this discourse in turn tends to influence how we interpret experiences and perhaps even our experience itself. This influence itself is an objective fact, about which we may construct true and untrue statements.

Second, my insistence on the objective fact of trauma does not mean that I dispute that experience may consist in the mere imagining of an event. As Chicago sociologist William Isaac Thomas famously put it, if people define situations as real, they are real in their consequences. So the idea of an event is an objective fact, even if the content of the idea clashes with the facts. Actors may experience their own impulses as threatening and these may therefore have a traumatizing effect. But the fact at issue in such cases is the *idea* of, for example, committing murder or abusing a child.

Third, it is certainly true that it is not only events that we have experienced personally that may traumatize us. But caution is advisable here. We identify with key reference individuals to such an extent that their experience may become our own. Our fear for the life of a loved one may become our own experience of mortal terror. Yet we may also have a straightforward, emotionally neutral knowledge of the dismay of those close to us or of our forebears. We are no doubt called upon to engage with their distress in such cases, but in this second case I think a concept other than that of trauma would be more appropriate.

Fourth, my emphasis on the objectivity of the traumatic experience does not mean that I wish to disregard the associated social dynamics, including the power-saturated nature of the interpretive event. It would be wrong to conceive of interpretations as simply emanating from experiences, and Alexander is quite right to apply to the interpretation of traumatic experience the arsenal of sociological approaches to the "social construction of everything."

Fifth and finally, it is beyond dispute that, as a scientific concept, "trauma" is neither timeless, nor has it even been around for very long. It is surely apposite to reflect on its history. Again, though, I fail to see why this should be an argument against the concept's reference to facts, which as such precede, and are independent of, their conceptual apprehension.

If it makes sense to preclude these potential misunderstandings, it should be clear that sociology too, however much it may acknowledge the realm of social constructions, has found no way around the question of what "actually" happened, who was "really" affected by an event, and so on. So it is quite impossible to merely reconstruct social constructions as often propagated and practiced these days in the form of "discourse analysis." Let's take as an example remembrance of the Vietnam War and its traumatic consequences. It is certainly worthwhile to reconstruct sociologically the history of social struggles over how the war is remembered. But how exactly do we deal with the fact that the trauma of the Vietnamese people receives practically no attention within the American memory? Is their suffering not trauma because it is not constructed as such? Or is this a disturbing indication that people rarely feel moved to incorporate others' suffering into their own construction of history? The impressive Vietnam War Memorial in Washington, DC, individualizes the suffering of the many by listing the names of all the more than 50,000 Americans killed in Vietnam. This monument would surely do far more to warn against the dangers of unjust wars, and for reconciliation, if it also listed the names of the 3 million Vietnamese killed in the war. But where would the motivation for this come from other than from viewing the suffering of Vietnamese survivors as something unarticulated and crying out for articulation?

Of course, a simple solution presents itself. This is simply to conceive as two different objects psychological trauma, whether individual or collective, along with its consequences, and so-called cultural trauma and its construction. We would then think in terms of traumatization that is not defined as cultural trauma, and cultural traumas without psychological traumatization (at present). The terminology would be confusing, but we would surely have to accept the legitimacy of studying both these objects. Alexander, however, has blocked himself off from this simple solution. Many of his statements make it very clear that he wishes to restrict the term "traumatization" to so-called cultural traumatization and considers traumatization without a culturally pervasive definition a matter of naive objectivism. Cultural classification, he writes, for example, is "critical to the process by which a collectivity becomes traumatized." And: "'experiencing trauma' can be understood as a sociological process that defines a painful injury to the collectivity, establishes the victim, attributes responsibility, and distributes the ideal and material consequences."[25] These statements cross the line into relativist constructivism. I think it is quite legitimate for Alexander to ask why certain events (such as the Japanese atrocities in Nanking) have been absorbed into the cultural memory to a far lesser degree than others. This continues to apply to most of the horrors occurring in the non-Western world. It is also true that the explanation for this cannot lie in the "intrinsic nature of the original suffering," as assumed, Alexander tells us, in "lay trauma theory," though he fails to identify the exponents of this theory.[26] But while it would be naive to consider the scale of traumatization the only variable in explaining the genesis of a cultural definition of trauma, it is merely an inverse form of this naivety to focus solely on cultural processes of definition and thus divert attention away from the difficult-to-reconstruct consequences of a suffering that has gone unheard.

This problem becomes apparent in connection with a particularly sensitive topic, when Alexander comments critically on the work of American historian Peter Novick.[27] In Alexander's rendering, Novick's well known hypothesis is that "the Holocaust became central to contemporary history because it became central to America, that it became central to America because it became central to America's Jewish community, and that it became central to Jews because it became central to the ambitions of Jewish organizations who were central to the mass media in all its forms." Novick, it must be added, is extremely skeptical about attempts to explain the awareness of the Holocaust in the United States in light of the dynamics of trauma processing. For him the evidence simply does not suggest that the majority of American Jews—let alone non-Jewish Americans—have in any sense been traumatized by the Holocaust. While Alexander bases his empirical statements solely on historiographical studies (rather than original documents) and in this way also mines Novick's work for information, he strongly opposes Novick's interpretation. He describes his analysis as tendentious and sums up the difference between his own approach and that of Novick as follows: "To employ the categories of classical sociological theory, Novick might be described as offering an instrumentally oriented 'status group' explanation à la Weber, in contrast to the more culturally oriented late-Durkheim approach taken here."[28] But the problem with this is that we cannot give an empirical question a metatheoretical answer. Alexander of course has no wish to deny the role of power, interests, and status groups; he merely wishes to prevent reductionism. But this antireductionist impulse has no effect in the face of the empirical hypothesis that interests are the key explanatory variable in a particular case. When Alexander goes on to claim that Novick is demonstrating an (American-Jewish) particularization of the Holocaust, while he is concerned with the process of universalization, we might describe this as two different topics (rather than theories). Novick would not reject Alexander's questions. But he disputes that the specific dynamics of American Holocaust remembrance can be understood in terms of the internal logic of trauma processes. And this objection cannot be refuted by references either to Durkheim or to an interest in processes of universalization. The provisional summary must be that Alexander fails to distinguish clearly between the psychological and social consequences of trauma on the one hand and the social construction of a phenomenon of cultural memory called "trauma" on the other. His interest in the latter topic causes him to belittle and shun the former. As this remains conceptually unclear, his text becomes ensnared in contradictions.

At this highly sensitive point, I believe we would have to distinguish between the level of the cultural construction of "trauma" as an assertion within public debate and the level of human experience, which is characterized by the difficulty of achieving expression within the available interpretive schemas. If we make this distinction it becomes apparent that there are traumas that are not legitimized as such, or not legitimized in cultural terms, and that there exist cultural claims to the concept of trauma despite the absence of psychological traumas.

If we fail to make this distinction, we cannot unlock the potential that psychological research on trauma holds for a historical social science. Here, culturalism gets carried away with itself. It must be reined in by an "experientialism."

THE ANTISLAVERY MOVEMENT AS MODEL FOR MORAL MOBILIZATION

Such an experientialist approach does not assume that we can access experiences without a symbolic medium. So it does not signal a shift away from the "linguistic turn" but instead underlines the fact that there are impulses at work within processes of cultural innovation that change publicly established situational interpretations. This may involve attempts to articulate experiences that the subject feels are not adequately expressed by public interpretations. But it may also be that the potential of an already available interpretive system is mobilized afresh; this often entails taking more seriously perceptions that were already possible, and indeed existed previously, but whose explosive force was suppressed by prevailing interpretations.

The narrow "culturalist" perspective consists in presenting people as prisoners of the cultures to which they belong. On this view their action is the mere execution of cultural programs that they have internalized or that they constantly come up against in others' normatively fortified expectations; so in reality they have no behavioral choices. This restrictive view contrasts with an emphasis on human action. But by the same token we should not imagine that actors have no internalized values and could relate to cultural expectations in a distanced and calculating way. The only way forward here is a more complex model, one that avoids the poor choice between a rational model of action or a model of cultural programming. Only by factoring in the irreducible creativity of human action can we resolve this problem.[29]

If we take this approach, then it becomes apparent that what is referred to in excessively holistic terms as "culture" is certainly not to be found at one single place within the space of action, but several. Many prevailing cultural elements are embodied in practices performed on a daily basis without every individual considering them or their justification. But there are also explicit justificatory discourses that deal with what is good or bad. We refer to values when statements of opinion take the form of explicit affirmation or denial of assertions about the good or bad. It would be quite wrong and a fallacious view of the role of consciousness in action if we were to understand actors' orientation toward values as a conscious orientation toward such assertions. A great deal goes unthematized by consciousness; it is embodied in practices without being highlighted or reflected upon. So there are likely to be tensions between practices and values. Prevailing practices may be called into question with reference to declared values, just as values may be revised with reference to lived praxis. Further, if we assume that, alongside the praxis of everyday life and communication about values, there are also institutions, in the sense of an action expectation that is detached from individual actors and has become obligatory, we begin to see a field of tension that has three poles: values, institutions, and practices. Institutions such as law may also deviate from values and practices. These institutions may thus be criticized in light of these, while conversely institutions may demand that values and practices be justified.

This means that processes of cultural transformation always take place within such a field of tension. Each of the three poles mentioned above may be central to the dynamics of these processes. It would be unhistorical to begin by assuming that any one of the poles is more important than the others, not least because it is only in retrospect that we can discern just how tensions were ultimately resolved. Processes of cultural transformation never occur in a vacuum; they are influenced by interests and power relations. Any notion of societies as systems or structures, as texts or discursive entities, merely distracts from this irresolvable tension to which human action gives rise. Unexpected events interrupt the flow of action; novel experiences find articulation; what were formerly demands or lived praxis become mandatory in institutions. Cases of institutionalization remain contested. They may lose their motivational bases gradually or suddenly just as they may get a new lease on life. None of the elements of such a field of tension is inherently stable and secured once and for all.

I now give these cursory and abstract assertions a more concrete form with reference to an example that is central to my theme in this book, a social movement that was surely the most important human rights movement of the nineteenth century: abolitionism, the movement to abolish slavery.[30]

The first point that must be underlined is how few eighteenth-century exponents of Enlightenment thought, including those who articulated an evolved sensitivity to the suffering of all human beings, expressed moral outrage about the institution of slavery itself or subjected it to argumentative critique. There were a number of impressive intellectual critics among French Enlightenment thinkers, but they had little real impact prior to the French Revolution and even in the first few years after it. Nonetheless, in 1794 the National Assembly decided to declare slavery abolished in the French colonies, while doing nothing at all to ensure the emancipation of the slaves. The chaos sparked off in Haiti by the Revolution provided Napoleon with welcome grounds for declaring slavery lawful again in 1802.[31] The issue was never really central in the minds of the revolutionaries; representatives of the colonial slaveholders still influenced the decision-making process in the revolutionary republic.

It is perhaps even more remarkable how little attention was paid in the nascent United States of America to the tension between the human rights proclamations that accompanied the struggle for independence and the institution of slavery. In America too there had long been outspoken opponents of slavery, above all among religious movements such as the Quakers. Even before the Revolution slave owners were sometimes expelled from such religious communities.[32] In their polemics against the British king, the revolutionaries themselves also made reference to "enslavement" as a rhetorical topos, but without expressing opposition to all slavery. Many of the revolutionaries—including Thomas Jefferson, the lead author of the Declaration of Independence, which was so important to the history of human rights—were themselves slaveholders. Some were prepared to grant some or all of their slaves freedom after their death, which suggests a bad conscience; but this stirring was still a long way from a fundamental rejection of slavery as such. Opponents of the Revolution were quick to point to the revolutionaries' duplicity. Even many opponents of slavery believed that emancipation was possible only if the emancipated were "returned" to Africa; given how radically they had been uprooted and how long they had been in America, this can only be described as a euphemism for deportation. In sum, with respect to slavery, the impact of the American Revolution was clearly ambivalent. In the states of New England, with their small black population, slavery disappeared; in the North as a whole, emancipation was soon to occur; while in the West slavery was never to be introduced. Certainly, numerous antislavery publications appeared in the revolutionary period, and these at least influenced the cultural atmosphere even if they failed to achieve any great political breakthrough. The southern states, meanwhile, were increasingly determined to retain slavery. Manumissions sometimes reinforced prejudices against blacks, so that slavery was more entrenched in the South at the end of the revolutionary period than prior to it. Its ideological justifications became ever more sophisticated.

Strikingly, the origins of the vigorous antislavery movement lay not in one of the revolutionary states that produced human rights declarations, but in Great Britain. From the 1780s on, a mainly religiously inspired movement developed there, its initial goal the humane treatment of slaves, then the limitation and prohibition of the slave trade, and finally the abolition of slavery itself. Some of the impetus for this movement certainly came from American religious opposition to slavery, but the movement was embraced by broad swaths of the population far earlier in Great Britain than in the United States. The situation in America changed dramatically only from the early 1830s on. As had occurred previously in Great Britain, but more radically, in fact fanatically, leading activists such as William Lloyd Garrison declared anyone who defended or even just passively accepted slavery to be in the grip of sin.[33] They were no longer willing to be fobbed off with promises that slaves would be turned into responsible citizens through a gradual process of education. These abolitionists dedicated their lives to their goal, demanding nothing less than the immediate, unconditional, and uncompensated abolition of slavery.

There is no space here for a broad narrative history of this abolitionist movement in Great Britain and the United States. What we need to do is explain how the mass struggle for the human rights of slaves could advance so suddenly, albeit at different times in the two countries. As with the origins of human rights declarations, it would be misleading to look for an explanation within the realm of religion or a (supposedly) antireligious Enlightenment.[34] It is true that in this case the movement was mainly religiously inspired, but this is the beginning rather than the end of the explanation. The movement's sudden breakthrough cannot be explained as the effect of a religion that also existed elsewhere without triggering a breakthrough and that was even used to justify slavery. For the most part no such breakthroughs occurred outside of the Anglo-American world; where they did, they were quickly repulsed or occurred only much later.[35] So what set this advance in the sacralization of the person in motion?

Two obvious explanations can be ruled out straight away. Some are swayed by the idea that social movements can be traced back to a gradual maturing of value orientations. On this view, if the American Declaration of Independence and bills of rights had already proclaimed the equality of all human beings, then regardless of the revolutionaries' inconsistency or duplicity sooner or later this textually enshrined conception was bound to come to fruition. But this idea clashes with the fact that abolitionism as a mass movement began in Great Britain. There were certainly links between this movement and the American and French revolutions, but these were far more complex than implied by the idea of the implementation of declarations. The Americans' struggle for independence prompted soul-searching among British Protestants, who wondered whether their own failings had caused this development. The conflict with the French revolutionaries gave rise to a new British patriotism "that wished to see the superiority of the British nation not just in economic productivity and military might but also in terms of its power to take a global lead both morally and legally."[36] The writings of American abolitionists such as Garrison certainly make frequent reference to the founding documents of the American Republic. But in the context of his statements this seems more like a rhetorical strategy to legitimize a cause to which he himself felt bound for other, namely religious reasons. There is no need to deny that specific actors were inspired by political documents; but this is a completely inadequate explanation for the rise of a social movement.

The second explanation can also be ruled out without further ado; skeptical of idealist teleologies, it goes to the other extreme, attempting to explain even a social movement such as abolitionism, based on profoundly moral arguments, in light of material interests. The most famous example here is the Marxian-influenced book by Eric Williams, *Capitalism and Slavery*, from 1944. Williams attempts to trace the abolition of slavery back first to the rise of modern industrial capitalism, with its institutionalization of free wage labor, and second to changes in the relative importance of the Caribbean economy within the British Empire. These ideas have been subject to a comprehensive debate that more or less ended in consensus: the slave economy did not come to an end due to lack of profitability. It was still efficient; it was in fact the early nineteenth century that ushered in the true flourishing of the slave-based plantation economy, as the Industrial Revolution led to increased demand for such things as cotton, the basis of the textiles industry. This drove the economic returns on slave-based production and thus the demand for slave labor to unprecedented heights. There may still have been links between abolitionism and an emerging industrial capitalism. But it is not the case that abolitionism killed off a mode of production already in its death throes or that the actors themselves acted out of economic motives.

But if we can rule out these two obvious possibilities, how do we explain the genesis of abolitionism? I would like to mention three elements of what I believe to be a more convincing explanation.

First, the religious character of the movement is in fact quite obvious. I am thinking first of all of the Christian self-understanding. The abolitionist movements in Great Britain and the United States were supported mainly by actors who were determined to at last make a reality of moral aspirations already inherent in Christianity. Slavery was declared a sin, while resistance to it signaled that individuals meant to live a life that truly reflected Christ's moral demands. They tended to be particularly outraged when slaveholders and their supporters opposed the evangelization of the slaves and thus Christ's Great Commission. The antislavery movement became part of the intermittent revivalist movements.

But these movements cannot be described simply in terms of their religious content; above all we must consider their specific dynamics. Here prophetic speakers castigated misdeeds as sinful and interpreted them as an occasion for repentance. Such discourse may set in motion major collective processes of moral reorientation that we cannot trace back to the interests of those involved. Indeed, through such processes they learn to completely redefine their interests. Here the adoption of religiously practiced forms of the public confession of sins and assurances of a moral rebirth helped politicize moral objectives. The call went out to people of all levels of education; women, whose role in the public sphere was heavily restricted, could become leaders of this movement.[37] The movement proved highly creative in its approach. The increased academic focus on abolitionism has even led to revision of the commonly held view that "new social movements" for which material goals are not dominant have arisen only under "postindustrial" conditions. This movement was neither predominantly interest led nor state oriented.[38]

So we can in fact regard abolitionism as a morally informed movement that responded to the call, which had always been inherent in the Christian faith, for a moral decentering, to see the world from the perspective of others and not just those with whom we are linked by established affective ties—which may be no more than an extension of self-love—but from the perspective of the "least of my brothers" (Matt. 25:40). So the first component of my explanation is *intensification of the motivation to put into practice a universalist morality that already exists in principle.*

But this intensified motivation for morality went hand-in-hand with cognitive shifts—and these make up the second explanatory element. Even if an intense moral motivation for decentering is present, our conception of our own moral responsibility depends on cognitive preconditions. If we are to feel responsible, we must make empirical assumptions about the connection between our actions and misdeeds elsewhere. Does what we consume really come from a country in which slaves or forced laborers are involved in production? Also lying on the cognitive level is how we assess our possible intervention. If we forgo consumption of this product or exhort others to join us in doing so, will this have any effect on the conditions under which it is produced? All of our moral positions are embedded in a context of empirical and thus fallible assumptions about the conditions, means, and consequences of our action and that of others and about causal connections between our action and that of others.

On the basis of these insights, American historian Thomas Haskell has ingeniously connected the rise of industrial capitalism and the concurrent advance of a "humanitarian sensibility," a connection of a quite different type than implied by efforts to trace moral action back to the covert pursuit of material interests.[39] From this perspective, increasing global interlinkage of social relations, on economic grounds, is a precondition for a movement such as abolitionism. The same process that, for example, allows businesspeople to expand their utility-oriented action across the world, in the slave trade itself but also other activities, enables others to relate a formerly consequence-free moral repudiation of abuses in other places causally to their own conduct. They thus experience a sense of responsibility for putting a stop to these abuses—as a realistic option for action and de facto moral obligation. So with the expansion of market relations, the space for moral responsibility becomes larger, and this is relevant to our actions. I call this second component a *sociostructurally induced expansion in the cognitive attribution of moral responsibility.*

Together, the first and second components open up a space in which it becomes possible to articulate experiences that previously went unheard. Those who are able and motivated to enter into a process of concrete moral decentering will listen to those who speak of their suffering and that of others. In fact they actively seek out witnesses to such suffering. For many people, it is this that makes experiences of oppression, injustice, and violence, in other words traumatic experiences, articulable in the first place. After the first surge of publicity in the revolutionary era, black churches provided a space in which the experiences of slaves could be expressed. Slaves' intermittent resistance, increased public awareness of their dreadful living conditions, and the autobiographical accounts of (escaped) slaves were fused with activists' moral motives in the abolitionist movement. Complaints were transformed into appeals and demands, helplessness into determination.

But a third component was needed for the abolitionist movement to be politically successful. This lies in its transnational character. The British abolitionists, according to Jürgen Osterhammel, "saw themselves from the outset as activists pursuing a global project. . . . The battle against the slave trade and slavery involved a transatlantic chain reaction in which every local action was endowed with additional meaning in light of a larger context."[40] Among political scientists the view has taken hold that the abolitionist movement represents the first manifestation of so-called transnational advocacy networks, which are hugely important at present in many fields of politics.[41] Individuals and small groups of activists gather facts, sometimes across borders, and find ways of presenting and publishing them. They open up new lines of communication between activists in various countries and those affected. They come up with new ways of expressing protest, disseminate these in other countries, or copy templates from other countries. They communicate about the best strategies for achieving their goals within a given national context. Despite all the transnational networks, the conditions for success often remain national.

But it is doubtful whether any of the national branches of the abolitionist movement would have achieved success without the creation of a global public sphere that made it possible to provoke outrage about violations of human dignity—without, in other words, a transnational network. Memories of the mass movement for abolition in Great Britain were rekindled there during the American Civil War, preventing the British government from granting the secessionist southern states diplomatic recognition, let alone intervening in the war.[42]

This made the transnational character of the movement important to the northern states' victory and to the success of the emancipation of slaves in North America proclaimed by Abraham Lincoln in 1863. So it would be quite mistaken—as sometimes happens in the context of human rights policies—to refer here to an international regime imposed on individual countries from outside. In fact these changes can be traced back to the social movements themselves. I call this third component *the practical transnational organization of moral universalism.*

These reflections on the genesis of the abolitionist movements in Great Britain and the United States are not exhaustive in historiographical terms. Nor do they make up a theory of social movements that comprehensively develops the pivotal idea of this book—that of processes of sacralization in general and the sacralization of the person in particular.[43] My aim in making these observations here was merely to describe in outline how experiences of violence can be transformed into actions guided by a moral universalism. But despite their historical and social scientific character, my remarks also have a moral philosophical purpose. This is to constructively oppose the notion that a universalist morality can only be consistently based on the force of "rational motivation." This oft-criticized Kantian notion has been reworked by Jürgen Habermas within the framework of his transformation of Kantian motifs by means of a theory of communication. Over the course of his intellectual development, however, he has increasingly conceded that rationality is a weak motivator of morality. For him, this makes it all the clearer that "the weak motivating force of morality must be supplemented by coercive positive law."[44] Without in any way wishing to minimize the significance of law in supporting demands for a universalist morality, my reflections here aim to complement the "weak force of rational motivation" in a different way.[45] My aim is to scrutinize the strong forces motivating a universalist morality, the kind of forces that may arise from cultural traditions such as religions and intensive experiences, both inspiring and traumatizing, and that may lead to individual and collective actions. We find such motivating forces, which facilitate decentered perception and moral-political action, in the sacralization of the person.

But my reflections on violence and human dignity not only have a moral philosophical point; they also imply a moral demand. If we understand human rights in part as a way of articulating the history of violence, then we must remain aware of this attempt at articulation. We can derive from this a demand to go further, to take account of as-yet-unarticulated suffering—but also a demand that we abandon any sense of cultural self-satisfaction. That which has binding force as a result of our history of violence must not symbolize a cultural triumphalism that makes human rights appear like a firmly established possession, one that demonstrates the superiority of one's own culture. In light of the ideas I have developed here on the sacralization of the person, this would be self-contradictory—in much the same way as when the cross, the central Christian symbol of suffering and sacrifice, has been used in "crusades" as a symbol of war and conquest.

NOTES

1. I got a bit carried away in my book *The Genesis of Values*; my emphasis on inspiring value-constitutive experiences was somewhat one-sided. I tried to make up for this by considering experiences of violence or powerlessness in the two following books *War and Modernity* and *Do We Need Religion?*

2. Otto, *Idea of the Holy*.

3. On the parallels between different types of experience, see various chapters in Joas, *War and Modernity*.

4. Vögele, *Menschenwürde*, 274–98.

5. Verfassung des Freistaates Bayern. Munich 2009, 29; Die Verfassung der Freien Hansestadt Bremen. Stuttgart 1996, 23.

6. Vögele, *Menschenwürde*, 290.

7. Preamble, Charter of the United Nations, UN, www.un.org/en/documents/charter/preamble.shtml; preamble, Universal Declaration of Human Rights, UN, www.un.org/en/documents/udhr/.

8. Morsink, *Universal Declaration of Human Rights*, esp. 36–91; Morsink, "World War Two and the Universal Declaration." In the literature on the genesis of the Universal Declaration there is controversy over the exact role played by the (uncontroversially implicit) reference to National Socialism, fascism, and war. I

forgo further examination of this topic here, as a more detailed analysis of this genesis appears in chapter 6. Here I am solely concerned with the significance of the history of violence as such.

9. Mills and Gerth, *From Max Weber*, 334.

10. See the outstanding essay by Mazower, "Violence and the State in the Twentieth Century."

11. See Baberowski and Doering-Manteuffel, *Ordnung durch Terror*.

12. Mazower, "Violence and the State in the Twentieth Century," 1164–65.

13. Arendt, *Origins of Totalitarianism*, 123–266. For an argument in the same vein, see Zimmerer, *Von Windhuk nach Auschwitz*; a contrary view is presented by Malinowski and Gerwarth, "Holocaust als 'kolonialer Genozid'?"

14. See Baberowski and Doering-Manteuffel, *Ordnung durch Terror*.

15. One of the main sociological texts of relevance here is Mann, *Dark Side of Democracy*. The most comprehensive collection of material on the history of colonial violence of which I am aware is available only in French: Ferro, *Livre noir du colonialisme*. It is striking that the terms "Holocaust" and "Gulag" are sometimes applied to phenomena in a quite inaccurate way, as for example in books on the extermination of Native Americans ("American Holocaust") or the brutal British crackdown on anticolonial resistance in Kenya ("Britain's Gulag").

16. Resick, *Stress and Trauma*, 14.

17. Leys, *Trauma*.

18. Kansteiner, "Menschheitstrauma, Holocausttrauma, kulturelles Trauma."

19. For interpretations, see, e.g., Kiesel, *Literarische Trauerarbeit*, 489–98; Sander, *Alfred Döblin*, 222–31.

20. Döblin, *Tales*, 20.

21. Ibid., 117.

22. Kansteiner, "Menschheitstrauma, Holocausttrauma, kulturelles Trauma," 110.

23. See above all Alexander et al., *Cultural Trauma and Collective Identity*, here 1. Alexander's own case study in this volume (196–263) has been stripped of most of the critical apparatus found in its first published version. But this is of much importance. For this reason, see also Alexander, "On the Social Construction of Moral Universals," esp. 72–80. For a more detailed critical examination, which I draw on here, see Joas, "Cultural Trauma?"

24. Mead, "Objective Reality of Perspectives."

25. Alexander et al., *Cultural Trauma and Collective Identity*, 15, 22.

26. Ibid., 26.

27. Ibid., 7.

28. Alexander, "On the Social Construction of Moral Universals," 73.

29. I have developed this idea in depth in *Creativity of Action*. For the kind of detailed critique of other theories that I merely allude to here, as it would be out of place in the present context, see Joas and Knöbl, *Social Theory*.

30. The following statements on the history of slavery and the antislavery movement are based on a broad range of literature, of which I shall mention just David Brion Davis, *Inhuman Bondage*; Bender, *Antislavery Debate*; Young, *Bearing Witness against Sin*; Brown, "Christianity"; Osterhammel, *Verwandlung der Welt*, 1188–213. Two articles provide helpful overall surveys: Drescher, "Trends in der Historiographie des Abolitionismus"; Gestrich, "Antisklavereibewegung." Readers are also referred to an article that fits methodologically with the ideas I present here as it considers the discursive processing of events and its contingent effect on processes of collective action: Ellingson, "Understanding the Dialectic of Discourse and Collective Action."

31. See Sieberg, "Französische Revolution und die Sklavenfrage."

32. Brown, "Christianity," 526.

33. Mayer, *All on Fire.*

34. See chap. 1 of this book.

35. Osterhammel (*Verwandlung der Welt*, 1189–90) makes the very interesting point that China and Japan rejected slavery earlier than Europe and America; in Siam it was not Western pressure that prompted the repression of slavery but the impact of a Buddhist revival.

36. Ibid., 1193.

37. See Gestrich, "Antisklavereibewegung," 249, and the literature cited there.

38. See the hypothesis put forward by Young, *Bearing Witness against Sin.* See also his earlier journal article "Confessional Protest," and the subsequent dispute with Charles Tilly (Tilly, "Comment on Young"; Young, "Reply to Tilly").

39. Haskell, "Capitalism and the Origins of the Humanitarian Sensibility."

40. Osterhammel, *Verwandlung der Welt*, 1191.

41. Keck and Sikkink, *Activists beyond Borders.*

42. David Brion Davis, *Inhuman Bondage*, 317–18.

43. For an excellent effort in this vein, see Pettenkofer, *Radikaler Protest.*

44. Habermas, *Inclusion of the Other*, 274 n. 51.

45. Habermas, *Between Facts and Norms*, 5.

4

NEITHER KANT NOR NIETZSCHE

What Is Affirmative Genealogy?

I briefly explained the concept of "affirmative genealogy" in the introduction to this book. In the following chapter, which presents a number of intermediate methodological reflections, I aim to flesh out this concept and thus the method used in this book. Within the context of contemporary debates in the philosophy and history of human rights, it is vital to explain why we should be attempting to produce a "genealogy" of human rights in the first place, as opposed to a rational justification for their validity claims or a simple history of their ascent and spread. We must also explain why, in sharp contrast to Nietzsche, we aspire to make this genealogy "affirmative." This dual explanation must set out why it is that only such an affirmative genealogy can do justice to the reality of sacralization, on which I place such great emphasis. However ready we may be to recognize the achievements of Kant and Nietzsche and to honor their insights, we must also clarify why the arguments presented here cannot take their lead from either of them.

To mention Kant and Nietzsche is not, of course, to exhaust the spectrum of possible views. I mention them here because their names symbolize two of the most significant and influential basic positions. The name of Kant is associated with the hope that we might get from him, or ourselves develop, a moral philosophical argument that entails an unconditional, universal validity claim entirely independent of history. Nietzsche's name signals the end of all such hopes, an understanding of the irreducible subjectivity of all evaluations and of the contingency of history, which would also dash any hopes of founding values through a philosophy of history.[1] Even most of their supporters would concede that there is much room for improvement when it comes to the specifics of each thinker's arguments, but for them this in no way reduces the appeal of their intellectual projects. It is no great stretch to interpret two of the most important thinkers of the late twentieth century, Habermas and Foucault, as attempting, respectively, to reformulate Kant in light of communication theory and flesh out Nietzsche in terms of cultural history. Because of the enormous symbolic significance of these two classical thinkers, the controversies surrounding the interpretation of their writings have become charged with an intensity that goes far beyond the philological and biographical. Did Kant, as typically asserted, erect his moral philosophy on the fact of human free will? This includes our capacity to formulate universally valid principles of action and tailor our freely chosen actions to these principles, demanded by reason, and thus gear them to a universally valid moral law. Or, however impressively it may elaborate the idea of the autonomy of the morally acting individual with respect to the conditions for and propensities of his action, is this interpretation of Kant untenable? Does it imply that Kant built his moral philosophy on a speculative-metaphysical or empirically fallible (anthropological) proposition that refers at best to a capacity whose normative status lacks clear justification? Is it not therefore more convincing, and more commensurable with Kant's intentions, to derive his moral philosophy not from the *fact* of human free will, but from the belief-like recognition of the *value* of human freedom, which would itself then lack any ultimate justification?[2] Much the same applies to Nietzsche. His idea is that consciously confronting the processes through which values arise removes the scales from our eyes, allowing us to see the contingent nature of their validity claims. Does this really serve only to let loose pure subjectivity? Or does this kind of genealogical analysis represent part of a project that is itself highly ethical and critical, one specifically intended to enable individuals to achieve authentic value commitments?[3] Everything one may say about these two thinkers falls within these often-heated disputes over how best to interpret them.

In addition, as noted above, the range of possible views on the relationship between history and normativity is much broader than these two names would suggest. We might also want to consider Hegelian and Marxian dialectics, historicism and positivism, the philosophy of life of Dilthey or Bergson, neo-Kantian approaches, including the celebrated arguments of Max Weber and Georg Simmel, analytical philosophy of history—as well as contemporary variants that build on the work of all these thinkers and schools of thought. I am keen to prevent my explanation for the approach adopted in this book from taking on encyclopedic proportions, but I also want to avoid creating the impression that I have simply disregarded existing argumentational models. I have therefore decided to use one single thinker as the foil for my account, the one who comes closer to my views than any other historical figure. This also fits with the generally hermeneutic approach of this book. The thinker I draw on here never himself refers to "affirmative genealogy," but comes very close to what is meant by this term. He also provided the very thing I aim to avoid here: an account of encyclopedic scope.

I am referring to Ernst Troeltsch, particularly his late magnum opus *Der Historismus und seine Probleme* (*Historicism and Its Problems*) and the posthumously published volume of essays composed shortly before his death, which complements his earlier book and places greater emphasis on certain aspects of it. This bore the title (not chosen by him) *Der Historismus und seine Überwindung* (*Historicism and How to Move Beyond It*).[4] Troeltsch's late work, which forms the foundation for the present book, had an unfortunate effective history. The titles of both books are ambiguous if not misleading. *Der Historismus und seine Probleme* sounds as though it is concerned with a special problem internal to a school of history found mainly in Germany, taking hundreds of pages to detail its aporias. No wonder that readers with such expectations were not drawn to the book. *Der Historismus und seine Überwindung* implies that Troeltsch is claiming to have found a way out of the aporias of this school, but seems unable to communicate this in any readily comprehensible form. Upon publication, the book met with a barrage of complaints from the younger generation of philosophers, historians, and Protestant and Catholic theologians, all expressing their disappointment that despite his stupendous erudition, Troeltsch had not managed to strike a path out of relativistic historicism. It was even rumored that Troeltsch himself acknowledged his failure. This notion of his failure and resignation has pervaded the literature ever since. Even in the work of authors who are fundamentally close to Troeltsch we find numerous attempts to distance themselves from this work that "is undoubtedly characterized not only by immaturity, inconsistency and contradictory elements, but also by categorial ambiguities, theological and philosophical vagueness and an avalanche of words solely intended to convey a sense of metaphysical reassurance."[5] An English translation of this work is at last in the offing (see n. 4); the lack of one so far has severely hampered its international reception.[6] As Gadamer has already pointed out, the debate on the work of Wilhelm Dilthey soon began to overshadow Troeltsch's impact following his early death.[7] Only in recent times have a small number of in-depth and sympathetic attempts to systematize his arguments appeared. It is no coincidence that these have been penned by Protestant theologians: it is impossible to formulate an appropriate approach to Troeltsch's late work if we lack sensitivity to the religious dimension of his key question and his attempt to answer it.[8]

Troeltsch's question was centered not on the problems of a particular intellectual school, but on one of the most profound problems of modern consciousness itself—to the extent that this consciousness is thought to have made us aware of the historical genesis of all belief, all claims to truth and value. Dilthey gave this its classical expression in a speech marking his seventieth birthday:

> A seemingly irreconcilable contradiction arises if we pursue the historical consciousness to its ultimate conclusion. The finitude of every historical phenomenon, whether a religion, ideal, or philosophical system, and thus the relativity of every kind of human conception of how things are, is the final word of the historical worldview; everything is fluid process, nothing endures. Conversely, thought requires, and philosophy strives to attain, a universally valid knowledge. The historical worldview has liberated the human intellect from the final chains left unbroken by natural science and philosophy—but where is the means of overcoming the anarchy of beliefs that threatens to erupt?[9]

Plainly, historical criticism of the Bible, and the unsettling effects of this criticism on Protestant Christianity in particular, were the first manifestation of this crisis; sooner or later, it was bound to envelop every timeless validity claim. Dilthey saw it as his life's work—within the context of this radical historicization of consciousness—to reflect on the possibility of universal validity claims, and gave expression to the hope that his "young companions," his students, would follow the path trodden by him all the way to its conclusion.

This is just what Troeltsch attempted to do and, I suggest, succeeded in doing. He sees the radical historicization of consciousness as itself a highly modern revolt against the modern naturalization of thought before and during the Enlightenment. He reminds us of the initially enthusiastic response to "liberation from the mathematical-mechanistic concept of nature" (178), how a historical perspective animated intellectual life as a whole, especially the understanding of art and literature, and the historical pathos that accompanied the creation of nation-states. But he also sees, without illusion, how quickly and inevitably this enthusiasm ebbed, giving way to a sense of "bad historicism." For Troeltsch, bad historicism is "unlimited relativism, a frivolous preoccupation with things, a paralysis of the will and of one's own life" (242), the sense of being held back from courageously shaping the future by the dead weight of historical knowledge, of having the solid ground of the present pulled from beneath one's feet by differing ways of constructing history. Many of the disappointed rejected historicism in this sense and returned to naturalism; the rivalry between the two generated alternating cycles of fashionability and—as in the discipline of sociology—attempts were made to create peculiar connections between them through theories of social change. Others went back even further, yearning for a return to the conditions that pertained before naturalism or historicism unsettled religious and other dogmas. For Troeltsch, however, there is no way back from naturalism and historicism, either to Church dogma or "its offspring, rationalistic dogma" (291). He saw this rationalistic dogma as particularly evident in the neo-Kantianism of his time. For him this dogma was a "a universal rational system which, thoroughly appropriated, would at least in principle make everything necessary and calculable, hence objective and certain, so that uncertainties would be solely a matter of enigmatic 'subjectivity.'" It seems to him straightforward to eschew this system of belief, as this is not a matter of "relinquishing something we once possessed," but of freeing ourselves from a phantasm that has dominated our thinking—"from all the kinds of conceptual phantoms that mislead us when it comes to forming standards—or that stunt the courage and vigor needed to produce them" (378). Max Weber's stark view on the relationship between real history and value systems not only fails to convince him, it horrifies him. He sees it as merely the juxtaposition of "ice cold, theoretically controlled, sociologically illuminated research into phenomena of the historical sphere. The aim is to clarify our situation and future possibilities, our room to maneuver, and the kind of resources with which we can construct the future. Alongside this research, in a manner quite abrupt and foreign to it, goes the selection of one value from the irreconcilable polytheism of values, one value to which people owe all their strength, one value which all historico-sociological knowledge thoroughly serves to realize" (354). For Troeltsch, Weber's position here is the "desperate solution of a heroic . . . positivism," which is impressive compared to the shallowness of "young people with their enthusiasm for romanticism, the utopians with their confidence in reason, or the emotionally starved students of classical humanism and of the older doctrines of the German state" (355). But rather than resolving the problem of how to mediate between history and normativity, it merely affirms its unresolved status.

But what is Troeltsch's solution? I will not attempt to adhere to the structure of his lengthy book, which is anything but clear. Instead, in six stages, I attempt to reconstruct his argument, which he only rarely clarifies analytically and mostly puts forward indirectly in his interpretations of other thinkers. These stages seem to me to form a complete chain of inference of great rigor and originality. But there should be no confusion about the fact that my reconstruction of Troeltsch's ideas—a justification of affirmative genealogy—is an interpretation that does not arise unambiguously from Troeltsch's work itself. The emphasis in what follows is not on the interpretation of a classical thinker, but on justifying the method on which this book is based.

THE FACT OF IDEAL FORMATION

The first step revolves around what I call the *fact of ideal formation*. "All life bears its ideal within it": this phrase from Leopold von Ranke's text *Politisches Gespräch* (*Political Dialogue*) of 1836 is a striking expression of this idea (407). I consciously intend my phrasing here to recall Kant's "fact of pure practical reason," but the different wording immediately points up a dual distinction from Kant. The concept of the ideal, first of all, is far broader and permits far more internal variation than morality, which was what Kant had in mind. Second, by referring to ideal *formation* rather than simply ideals or morality, we draw attention to the unpredictable genesis of values rather than their everlasting validity. And we underline the importance of intellectual contemplation of this genesis if we wish to comprehend what a value that has taken hold actually is.

Troeltsch both expresses appreciation for Kant and delimits his own concerns from those of Kant and especially neo-Kantianism, and this plays a key role in how he positions himself intellectually. His point of departure is that if we wish to mediate between history and normativity we cannot restrict in advance the dimension of values and norms to a timeless morality; "in any event, from the moral dimension alone, no understanding or logical construal of history is to be attained" (269). Terminologically, Troeltsch uses a rather traditional distinction between the "moral" and "ethical" to express his ideas. "Ethical" values or "cultural values are admittedly imposed values, mandated values. They do not correspond to nature or to the flow of life but arise from autonomous spiritual creation. They share the normative character of moral values, but are not moral values themselves" (391). It is these ethical values that arise and wither away over the course of history and that we can glean from history itself. But Kant took a different approach. In the case of the natural sciences he certainly attempted to glean the criteria of evaluation from reflection on their presuppositions and methods. But he did not do so with respect to empirical historical research, which of course for him was not strictly scientific in character anyway. Instead, he obtained the criterion of evaluation from a realm that is not itself historical and merely applied it to history. This realm is that of moral reason; it "signified a perfect human community based on moral freedom and self-determination. For the purely spiritual and dispositionally-formed core of this community, he [Kant] called for a nucleus of constitutional order that would make freedom for individual persons mutually possible. In the final analysis this was to be a constitutional, worldwide federation of free peoples" (316). Inevitably, if we obtain an ideal through a nonhistorical moral philosophy, our relationship to history can only consist in evaluating all historical phenomena according to the degree to which they approach this ideal and to urge all actors to ensure that their impact on history accords with this ideal.

Writing one hundred years after Kant and at a time when the historical humanities disciplines and *Staatswissenschaften*, or sciences of the state, were at the peak of their development, Troeltsch is unconvinced by Kant's approach to the problem of history and normativity.

For him the only indisputable merit of contemporary neo-Kantians is that they have made progress toward formulating a logic of the constitution of historical objects; but precisely because of this they have transformed the historical diversity of ethical values into a diversity of subjective perspectives and can tell us nothing about their genesis. If they are bold enough to explain this genesis itself in causal terms, then ethical values become epiphenomena of processes that must be explained in biological, psychological, or sociological terms. But if explaining the genesis of ethical values is considered impossible, then all we can do is place them within formal schemas or "an unwarrantable antilogical standpoint of arbitrary selection and relationship" (269). For Troeltsch, this is the dead end in which Max Weber also found himself as a result of his neo-Kantian position.[10]

At this point there is a risk of two serious misunderstandings. The reader might understand the arguments presented here as disputing that there is any possibility of a culture-independent morality or even as rejecting the moral claims championed by Kant. Yet neither of these objections follows from what has been said. It is beyond question that the formal character of moral oughts itself allows the formulation of moral norms, and that these "apply to us with the force of pure normativity, all the more powerful for having been freed from all content: the individual values of autonomy, strength of character, determination, dignity, virtue, and truthfulness, along with the social values of mutual respect and fairness, and finally, in the common relationship of all people to the society that overarches them, the values of solidarity and mutual interconnection." It is beyond dispute that "these formal values, because of their formality and because they flow from normativity itself, possess a universal, rationally necessary validity. This validity obtains wherever obligation is recognized at all, and to the degree that it is clearly articulated and made independent in its own right" (391). But as a consequence of this unhistorical formality, every "application" of these formal moral criteria, whether in the moral action of individuals, or in the evaluation of the moral action of others or the moral qualities of entire epochs and cultures, remains dependent on an injection of content, on translation into "ethical" values. In the action situation, irreducible orientations toward the "good"—to use a different terminology—come up against the testing authority of the "right." The right can only ever be a testing authority, a "sieve of norms" (Paul Ricoeur)—unless it itself becomes a specific good, the value of justice. Whole societies and cultures also exist within a field of tension between their particular material value systems and the potential of a formal morality that aspires to universality. Every culture hedges in this potentially universal morality in a specific way by defining its field and conditions of application. The inclusion or exclusion of people of other nationalities, ethnic groups, races, religions, gender, age, mentality, and morality are justified in various ways. Both in the case of the moral action of individuals and in the evaluation of entire cultures, it would, however, be a mistake to get carried away with calls for a universalist morality to the point where we imagine that any culture can do without a specific, particular value system and without a specific, particular interpretation of the world. But "particular" does not mean "particularistic." The fact of the cultural specificity of value systems does not exclude the possibility of taking account of universalist perspectives. On the contrary, it opens up the question of which specific cultural traditions interface best with the universality of the right.[11]

Between Kant and Troeltsch, however, lie the perhaps most ambitious attempts to mediate between history and normativity ever made—Hegelian and Marxian dialectics—and it is worth mentioning, at least briefly, why Troeltsch does not embrace them. He subjects both to in-depth and highly erudite analysis—by no means a matter of course at the time. He defends both against a range of fashionable simplifications and polemical distortions. Ultimately, though, he criticizes not just Kant, but also Hegel, as overly rationalistic. "Hegel sought an absolute, rationally grounded value system, but one with the property of presenting historical individualities out of its own resources, in terms of logical sequence, combination, and consummation" (319). This gives rise to the rationalization and teleology of historical becoming, not in the sense of a crass justification of all that is real as rational, but of the selection of historical material that allows us to perceive the ultimate identity of the real with the rational: "Only the high points of becoming, where self-understanding and the developing consciousness of reason shine forth together with their presuppositions and preconditions, constitute the object of historical study. These high points constitute a path of light radiating from huge clustered masses, alongside which there are plenty of things that remain obscure, things marked by apathy and dullness, accident and wickedness" (459). The relationship between these high points is by no means necessarily empirical-causal; it is in fact dialectical-logical, and here this is meant to imply teleological necessity. Contrary to criticisms often made of Hegel since the days of the Young Hegelians, this necessity is by no means simply constructed a priori. Hegel was undoubtedly geared toward empirical knowledge as the precondition for constructive description, and if the criticisms of Hegel's historical vision made by empirical historians, sociologists, and Marxists are correct—namely, that it fails to "do justice to the complexity, the essential relativity, or the real and manifold interests of the historical life. Instead, in a violently monistic tendency, it partly blurs all such things and partly overlooks them entirely" (479)—then in the first instance this applies only to the way in which he realized his great project of synthesis, rather than the intention behind it. These shortcomings do not in themselves invalidate the idea of identifying historical goals.

More relevant is the other objection raised since the time of the Young Hegelians, according to which Hegel's entire method, as he himself conceded, presupposes that the owl of Minerva takes wing at dusk—that we can only reconstruct the totality of a process in this way if the process is completed and we can infer the preconditions for its occurrence entirely from the outcome. Troeltsch denies that this shortcoming of Hegel's method has anything to do with reactionary enthusiasm for Prussia, a quietist mentality, or intellectual hubris. Nonetheless, he regards inadequate reflection on the relationship between historical teleology and unanticipatable historical innovation as Hegel's crucial and irremediable failing. For Troeltsch, Marxism is of no help here as it makes the same mistake in an even more extreme form. Troeltsch recognizes the important economic-sociological revisions of Hegel by Marx and Marxism (I come back to this point in the sixth stage of this reconstruction of Troeltsch's arguments). But the values of Marxism, the utopia envisaged by the Marxist movement, are, Troeltsch believes, in no way gleaned from history; indeed, they would confront history with "an utterly messianic grotesqueness" (341). If all historical value and meaning constructs are "simply reflections of class interests and class viewpoints projected into the realm of a merely ostensible and illusory universality" (340), this cannot be otherwise. On this view, there is no metaphysical, transcendental, or historical justification of values in Marxism. There is only a utopian hope of constructing the future and a contemporary enthusiasm for those values claimed to be the "correspondence to the definite historical situation of an oppressed class suffering under these conditions" (341).

Troeltsch sees no easy way to align oneself with Kant, Hegel, or Marx: they have failed to overcome the restriction of ideals to morality in the narrower sense or show convincingly how to mediate between history and the diversity of values; he therefore turns to other traditions. With respect to the growing consciousness of the diversity of culturally vibrant ideals, he mentions Schleiermacher and Humboldt, as well as the whole broad current of historically oriented nineteenth-century sciences of the "state, law, economy, art, religion, science" (397). But this consciousness is necessary not just to measure peoples, states, and cultures against criteria alien to them, but to understand them in terms of the value relations they themselves experience as valid. Only then can we fully acknowledge the fact of the diversity of lived ideals. While we might capture this diversity, as existent phenomenon, through a systematization valid for all time, another insight compels us to abandon this aspiration as well. This is the understanding of the future production of new ideals of which the present cannot begin to conceive, "the generating of the ideal of every epoch out of its own resources through creative, spontaneous, and independent critical judgment and penetration" (325). Troeltsch rightly calls this far-reaching insight a new idea.[12] But in terms of its significance, this new idea goes far beyond the abstract admission that innovations in the field of values cannot be ruled out in the future. It places the formation of ideals, the genesis of values, at the center of our attention when we consider the mediation of history and normativity, and with far-reaching consequences.

Against all efforts "to reduce spontaneous and powerful intrinsic ideals that emerge from self-confidence to mere psychological illusions, productions, or reflexes" (359), Troeltsch thus highlights the fact of ideal formation and the irreducibility of the ideals it generates. It is the self-delusion of an uncreative age to assert that "its own present age possesses an illusion-free knowledge that explains everything, [while construing] the past as the romantic age of illusions" (360). In reality, the production of criteria never ceases. Emphasizing the fact of ideal formation, then, is not a matter of rejecting an evaluative assessment of historical realities. Troeltsch's efforts to differentiate his work from that of Kant and other forms of rationalism were open to this misunderstanding. In fact, the aim here is to do without criteria that are assumed to be nonhistorical, as their use only reveals the historical self-forgetfulness of the subject proclaiming them. What we must forgo is "that feature of standards which is incompatible with the individual nature of all actual historical formations. Likewise abandoned must be the feature incompatible with the inherently transitory output that also characterizes history and therefore must be individual. What has to be abandoned, then, is the universality, timelessness, absoluteness and abstractness of these standards and their simple identification with reason as such or with the divine essence of the universe." It is not, therefore, criteria that we must forgo, but the claim that these criteria have not been obtained from history. "Self-certainty without timelessness" is how Troeltsch puts it (ibid.).

During this first stage of the argument, it is vital to grasp that, without making any claim to timelessness, this self-certainty presupposes that ideals that have been formed, values that have emerged, are not subjective whims or hypotheses regarded as useful, which could make no claim to certainty. These ideals are not chosen or the outcome of a decision. As I tried to show in my book *The Genesis of Values*, such ideals are typified by a sense of subjective self-evidence and affective intensity. It is experiences rather than justifications that are constitutive of intensive value commitments. Troeltsch too refers to the "sense of proof" (373) or "subjective absoluteness."[13] We do not seize our values, we are seized by them, or—as Troeltsch puts it—in such a case this seizing is an "act of generation that recognizes itself as obedience" (374). Such ideal formation is therefore accompanied by the awareness, not of having posited something in an arbitrary way, but of having grasped "within this whole an inner course of development, an inner movement of life on the part of the universe, or the divine" (361). "Revelation" is the phenomenologically appropriate term for this experience—the sense of having partaken in a revelation that itself prompts feelings of obligation, an "obligation inherent in our being, the obligation to realize intrinsically cogent values" (312). Kant has said all that needs to be said about this sense of obligation. Yet this experience does not simply appear in association with an eternally valid morality or a single "value," but with respect to the individual totality of an overall cultural formation.

THE SPECIFIC INDIVIDUALITY OF HISTORICAL PHENOMENA

Mention of the individual whole of a historical phenomenon brings us to the second stage. For Troeltsch, the fact of ideal formation, the systematic foundation of his argument, constitutes the *specific individuality of historical phenomena*. Individuality in this sense is not, of course, a merely numerical phenomenon. A single inanimate object, plant, or animal may also be individual in the sense of its distinctiveness and noninterchangeability. But the concept of individuality takes on a far more sophisticated meaning if the individuals involved have ideals or, better, have the capacity for ideal formation. If this is the case, we cannot do justice to their individuality if we understand them as merely factual; that is, without taking account of the immanent relationship between the facticity of such an individual and his highly individual values. We cannot understand a human being if we are unfamiliar with his values and judge him only by his actions, which will never represent the total realization of his ideals. We are particularly keen not to be judged by others solely in light of our actions, certain that we ourselves amount to more than these actions. Understood in this way, the concept of individuality "not only signifies the purely factual particularity of a specific historical and spiritual complex but also simultaneously implies the individualization of an ideal, or of what ought to be. This ideal, moreover, is never exhaustively realized in what is always a particular form. The ideal is something that is aimed at and, depending on circumstances, more or less happily embodied" (394). For the theory of values, then, the concept of individuality "in the sense of a union of the actual and the ideal, a union of what is given by nature and circumstance and of what is at the same time ethically required" (404) becomes the key concept. But it is key not just to this theory, but also to constituting the object of the historical sciences. Their fundamental category is that of the "individual totality" (205) in the sophisticated sense set out above.

Individuality in this sense is not limited to the individual human being. Because the historical object is constituted through the concept of the individual totality and this in turn "by the concept of an immanent value or meaning" (245), "collective individualities" may well be the object of historiography: "peoples, states, classes, social estates, cultural eras, cultural trends, religious communities" (206).

Troeltsch even declares "complex events of every kind such as wars, revolutions, etc." to be such meaningful totalities (ibid.). This should not be misunderstood as the false application, to mystified collective entities, of categories that are meaningful only with respect to individual persons. It is just that, as a rule, lived ideals are not perceived as orientational only by a single individual, let alone created or discovered by those individuals who take their lead from them.

More long passages of Troeltsch's work are devoted to intellectual history, first with respect to the question of how this sophisticated understanding of individuality came into being and developed, and second, why it meets with incomprehension throughout much of the sciences and philosophy. We have already seen that Schleiermacher was an important source of inspiration here. Dilthey and Simmel, Windelband and Rickert are among the key thinkers who declared the individual in this sense a specific feature of the historical world. Troeltsch provides a brilliant analysis of the complexities of the arguments found in their work and that of others. From this perspective, thinkers such as Hermann Lotze, generally treated as mere epigones of German idealism, appear as "forerunners" (736) of a new way of thinking that is no longer captive to the rationalism of classical German philosophy, but that ultimately lacked the audacity to combine the concepts of individuality and value in the way I have outlined, and make them the foundation of the historical sciences. Troeltsch's greatest sympathies lie with Dilthey. Without in any way reducing the "spirit" to mere "life," Dilthey managed to get beyond the Hegelian notion that the spirit obeys laws governing its logical self-movement, let alone that "nature" and "spirit" are subject to the same laws. Dilthey instead privileged the "experiential diversity, an abundance of contradictions, practical orientation and irrationality" (716) of life, which can only ever be processed intellectually, but never overcome. Though certain neo-Kantian thinkers—Windelband more than Rickert—at least come close to this understanding of individuality, in their work history falls between the stools of a historical science that is alien to values and an unhistorical world of values. Even more starkly than Rickert and, for Troeltsch, even less plausibly, Max Weber wrenches apart studies of causality and "a science-free value position liberated from all value-rationalism and any metaphysics as well as from all religion and speculation" (853).

Troeltsch sees the real lack of understanding for the specific conception of individuality found in the Schleiermacher-Dilthey school—the hermeneutic tradition, in other words—as lying in an intellectual tradition that he regards as the complete opposite of this school. He refers to "Anglo-French positivism" (333). As this positivism does not recognize the concept of individuality that emerged in the romantic period or, if it does, condemns it polemically as "mysticism," the psyche of individuals appears here as an aggregate of isolated elements, just as groups of people and whole societies appear as mere aggregations of their members. This makes it appear impossible to build a bridge between the facticity of these aggregative phenomena and universal values. From this perspective, we can build such a bridge only via a detour through supposed psychological, economic, or sociological (quasi-) natural laws, which are then also interpreted as value-like laws of historical development: "The development toward pacificism and industrialism, or toward democracy and the organization of humankind, or toward rational, scientific hygienics for peoples and for the human race, or toward the greatest good for the greatest number, or toward a planned world socialism that would systematically heal the ravages caused by modern exploitation of nature, or toward the survival of the fittest and the free competition of Manchesterism: this, then, seems to be the essence of this sort of natural law" (334). Guided by the model of the natural sciences even when investigating individual-historical objects, statistical analysis of the relationships between isolated elements gains an importance it could never have within a hermeneutic tradition geared toward the comprehension of meaningful totalities.

If we place the possibility of ideal formation, as described earlier, at the heart of how we define specifically historical phenomena, this has a whole number of consequences. Methodologically, this idea directs our attention to the "analysis of creative junctures and the tendencies that originate within them" (945), as it becomes hugely interesting, for the purposes of historical analysis, to determine the timing and context of the genesis of values and value complexes. Philosophically, a focus on the emergence of ideals throws up the question of whether anything new can in fact emerge over time and to what extent such novelties merely result from a necessity that is itself immutable or whether they go beyond this necessity. On this question, with which German neo-Kantianism could offer him little help, but which had gained dramatically in importance because of Darwin and the new theory of evolution, Troeltsch is prudent enough to refer to the French neo-Kantians, such as Charles Renouvier, whom he asserts "clearly illuminated the problem of new beginnings and of creation" (936).[14] But much more even than them, "freedom, creation and originality" prompted Henri Bergson to take an entirely new approach: "Thus he, more than anybody else, ushers us into the heart of our problem" (937).

This remark clearly shows that Troeltsch would like to provide a broader basis on which to justify his conception of ideal formation and historical individuality, which is gleaned essentially from reflections on problems of historiography. We might say that he is eager to give it first an anthropological and then, in addition, even a metaphysical foundation. His many references to the creativity of action may be viewed as an anthropological foundation. Particularly in his remarks on a "formal logic of history," Troeltsch discusses the "creative originality of separate individuals" (219) and its relationship to the pregiven conditions of their action. In the contemporary philosophy of history, this dimension of human action came into play above all with respect to the great individuals, not to say the great men. Troeltsch is aware that the problem took on this form only "from the omnipotence of the concept of naturalistic causality, or from a psychology that follows exclusively from this concept" (219–20). For the historian in his everyday praxis, but also for the theorist of science not guided by naturalism, meanwhile, it is obvious not only that "great men" rise above their conditions, but also that there is an indissoluble element of originality in all human beings and all their social and cultural constructs:[15]

> This personal originality, however, has the power to exert transforming and decisive influences on the whole, influences which are not merely a given, but which we observe particularly in their surprising and unpredictable productivity. This is the element of the creative, which is not reducible to individual acuteness and singularity, but from them produces the great transformative impulses that constitute a particularly important, if not the only, theme of the historian. It apparently exists in every single person, but can increase by degrees from a preponderant passivity to a powerful impact. This element signifies the decisive role of novelty, of

> what is not yet included in antecedent elements but asserts itself by uniting with them, and constantly enhances reality by introducing new creations, new energies, and new beginnings into it. (220)

But if the action of all human beings always generates something new in this way, and outstanding feats of creativity are embodied in "institutions and spiritual forces," then the logic of historiography should not marginalize this fact. Quite the opposite, it is "the incalculable newness and actuality of what is produced" on which it should focus. This is not a matter of rejecting causality and rationality, but of formulating a concept of causality and rationality appropriate to the facts of human action and the constructs to which this action gives rise. For Troeltsch, immersion in historical realities leads to a "logic of the novel and creative," which seems irrational only to those who defend a constricted conception of rationality against all the evidence (221).[16]

Beyond the thesis of the creative character of human action, this anthropological foundation also includes the problem of intersubjectivity or—in Troeltsch's terms—of "knowledge of other minds." He sees this as a key problem of the epistemology of history and a central object of philosophical reflection in general, for the simple reason that "the possibilities and difficulties of common thought, philosophizing, and action really depend" (991) upon knowledge of other minds. But this relationship to the other person is far more than just a precondition for coordinated action; it brings constant change and enrichment to every actor, because "fresh elemental forces overflow from the ego of the other into one's own" (997) through interaction with others. As with Ranke and Dilthey, Troeltsch's descriptions of historical understanding also take on frankly erotic overtones, when he refers for instance to the "capacity for surrender to and penetration of the mind of the other." His remarks here are animated by the passion of the historian, the passion inherent in all understanding. At the same time, however, through the self-restraint of those trained in its praxis, this understanding must also be kept free of all "fanciful mysticism." The possibility of pure intuition is explicitly denied. "What remains constant is the binding of such intuitive knowledge to ordinary or inferred sensory mediations" (998). Knowledge of other minds is necessarily mediated by symbols.[17]

Troeltsch goes further than this, hinting at a number of points in his text that for him the thesis of the creative character of action, of knowledge of other minds, and of ideal formation must also be reflected on the metaphysical level. Here he bases himself on his interpretation of Leibniz's theory of monads and Malebranche's philosophy of participation. This I leave to one side. I will merely mention that Troeltsch inclines toward this metaphysical foundation because he views it as a means of avoiding interpreting human creativity in an antireligious way, of seeing it instead as a form of participation in divine spirit.[18]

If, therefore, individuals, collectivities, and institutions are inconceivable without ideal construction and if their specific meaning- and value-oriented historical individuality, which goes way beyond biological individuality, is constituted by this very fact, then this also means that we can never view the objects of historical contemplation as dormant. If someone has an ideal, she cannot avoid locating herself in relationship to it; she will also inevitably be located by others within the imaginary space thus generated. In contemporary philosophy, Alasdair MacIntyre, Charles Taylor, and Paul Ricoeur have elaborated the narrative structure of our self-understanding with particular clarity.[19] Taylor especially sees that we must interpret our action as the attempt to live up to ideals, evaluating it, as such, in terms of the success of our efforts. We examine how our life has gone so far, and whether the action we are preparing to undertake takes us closer to or further away from our ideals. It seems to me that Troeltsch is intuiting the same thing when he asserts that the basic concept of the historical individuality gives rise to that of the "continual context of becoming." The third stage thus introduces the concept of *development in the sense of a continual context of becoming.*

HISTORICAL DEVELOPMENT

The concept of historical development is open to misunderstanding in a range of ways. It does not mean "progress" or "evolution" or a Hegelianizing process of reading developmental trends into values on the basis of a blend of science and belief (854). Like subsequent influential thinkers (Karl Löwith), Troeltsch interprets the philosophy-of-history concept of progress straightforwardly as "secularization of Christian eschatology" in the sense of the idea of "a final, universal goal to be attained by all humankind, a goal transferred from the sphere of miracle and transcendence to that of immanence and natural explanation" (230). But for Troeltsch this concept of progress is only comprehensible in specific historical periods of palpable advance and only ever through faith. The historical concept of development, meanwhile, merely refers to individual developments in which we may identify convergence on (or remoteness from) given ideal formations. Such developments may fuse together to form a whole; often, though, they simply exist in parallel or occur in succession. As unavoidable as abstract concepts ("Protestantism") are, the historian must strive to reestablish the fluidity of action and experience congealed by such abstraction. This undoubtedly includes reconstruction of developments ascendant in a given case that articulate and realize meaning, "except that this ascent is invariably succeeded by disintegration, exhaustion, or disorder that in turn appears as an abrupt or gradual breakdown. There can be no question of a continual, all accumulating and expanding progress, simply stretching out forever in an overall progression" (232).

The concept of evolution, as introduced in the cultural and social sciences by Herbert Spencer, must also be understood in a very different way than that of historical development. This is merely to highlight a difference rather than judge the value of evolutionary theory to the cultural and social sciences. It may be possible to apply this theory in all kinds of ways, which I do not consider here. The difference lies in the fact that the concept of evolution is not concerned with the continuity of meaning; that is, with the creative linkage of present action with a past to which orienting ideals always remain related. The theory of evolution, of course, remains captive to a natural scientific conception of time, while historical time arises from the subjective experience of action, and for that reason "determining boundaries is quite impossible; caesuras are simply inserted more or less arbitrarily in accordance with configurations of meaning and major changes of meaning" (230). Because of this, theory construction here never means an advance to universal laws; if it wishes to avoid dissolving into empty abstractions, such theory construction can never divorce itself entirely from the "description of compared individualities" (236).

But as convincing as it is to mark it off from "progress" and "evolution," is this idea of development not merely a weak echo of Hegelian metaphysics—"romantic humbug," as Max Weber put it with his customary acerbity, probably during a conversation with Troeltsch (382)? In the first instance, Troeltsch believes Weber has simply misunderstood his concept of development. For him, Weber, his long-term friend and rival, is guided by strong values, ones that he personally espoused; these are "a belief in human dignity, from which it followed that democracy was the relatively most just and most moral system of government, and a belief in Germany's political future and grandeur" (854). But just as characteristic of Weber as these two value orientations is the iron discipline with which he rejects any attempt to "read these values back into lines of development" (ibid.), allowing such values to prejudice scientific explanation or combining the two. The "basic dichotomy between causal givenness and obligatory value, which are never . . . to be viewed synoptically in terms of growth and value realization" (853), is something Weber shares with Rickert and neo-Kantianism as a whole, but it is Weber who expresses it most starkly.

The misunderstanding lies in the fact that the idea of development, in the sense described here, is not intended to circumvent the stating of one's personal opinion or covertly declare this task dealt with. When we identify moves toward or away from historical ideal formations within historical processes, this task of self-positioning remains to be done—however close to or distant from our own views these ideal formations may be. What counts here is the investigation of historical developments in terms of their relation to ideals and the "sense for evidence and reality" (854) experienced by the researcher as he carries out this investigation. Of course, the feeling that we have not just constructed a historical tendency but factually apprehended it cannot in itself be the decisive factor in our arguments. But we cannot entirely disregard it either if we really want to elucidate the logic of historical research in light of the historian's praxis.

Unlike Weber, Troeltsch therefore draws not so much on neo-Kantian criticism or on "experimental psychology based on universal, causal-genetic laws," but rather—recalling Dilthey—on "empathetic and understanding psychology. In the end, understanding psychology always had to take into account aptitudes, dispositions, and formations of higher value and had to immerse itself in the flow of their becoming in order to reach understanding retrospectively and to make meaningful interpretations" (715). This is another reason for Troeltsch's obvious, if by no means uncritical sympathies for Henri

Bergson. In Bergson's work, the relationship between action, freedom, and metaphysics

> is the exact reverse of Kant. It is not the intellect and mathematics that constitute the pure understanding independent of everything practical, and it is not only the practical and ethical that reveal freedom and the absolute. Instead, understanding is conditioned by the practical life situation, and freedom and the absolute constitute the immediate experience and certainty of the metaphysical ground of things, of the free, creative, illimitable will and life in itself—and for Bergson, the ethical element certainly does not retreat innocuously behind freedom, creation, and perpetual movement. Intuition and metaphysics, our life and global life are essentially identical. What flashes into view here is not primarily a closed system of rational values related to the presumed necessity and independent validity of mathematics, but rather the boundlessly creative productivity of global life per se. We experience this productivity in our own relative freedom and historical regeneration, but it can never be recognized from intellectual concepts oriented to identity, repetition, and a closed system, even if these concepts really were what they are usually taken to be. Intuition is liberation from intellectualism and mathematicism, the ascent into metaphysics—not the closed and rationally necessary metaphysics of purpose and absolute value again, but a metaphysics of completely unpredictable and constantly innovative productivity and freedom. (939)

From this perspective, based on Dilthey and Bergson, and also closely related to American Pragmatism, Weber's skepticism about the concept of historical development in this sense appears unfounded, if not self-contradictory. It is true that Weber eliminated "every remnant of a general, universally historical and teleological tendency" from his comparative sociology, and for good reason, but, taken together, his brilliant studies—firmly grounded in reality—in agrarian and commercial history, on the genesis of modern capitalism, on the history of city and state, on the economic ethics of the world religions represent "fragments of a grand, comprehensive outlook oriented to sociology and developmental history" (595). We cannot, therefore, avoid the question of whether the historical picture emerging from his analyses was really derived "in an essentially causal-genetic way from law-based connections among elemental components" (854), as he proclaimed with regard to methodology, or whether his major claims of historical tendencies—from "disenchantment" to "rationalization"—do not in fact entail assumptions of historical development that Weber is unable to consistently acknowledge.[20]

Troeltsch laments Weber's switch to positivism with respect to these issues, even if it is a positivism sensitized to historical research via instruments such as the "ideal type" and the concept of the "objective possibility"; as far as his contemporaries are concerned, he positions himself far more closely to Georg Simmel and Max Scheler. Both retain the concept of development founded in the historian's praxis, while also purging it of teleological assumptions. Nonetheless, Troeltsch is not satisfied with either solution. He is unhappy with the dualism of Platonic ideas of values and a philosophy-of-life conception of the vital force (*Lebensstrom*) found in Scheler's work. On the basis of this dualism, "development" can only mean that "a system of ideas, in itself free of development, is appropriated and extended into an endlessly flowing, continuous stream of life with an increasing will to live" (911). As sensitive as Scheler is to the phenomenology of moral feelings and to history, he ultimately removes values themselves from history. He is "protected from Simmel's incorporeality and egocentrism, from Dilthey's brooding uncertainty, from Windelband's and Rickert's purely formalistic objectivity, and from Nietzsche's arbitrariness" (915), but at the same time his dogmatic limitations prevent him from fleshing out the concept of development in relation to the fact of historical ideal formation in a truly consistent way.

The last quotation already tells us that Troeltsch also found Georg Simmel's solution unsatisfactory. To clarify the reasons why, we must examine the inverse risk that results from renunciation of a teleological concept of development. We might call it the risk of historical episodism. If, in contrast to notions of progress and the work of Hegel, there is no universal historical context of meaning, then history may fragment into disconnected parts; it may be possible to compare these parts, but no connecting thread runs between them. If we assume the fact of ideal formation, then in the first instance we must obviously assess all historical constructs in light of themselves, in light of their own ideals. Even if, in taking this step, we disregard the fact that the historian cannot help but place himself and his values in relationship to the individual immanent value of a historical construct, we come up against the limits of an immanent perspective of this kind. This perspective could only speak to us by presenting "depictions of the past [as] mere examples for edification and encouragement, or perhaps for warning and deterrence" (246). But this becomes impossible as soon as we introduce the concept of continuous development in the sense described here, even if we do so only within the individual historical construct. Quite regardless of how the historian may view things from his historical period, development within this construct itself

> never takes place in isolation but always in interaction with other totalities, and it is precisely from their minglings and cross-fertilizations that the richest and most important formations arise. The Greeks and the Near East, the Teutons and antiquity, the Middle Ages and Islam are well-known examples of such interaction. But this already requires us to locate the development of a particular totality in the reciprocal contact and movement of adjacent totalities. There is no such thing as an isolated history of development. But if not, then any comparatively penetrating analysis must always cover the interlacing of different totalities and thus eventually extend its scope to the ultimate limit: the human race. (ibid.)

Even if we weld together the development of all these totalities, we cannot simply separate this from the question of the development of meaning. The problem of universal history emerges of necessity from the concept of development (see 963).

The universal-history perspective is unavoidable the moment we take the concept of historical development seriously, but in practical terms universal history is only ever realizable within limits. However much he may focus on universal history, Troeltsch wishes to avoid a merely abstract concept of humanity. As a result, he suggests that initially we consider only "closed, perceptibly and objectively causally connected groups of events that are already completed at the time" (1002). He is highly skeptical of any universal history not grounded in this way. We need not pursue here the empirical question of the extent to which, in Troeltsch's day or our own, "humanity" refers to a de facto event continuum rather than merely an abstract concept. All that matters here is that for Troeltsch the idea of universal history is of necessity derived from the notion of historical development, whether or not it is practically realizable.

This idea had already been conceived even without the specifically historical concept of development—for example, in Jewish messianism, the Christian doctrine of salvation or redemption, and Stoicist natural law: "People did not yet need the concept of development because they had universal, ahistorical truths, and the relation of this universality to historical diversity and to individual persons merely presented difficulties that were easily overcome. They had a goal, and in one way or another quickly made it compatible with history" (1003–4). Attempts to construct universal histories then appeared in the Enlightenment and the work of Herder, Hegel, and Comte, a number of thinkers inspired by the philosophy of life, and a few professional historians. But after Hegel and Comte, skepticism about the purpose of such an endeavor increasingly held sway. Dilthey, for example, feared that any attempt to go beyond the reconstruction of specific historical structures would make history the mere "outlet for an abstract idea, or into a puppet show" (799), in which actors merely implement a transhistorical plan. In much the same way, Benedetto Croce aimed to dispose of "the puppetlike character of the individual, incontestable in Hegel's system," and get beyond teleologism, "the a priori value system that culminates in the state and the absolute spirit together with its ultimate, complete realization that draws everything out to the end" (923). But particularly instructive with respect to recovering the concept of historical development—against Rickert and Max Weber—and the dangers that this involves is Georg Simmel, with whom Troeltsch grapples in particular depth. He praises Simmel for coming up with a conception of history and historical individuality richer than that found in neo-Kantianism. But while Simmel was brilliant at recognizing individual creativity within history, which enabled him to produce his monographs on great thinkers and artists, he was entirely captive to a perspective that privileged "an individual imperative for certain cultural circles, or, better, for certain personalities": "There is not even a history of philosophy, but only ad hoc analysis of the philosophical 'attitudes' that emerge from the current of mass thought" (884). An outstanding epistemological sensibility but without the religious background of Ranke and Humboldt, a Kantianism "with neither God nor the soul" (886–87)—this is Troeltsch's view of Simmel. Here, the idea of development is honored with respect to individual phenomena, but eliminated the moment we wish to apply it to the relationship between historical individualities.

THE INEVITABLE SELF-POSITIONING OF THE HISTORIAN

But this relationship becomes totally unavoidable if we factor in the stance of the historian herself. The fourth step is therefore to demonstrate the *inevitable self-positioning of the historian*, who has her own ideals in relation to historically effective ideal formations. The fact of ideal formation is not just of significance to defining the object of historical analyses, but also to the present and the situation of those carrying out historical analysis. A simple thought experiment may serve to demonstrate this. We may do everything we can to recognize and defend enduring truths and timeless values, but we can be sure that subsequent generations ("future historians" [394]) will treat us as historical individualities as described in the second argumentational stage. But if we anticipate the future historicization of our thinking and evaluations, then we ourselves can clearly see the fundamental contingency of our own opinions and validity claims. To refuse to take this step is to evade the full force of historicization. Troeltsch sees such refusal at work whenever one's own actions appear as the overcoming of history, as the mere disposal of historical ballast.[21] He is thinking of the "natural system" of the Enlightenment, for which "historical study essentially consisted in the critical clearing away of the past and, if necessary, in demonstrating the ever-present *consensus gentium* of the truths of natural reason—unless, for such truths, people preferred to restrict themselves to the Chinese or to primitive peoples" (281). A historical consciousness that incorporates the self-reflection of the present and one's own doings makes it clear that rejecting current values is just as much a historical deed as upholding them, that one way or the other one's own ideals have a history as do all other ideals, a history, moreover, that we must relate to the history we are analyzing.

We never "choose" our values outside of historical situations to which we might then subsequently apply them. So Kierkegaard's notion of a "leap of faith"—which "led him into a vehement, exaggerated, absolutely individualistic pietism" (383)—is an exaggeration of the indisputable element of decision and daring that is always present when we have the will "to shape responsible ideals of our own" (382) and thus consciously commit to values whose claim to validity we have experienced as subjectively self-evident. Eduard Spranger has come up with a felicitous term for Troeltsch's stance here: "existential historicism."[22] Indeed, Troeltsch does not conceal the element of existential decision through teleological or evolutionist conceptions of history; but neither does he rip this element out of history, as if we could simply overcome history through some kind of decision. Further, he does not misleadingly portray what occurs in responsible ideal formation as if the experience of subjective self-evidence itself originates in our will; in fact this experience eludes our will.[23] We experience values as a demand made of us, or not, and this applies both to the present and to our encounter with the ideals of times past and unfamiliar cultures that speak to us through historical objects.

Many authors have conceded that the constitution of the historical object is dependent on our comprehension of its immanent values and that we cannot in fact relate to the values of other eras or cultures without reflecting on our own values. But they sometimes come to a different conclusion than that found in Troeltsch's existential historicism. They demand that we present the relationship between present and past ideal constructions in "purely theoretical terms, without taking any position and without tailoring the entire process to a meaning to be realized in the present or future, thus severing completely the threads that connect historically perceptible contexts of meaning with all present-day decision about meaning and shaping of meaning. Such demands are not lacking, and some historians see the dignity peculiar to the discipline of history specifically in them." But for Troeltsch, unless we are talking about such things as editorial work, the purposelessness demanded in such research is a mistake, one that leads to "bad historicism." Since Nietzsche's polemics this means "unlimited relativism, frivolous preoccupation with things, paralysis of the will and of one's own life" (242):[24] "Then the particular interest of the observer and actor is no longer completely ruled out, but turns into taking pleasure in the play of phenomena, in the diversity of the real. It turns into an outlook that embraces everything and excuses everything, into interest in mere form, or even into skepticism with all the moral effects of an elegantly cultivated irony. In tough-minded intellects this irony turns into sarcasm, in mild and gentle ones, into humor" (ibid.).

But Troeltsch not only considers the psychological consequences of a contemplative ethos and an ascetic attitude toward our opinions as problematic. He also sees it as "logically quite impossible not to go beyond that realm of historically broadening and stimulating possibilities to the shaping of independent meaning, and it is logically impossible not to make use of historical perception for independent decision and creation" (243). All historical meaning is potentially current meaning. We always feel called to endorse or oppose it. If we do not feel called in this way, this meaning remains dead to us—as historians, we have failed to bring it to life. But if we feel called, then this call goes way beyond research, affecting our present, future-directed action. Then we see ourselves as actors who assimilate specific pasts and particular developments and carry these on into the future. This is a matter of "an unfolding of the data in the movement toward what ought to be, as the observer perceives it from his or her situation. It is not . . . the most factually substantiated tendencies of the past and present, but . . . the tendencies of the greatest possible value" (251) that we draw on. We then incorporate historically originating ideals into our action and attempt to realize them beyond their historical manifestations, perhaps even beyond their past potential for realization.

This radically changes the meaning of historical teleology. The construction of history as the progressive achievement of an ultimate goal, in which acting subjects play no role or are mere marionettes, becomes a "teleology of the will that molds and shapes its past into the future out of the present." But because this will itself reflects on the conditions of its genesis, this action-oriented and nonobjectivist teleology is not voluntaristic. Will formation and historical construction correct one another in this way. "This is the only possible way to master historicism philosophically" (299). This philosophical mastery does not mean that we have achieved a foundation on which the disciplines concerned with historical objects, including the present, might now progress forever in a continuous and cumulative fashion. On the contrary, this insight teaches us that differences in historical construction are inevitable and—because of historical change, new action situations, and new ideal formations—will always remain inevitable.

"A Christian and a humanist, a pessimist and a might-makes-right realist, even with the strongest devotion to and critical ascertainment of the facts, will always construe them differently, for the events deemed cogent and decisive will necessarily seem different to each"

(1012). So present-day evaluative reactions on the one hand and historical processes on the other become intertwined in a way that cannot be conveyed by a simple distinction between is and ought, facts and values.[25] In cases where the *is* in question itself contains an ought, as with historically originating norms and values, we position ourselves not only with respect to facticity, but also the validity claims of historical constructs. To declare genesis of relevance to theories of validity is not to replace the discussion of validity with the discussion of genesis.[26]

AFFIRMATIVE GENEALOGY

This brings us to the fifth stage, which is where the concept of "affirmative genealogy" must be introduced. My explanation of why the scholar working historically has inevitably to position himself vis-à-vis the meanings found in individual historical constructs and their developments referred to the way in which historically embodied meaning calls upon us; this is something that we can close ourselves off from only through false self-constraint or by failing to allow this historical meaning to come fully alive to us. We hear this appeal in a particular historical present and within this present it is oriented toward new action geared toward the future. In the preface to his great work, Troeltsch draws attention to the "problem shift" that had become undeniable in his day: "In place of the objective teleology and contemplation of the overall progression of humanity founded on laws of nature, spirit or the world, we have the contemporary cultural synthesis produced by the [thinking] subject" (163–64). This is not a matter of an alternative between a historical or present-day orientation; instead, gaining a historically grounded understanding of the present helps solve contemporary orientational problems. On this logic, the graver these contemporary orientational problems are, the greater our need for a historical grounding. We must not allow the desire to shake off history in order to free ourselves for the present and future to gain traction.

Unmistakable in Troeltsch's work here is an argumentational trope that goes back to the Protestant historical-critical Bible interpretation.[27] As in this tradition, in light of orientational issues of a given present, and repelled by the fact that particular interpretations of historical texts have become dogmatically ossified, the initial impulse is to breathe new life into these texts by reembedding them in the historical contexts of their emergence. In the first instance, this historicization increases these texts' unfamiliarity, their cultural and chronological distance from the investigators' present. But by opening themselves to the appeal inherent in this vibrant other, they also experience something new that does not remain exoticized in the past but instead reorientates them, both individually and collectively. In the argumentational trope described here, this perspective, which is theological in the first instance, a perspective that involves seeing historical thinking not as an attack on faith but as the royal road to the revitalization of faith, is declared the model for any productive conception of history—beyond the realm of faith and theology.

Troeltsch defends Dilthey himself against the preconception that he had merely wandered around aimlessly in history attempting to understand everything, dooming himself to an epigonism characterized by a lack of creativity and resulting haphazard enrichment through the creative achievements of others. On the contrary, for him "the immediacy of experience [was to draw] all the energies and powers of history into a living cycle" (802). But Troeltsch lays claim to a methodologically far more conscious balance between historical reconstruction and present orientation. His forceful assertion is that a culture that remains vital "must repeatedly demolish mythical and conventional history in order, like Antaeus, to achieve contact with the maternal ground of its formation" (1042). Of course, that which is generated in this way will be

> destroyed and displaced again for the same reasons. This will continue as long as the sovereign power exists to recast, simplify, deepen, and revitalize our historical heritage, to draw forth primal powers ever anew, and to discard the constantly accumulating ballast. If this power is lost, history itself loses meaning and interest. No one would desire to study history merely to gain knowledge of bygone things. If they did, the study of history would turn into scholasticism, and with it would be forgotten, for there would be no need for history in a world of barbarism or neoprimitivism. (1043)

It is not just Christianity that could be revitalized by historical self-investigation. The same goes for the always new, historicizing, and thus revitalizing relation to antiquity, the Middle Ages, or whatever past it might be. But these historically obtained orientations to the present are of course necessarily contested. Each of them is itself a historical individuality. But individual positions are not simply "a harmless variation within a homogenous whole. No mere play of various individualities, with a final levelling of all in one common mean is possible; it requires a conflict."[28] As much as historically oriented sciences might progress, they will never simply accumulate knowledge about history, but always acquire and espouse historical meanings in new and contentious ways.

I have described the existential historicism exuded by all these reflections as the method of affirmative genealogy. This method is genealogical because it has freed itself radically from the idea that we might contemplate an objective teleology, and this indeed was Nietzsche's achievement. Troeltsch is well aware of Nietzsche's pioneering role here methodologically, though he does not comment specifically on his concept of "genealogy." According to Troeltsch, Nietzsche is the main source of "the crisis and self-awareness of modern historicism" (332); he has "really understood and had a feeling for the problem of offering proof for values from history" (331). "The elements for a theory of history" (764) are all present in Nietzsche's work: the problem of historical time, the relationship of the concept of development to values, their connection with shaping the future. But Nietzsche in no way resolved the problems he highlighted so brilliantly. We find an intersection of deterministic and voluntaristic propositions, but no link between transvaluing contemporary creativity and a tradition anchored in the past but still vital, impactful, and worth maintaining. For Troeltsch, it is Nietzsche's atheism that is responsible for his dissatisfying inconsistency; this is the logical precondition for "the sovereign and original proclamation of a vigorous individuality that constitutes its own peerless god" (330). Strikingly, at a time when the widespread and seemingly unquestioned assumption was of an advancing and irreversible secularization, Troeltsch appears to have regarded the atheism of Feuerbach and Schopenhauer, Marx and Nietzsche, as a historically temporary phenomenon. He defends their achievements by stating that they will retain their significance even if "the atheism from which they first arose will someday belong to history" (763).

This genealogical, that is, contingency-conscious reconstruction of the past is described as "affirmative" because recourse to the processes of ideal formation, the genesis of values, rather than negating our commitment to them or endowing us with the sovereignty to assess our value commitments, opens our minds to the way in which historically embodied meaning calls upon us. This recourse is not a matter of vain reference to a series of eminent forebears in order to back up what we already think anyway—as often happens amid the battle of opinions as we emphasize the superiority of our own traditions. This would be no more than a struggle for distinction in which we try to enhance our own status by highlighting our background. "Affirmative" does not involve affirming a factual reality in the present, but affirming the way in which historically formed ideals call upon us, the willingness to realize erstwhile values or perhaps even those that are supposedly valid now, values with which social reality adorns itself but from which it in fact deviates. In this way, we can examine the historical genesis of values experienced in the present with a sense of subjective self-evidence and with affective intensity—as with the value of universal human dignity in the context of this book. The methodological focus of affirmative genealogy is on the "creative junctures and the tendencies that originate within them" (945). But none of these tendencies are assumed to entail a teleology culminating with us. What produces the teleology is our revitalizing recourse to the appeal made by historically generated ideals. Through the same process, what started out as mere subjective self-evidence is refined until it achieves a state of historically satiated argumentational clarity, though this can never be a matter of pure justification of validity removed from history.

The call that goes out from historically embodied meaning must be heard and absorbed individually. Does this mean that its impact is in a sense transmitted only between historical individualities and that all claims to universality must vanish in the ocean of historical particularities? This would be a complete misunderstanding of my arguments as well as Troeltsch's intentions, in two respects. First, Troeltsch was enough of a Kantian—as I pointed out in the first stage—to acknowledge the scope of a formal moral universalism, though he believes we come up against its limits whenever we are dealing with specific cultural ideals. In his view, we cannot construct such a cultural ideal solely on the basis of a formal moral universalism. Though Kant's instincts have now received empirical support from the psychology of moral judgment and the social abilities of children and adolescents, the boundaries marked by Troeltsch remain in place. We cannot answer the question of which actions can be justified in universalist terms, which cultural traditions and which institutions ought to be carried on or transformed, without addressing historical particularity.

Second, the call that goes out from historically embodied meaning is not merely an appeal to us on the subjective level but to everyone, an appeal that makes sense to us because it entails a claim that is valid independent of us. When we experience a value, we experience it as valid in itself, and when we experience it as such we have an obligation to recognize it. Individuality in the historical sense is not subjectivity in the sense of the opposite of objectivity and universality. Instead, this term expresses the insight that on the level of values (or "cultural ideals") every attempt to achieve timeless validity must always remain a temporal phenomenon. So what we need to do is not oppose universal validity claims or negate their possibility, but to consistently take account of the necessary situatedness of these claims' emergence, espousal, and recognition. This is not to give up the idea of universal validity but to transform it in light of a radical awareness of historical contingency: "True universality does not apply to humankind. It neither makes possible the idea of humankind nor yields a universally identical form of autonomous, rational, liberated or enlightened reason. True universality does apply, however, to individual formations by virtue of the penetrating, animating power of life as a whole. The rationality of this power rests on an inner correspondence with the developing basic direction of the divine will to live, intuitively grasped and surmised from history, verified in comparison and in practical encounter" (379).

Many present-day readers who sympathize with the basic thrust of this radical historical awareness of contingency will have winced when they got to the end of the last quotation, as a statement they probably found quite plausible suddenly laid bare, through reference to the "divine will to live," the theological meaning it held (in part) for Troeltsch. It is a specific idea of God that inheres in Troeltsch's existential historicism, the notion of a God revealed historically and in history not just at a single point of time or once and for all, but in human action.[29] He is guided by this idea when he analyzes the European Enlightenment as a period of transition between the unquestioned validity of Christianity and the emergent historical and cultural relativization of all certainties as a time of "a flat denial, or certainly a restriction, of the historical through rational construction . . . the last barrier against the nascent historical consciousness to which, unwillingly, rational construction often adapts itself" (185). In his view, Kant's rationalism is the "secularized echo of religious absolutism."[30] But sharing Troeltsch's religious motives is no more a prerequisite for accepting his methodological arguments than is agreement with the religious motives of Kant and Hegel or agreement with the antireligious motives of Marx and Nietzsche with respect to their arguments.

It does follow necessarily from his arguments that a moral or legal universalism is dependent on the historical and cultural sources from which its motives and ideas take their sustenance. But this does not mean that we should construe the history of humanity as oriented toward a fixed normative standard—fixed because it is considered justified. As Troeltsch argues: "The only direction open to us is to wrest from a distinct, individual sphere of culture and its development the cultural synthesis that encapsulates and continues it. The synthesis itself, in accordance with this overall assumption, must necessarily be something historical and individual" (392–93). In concrete terms, for him this means that in the Europe of his day there can only be "one world history, the history of the European world" (1025). This history is not meant to close our minds to universal history, but to confine us to the realities of de facto processes of universalization. The reasons put forward for this are of course empirical ones. In retrospect, they seem strangely out of touch with the very real universalization that had already begun. Troeltsch seems to underestimate the embedding of the European economy in a world context, the significance of colonialism and imperialism, and the global character of the world war. He wrongly predicts that America will move ever closer to Europe (1048), and against the objections of leading Orientalists, he excludes Islam from the universal history of Europeans (1045). Contrary to his own earlier text on the social teachings of the Christian churches and groups, he now underlines Christianity's character as "the religion of Europe" (1037). There are good historical reasons to argue against all of these limiting views.[31] But such a critique only goes to demonstrate the correctness of Troeltsch's methodological claims: a less Eurocentric conception of Europe is itself dependent on the kind of arguments I have referred to here as "affirmative genealogy."

The first stage of my argument, which emphasized the fact of ideal formation, might already have raised the suspicion that a method for analyzing historical phenomena that begins on this basis is "idealistic" in a touching or risible sense. Does such a method not disregard material interests, the significance of economy and power, hypocrisy and repression—every disillusioning analysis produced since Feuerbach, Marx, Nietzsche (and Freud) and their hermeneutics of suspicion? As a history of ideals, is such a view of history not damned to remain a mere history of ideas or alternatively to follow a path across the peaks rather than entering the valleys of everyday struggles?

SOCIOLOGICAL REALISM

Now there are good reasons for viewing all the hermeneuticians of suspicion themselves with plenty of suspicion, but this does not mean we can learn nothing from them. The sixth step is therefore concerned with defending affirmative genealogy *against the suspicion that it lacks realism*. Just as Nietzsche's historical awareness of contingency with respect to the genesis of values, as entailed in his genealogical method, is constitutive of my argument here, the opening and turning of Hegelian historical dialectics to the sociological and economic dimension as a result of Marxism is central to any empirically grounded affirmative genealogy.

Troeltsch leaves us in no doubt about his high regard for Marx and Engels and quite a number of their continuators. Though the problem of how to justify the criteria of historical value judgments, as mentioned above, is left entirely unresolved in Marx's work, he at least finds in Marxism "greater regard for the real and historical than in the purely rational solutions, to say nothing of the pessimistic-nihilistic solutions" (341–42). Troeltsch acknowledges Marx's scientific significance, his achievement or at least his role as source of stimulation even more clearly when he attributes to him "a new concept of the interdependence of all social structures and of the inner movement of history" and emphasizes that "the greatest achievement of Marxism" was "the discovery and analysis of modern capitalist society itself as a completely singular historical phenomenon" (541). He regards two of Marx's reasons for breaking away from the Hegel school as epochal advances in historical thinking: "the thirst for the immediacy of concrete physical life in opposition to the completely overconceptualized spirituality of the Hegelian system, and the need for rationally necessary objectives for the future instead of mere contemplation and comprehension of the completed process" (542). Troeltsch even describes the *Communist Manifesto* as a captivating demonstration of the potential of Marxist dialectics: "This again was ultimately an outline of universal history, firmly connected to a general social aim, but free of all unrealistic abstraction and all sentimentality. This was the basis of its magic" (552).[32] Marx was a thoroughly historical thinker who wished to explain history not through quasi-natural scientific laws but through the identification of historical-individual structural laws and the tensions to which these give rise, which drive things forward. From a purely philosophical point of view, Marx's changes to Hegelian dialectics are "cruel ravages of its original and only possible meaning, of its metaphysical and logical foundation, of its utterly indispensable connection to the analysis of consciousness and its combination of being and value" (557–58). But these philosophical "ravages" also represent a process of intellectual unshackling and increased historical realism.

"Of course there is more than enough of the one-sided, the forced, the tendentious, and the inflexible, not to mention the darkness of a godless and vacuous background which is applied to this depiction of history, which mingles economic realism, fatalism, and even ethical revolutionism" (556). The benefit lies in the insight into the importance of focusing on the investigation of historical dynamics, "the interpretable, depictable, concretely individual unity of all historical formations; the sense of oneness and teleological direction in all individual historical totalities as well as in their presumed connections, both mutual and successive" (566). But the price that Marxist dialectics pays for enhanced historical realism in comparison with Hegel is very high. Particularly in the work of Engels, this dialectics is partly naturalized, partly transformed into a naive teleology of a world history on the way toward communism, a teleology whose relationship to the pathos of revolutionary action is anything but clear. However much we might sympathize with some of its motives and respect some of its achievements, we are left with the impression that the Marxian transformation of Hegelian dialectics represents more of an aporetic entrapment in its unresolved problems than a solution to these problems. Neither Marxian nor the original Hegelian dialectics provides a solution to the problem of how to mediate between a realistic analysis of history and the reflective justification of values.

Marxism retained an inherent tension between a desire to produce criticism of ideology and its own truth claims. On the one hand "all values, truths, and general feeling independent of the economy appear impotent, and in their impotence are exposed as a sham" (572), while on the other at least the natural sciences, great art (on the margins of Marxist thought), and of course unequivocally its own social theory are claimed not to involve self-deception. This tension is resolved only through the notion that a kind of definitive historical breakthrough is in the offing, after which the self-alienation expressed in ideological constructs will be permanently overcome. As a result, the profoundly historical inclinations of the founders of Marxism are marked by their perspective on the overcoming of all the history that has gone before, while their own theory is regarded as anticipating something not open to historical revision. The utopian invalidation of radical historicization thus quickly reverses the gain in realism over "idealist" dialectics.[33]

If we want to achieve realism, we must therefore take a different approach and break with Marxist dialectics. Nonetheless, Marxism can still serve as a rich source of stimulation. Troeltsch clearly believes that Marxism had an impact on leading historians and historically oriented social scientists of his day, such that he deals with several of them—Tönnies, Plenge, Bücher, Sombart, and Max Weber—in the chapter on Marxism. He sees the unmistakable impact of Marxism in Hans Delbrück's great history of war as well (588). Most important for him are the attempts by Sombart and Weber, while conceding that Marxism is right to emphasize the economy, to avoid the false conclusions that result by elaborating just how much, in the so-called base of all cultural-social life, "there inheres from the outset a certain inner disposition peculiar to the cultural sphere in question—a disposition that has given certain colors and directions to the most elementary organization of life—or [to the extent to which] certain economic upheavals receive their force and significance only with the appearance of spiritual attitudes" (575). Max Weber's studies of the genesis of a "spirit of capitalism" are especially pertinent here, as are his comparative studies of the economic ethics of the world religions, which demonstrate that the kind of general statements on base and superstructure found in Marxism are ultimately of little use. The nature of the problem here—namely, the relationship between economic and cultural-historical developments—is such that it "admits of no general solution, but in relation to particular circumstances always and everywhere presents a picture that is unique and individual" (595). So however much Troeltsch distanced himself from Max Weber's views on the justification of historical criteria, his thinking closely matches the sociological-realist turn that Weber represented.[34]

We should certainly view the affirmative genealogy that I aim to defend here as an attempt to justify values through historical reflection. But it must still provide a sociologically realistic historical analysis. Without one, it would itself become an ideological construction. If we take the fact of ideal formation as our point of departure, we will resist all attempts to conceive of historical dynamics as processes determined by laws of nature or explain them in terms of mere interests. To do so is not to close our eyes to the role of interests, power, and ideological delusions in history. Prominent in the work of Troeltsch is a task significant to such a realistic affirmative genealogy; namely, to provide a sociologically grounded historical periodization.

Troeltsch shares Marxism's skepticism about every periodization constructed chiefly in terms of cultural facts. For him Hegel is the epitome of such a "purely ideological" periodization of history. "For his state is the juridical self-construal of a universal spirit or realm of soul that is ultimately defined by a religio-metaphysical self-consciousness. This self-consciousness comes into being in the course of the destinies of peoples and nations" (1054). But Hegel is certainly not the only one to make such an attempt. Right up to the present, many authors have tried to make universal historical periodizations out of what are in fact periodizations of the history of art ("postmodernity"), history of philosophy, or history of religion. It was long typical of the German tradition of historical studies to use stages of state development as the principle of historical classification and to take this to be more realistic than ideological periodization. Yet even then, partly in the wake of Hegel, the state itself was often viewed in quite ideal terms and less "as a formation with very real powers and material needs. Only with the satisfaction of these needs is the foundation prepared for a relatively independent, vigorous coming to consciousness and self-shaping of the spirit that infuses a brief span of time and space" (1063).

Interestingly, though, in Troeltsch's case it is not—as in Marxism and in the work of many other apparent realists—a belief in the ultimate irrelevance of religion or metaphysics or of their merely epiphenomenal character that prompts him to reject a historical periodization founded in religion or metaphysics. On the contrary, he thinks it is true that major cultural periods are characterized by "a distinctive metaphysical consciousness." We must, however, make a sharp distinction between an elusive foundation of lived religiosity and institutionalized religions formalized as religious doctrine: "The religio-metaphysical dimension leads in the direction of stable periods, but as a means of objective periodization, it cannot be applied to official, organized religion because of its elusiveness and because of its nonidentity with the tendencies" (1054). This view is—correctly, I think—based on the fact that all institutionalization of religious experience and articulation, and all attempts to fix these in doctrine, lead ineluctably into the field of economic, political, and social interests and forces and therefore cannot be used analytically as if they were independent of these. These ideas chime with what I said while introducing the concepts of the sacred and sacralization.[35] The interesting things here are the dynamics of sacralization processes and the constant shifts in the content of the objects to which the quality of sacredness is attributed. These processes of the emergence and shifting of sacrality occur within "the great, durable sociological-economic-political forms that present themselves individually and allow conceptual analysis." Every reconstruction of ideal formation, of value genesis, will therefore construct periodizations in accordance with the creative nodes of this particular development; but for a history that is not constructed as the affirmative genealogy of a particular value, a "somewhat more external conception of periodization" will prove more appropriate (1079).

We do not need to produce a historical-sociological analysis of the genesis of the appeal that rings out from historically embodied meaning in order to open ourselves to it. But if this meaning, if historically generated ideas and values have become abstract, dogmatic, or rigidified by convention, then historical research in the form of affirmative genealogy is the best way to breathe new life into them: only an encounter with their original vitality makes such meaning, which always already points beyond its conditions of emergence, newly perceptible. Right at the end of his wide-ranging reflections, Troeltsch comes up with a metaphor to convey the tasks of the present, which is of course what such historical reanimation has in mind: "to provide a new sociological matrix for the ideological material, and to give life to the sociological matrix with a new and fresh way of thinking, with a new conjoining, adapting, and recasting of the great historical components" (1097–98).

So reinterpretation of historically embodied meaning is just one part of the picture; if we are to do justice to this meaning, if we wish not just to hear its call but to realize it, then we must also achieve a realistic picture of present conditions for the realization of historically generated ideals and their unfulfilled potential. Values cannot remain mere values. They come alive only if they are defended argumentatively as values—but above all if they are upheld by institutions and embodied in practices.[36] In its historical analyses, an affirmative genealogy of human rights must therefore take account of the dimensions of values, institutions, and practices and the interplay of these dimensions. But it must also be geared toward the opportunities and risks of realizing values with respect to all these dimensions and their interplay today.

NOTES

1. Joas, *Genesis of Values*, 20–34.

2. Particularly instructive in this regard is the discrepancy between the concise summary of the typical point of view by Jerome B. Schneewind and the "value theory" alternative outlined by Paul Guyer. See Schneewind, "Autonomy, Obligation, and Virtue"; Guyer, *Kant on Freedom, Law, and Happiness*; Guyer, "From a Practical Point of View."

3. On the "destructive" interpretation, see my own interpretation of Nietzsche in *Genesis of Values*, 20–34; on the alternative, see, e.g., Owen, *Nietzsche's "Genealogy of Morality,"* and—going too far, in my view, to bring "genealogy" and "criticism" together—Saar, *Genealogie als Kritik*. For other important insights into genealogy in Nietzsche and Foucault, see MacIntyre, *Three Rival Versions of Moral Enquiry*, esp. 32–57 and 196–215.

4. Troeltsch, *Historismus und seine Probleme* (1922) and *Fünf Vorträge* (published in 1924 as *Der Historismus und seine Überwindung*). Page numbers in the text refer to the large *Historismus* book from 1922, with translations kindly

provided by David Reid and Garrett Paul. As their forthcoming translation of the book is still at the revision stage, these translations may differ slightly from the final published version. The publishers of the Troeltsch *Gesamtausgabe* (*Collected Works*) sensibly abandoned the 1924 title. The English version of the 1924 text was published in 1923 under the title *Christian Thought: Its History and Application*.

5. Ruddies, "Geschichte durch Geschichte überwinden," 217.

6. On the (non)reception of this work in the United States, see Paul, "*Der Historismus* in North America."

7. Gadamer, *Truth and Method*, 462.

8. Schwöbel, "Die Idee des Aufbaus"; Rendtorff, "Geschichte durch Geschichte überwinden."

9. Dilthey, "Rede zum 70. Geburtstag," 9.

10. This is also the reason why I treated neither the neo-Kantians nor Max Weber as contributors to the debate on this problem in my book on the genesis of values.

11. Here I draw on statements that I have made elsewhere—unconnected with Troeltsch and drawing on Pragmatism and Paul Ricoeur—to clarify the relationship between the good and the right. See Joas, *Genesis of Values*, 175–82. Very similar points are made in Troeltsch, *Fünf Vorträge*, 83.

12. He attributes it (325) to Rudolf Eucken. It seems clear to me, though, that Nietzsche and the American Pragmatists had already thought this thought before Eucken. Émile Durkheim also moved ever closer to this idea of the contingent genesis of new moral ideals. See esp. his last (uncompleted) text of 1917, "Introduction to Ethics," esp. 81.

13. Troeltsch, *Fünf Vorträge*, 117. The English translation (*Christian Thought*, 147) is flawed, referring to "subjective validities." With the concept of "subjective absoluteness," Troeltsch seems to me to be getting at the same thing that Max Scheler—through his critical engagement with Georg Simmel's theory of the individual law—expressed brilliantly as the self-evident recognition of the "good-as-such for me." See Scheler, *Formalism in Ethics*, 490. On Simmel and Scheler in this regard, though without yet considering Troeltsch, see Joas, *Genesis of Values*, 92.

14. Renouvier's thought was of constitutive significance to the intellectual self-discovery of both William James and Émile Durkheim. See James's early article "Bain and Renouvier," but above all his journal entry from 1870, prompted by Renouvier: "My first act of free will shall be to believe in free will" (quoted in Henry James, *Letters of William James*, 147). On Durkheim and Renouvier, see Durkheim's statement as quoted by René Maublanc (1930): "If you wish to develop your mind, commit yourself to the careful study of a master; get to know every last corner of a system of thought. This is what I did and my teacher was Renouvier" (quoted in Fournier, *Émile Durkheim*, 52).

15. I have attempted to develop a theory of action that draws broadly on this idea in *Creativity of Action*.

16. No comprehensive comparison of Troeltsch's ideas with Pragmatism has yet been produced. For an important first step in this direction, however, see Jaeger, "Ernst Troeltsch und John Dewey."

For many people today, the image of Pragmatism has been shaped by the writings of Richard Rorty, and he has contributed an original and influential text on the debate on human rights ("Human Rights, Rationality and Sentimentality"). I therefore want to briefly set out the difference between his thesis and my arguments in this book. I share Rorty's skepticism about the motivating force of reasons put forward through rational argument and thus about the role of fundamental philosophical justifications in the history of human rights. But I do not share his view that reasons lose their argumentational power as soon as they attempt to move beyond a particular cultural context. So I also think it is wrong when Rorty proposes that we abandon argument entirely in favor of narration. My proposal for an affirmative genealogy, meanwhile, defends a specific context-transcendent interleaving of narration and argument. Rorty spectacularly fails to grasp one of Pragmatism's key ideas; namely, that of experience and its articulation. This is what makes his reference to the "invention" of new metaphors, "conversion" to a new vocabulary for describing self and world and the manipulation of others' feelings, sound so voluntaristic. It is incorrect to state that when we answer the question of why we feel committed to particular values or a particular worldview, we draw on the pure contingency of our socialization. In fact we perceive these values and worldviews as appropriate articulations of the experiences that we or others have been through; we embrace new ones not through a decision but because we have encountered an articulation experienced as even more appropriate. Rorty has as little feeling for the specific truth claim that this entails, which does in fact differ from cognitive validity claims, as he does for the necessity, rather than simply abandoning philosophy in favor of literature, of instead developing an affirmative genealogy featuring as much empirical history and social science as possible.

17. There are exciting parallels, which merit closer attention, between Troeltsch's ideas here, which are a result of historicism, and George Herbert Mead's philosophy of temporality, rooted in Pragmatism. See Mead, *Philosophy of the Present*, and Joas, *George Herbert Mead*, 167–98.

18. For an excellent account, see Schwöbel, "Idee des Aufbaus," 276.

19. See MacIntyre, *After Virtue*; Taylor, *Sources of the Self*, esp. 46–47; Ricoeur, *Oneself as Another*. See also Joas, *Genesis of Values*, esp. 130–32.

20. Weber's latent conception of development is the starting point for Wolfgang Schluchter's oeuvre. See esp. Schluchter, *Rise of Western Rationalism*. Wolfgang Knöbl has put forward the interesting idea that the gap between Weber's contingency-sensitive constellation analyses and his contingency-resistant

processual categories arise from his failure to resolve the question of how to justify values. See Knöbl, "Makrotheorie zwischen Pragmatismus und Historismus," 287–93.

21. This corresponds to Charles Taylor's vivid term "subtraction story." See Taylor, *Secular Age*, 22, 26–29, 267–68, and 567–79.

22. Spranger, "Historismusproblem," 434. There can be no doubt that Troeltsch's writings, particularly those dating from before the First World War, still contain traces of a teleological philosophy of history. "Existential historicism" rests upon a strengthened awareness of historical contingency.

23. William James put forward the classical argument in this respect: James, "Will to Believe"; see Joas, *Genesis of Values*, 40–43.

24. Nietzsche, "Use and Abuse of History."

25. For an excellent account, see Putnam, *Collapse of the Fact/Value Dichotomy*.

26. I return to the consequences of this argument for communication about values in chapter 6.

27. This has been recognized and described with great clarity by Rendtorff, "Geschichte durch Geschichte überwinden," 301. In Troeltsch, see 1042.

28. Troeltsch, *Christian Thought*, 180.

29. On the theological dimension of Troeltsch's arguments, see the interpretations by Rendtorff and Schwöbel mentioned earlier. I myself have gone into these aspects in "Deutsche Idee von der Freiheit?"

30. Troeltsch, "Zufälligkeit der Geschichtswahrheiten," 557.

31. In grappling with Troeltsch's definition of "Europeanism," I cannot help thinking that what we are seeing here is an exaggerated attempt to legitimize the material limitations of his next planned book, "Cultural Synthesis." In contrast to many interpreters, but in line with the views of the editor, Hans Baron, I believe that his posthumously published volume of essays in intellectual history and sociology of religion (*Aufsätze zur Geistesgeschichte und Religionssoziologie*) gives us a good idea of the content of this unwritten book. For my own views, see the introduction in Joas and Wiegandt, *Cultural Values of Europe*, 1–21. Comparison between Troeltsch's "Europeanism" and Jaspers's theory of the Axial Age is instructive. See Cho, "German Debate over Civilization."

32. My attempt at a social scientifically informed retrospective on the *Communist Manifesto* is rather less euphoric: Joas, "Globalisierung und Wertentstehung."

33. As early as 1924, with brilliant insight, Karl Mannheim called for a comparison to be made between Troeltsch's great book on historicism and, as he puts it, the "most profound and significant" of all attempts to reformulate Marxist historical dialectics, Georg Lukács's *History and Class Consciousness* from 1923. As far as I know, no such comparison has yet appeared. In view of the enormous importance of Lukács's book to the so-called critical theory of the Frankfurt school, this continues to represent a profound challenge to the dialogue between this

tradition and a Christianity-inspired historicism. See Mannheim, "Historicism," 124 n. 1.

34. It is only consistent when Troeltsch compares and contrasts his own major account of the history of Christianity as "sociological-realistic-ethical" with Adolf von Harnack's "essentially ideological-dogmatic account" in a footnote (596 n. 190). It is odd, then, that an author such as Hans Rosenberg, so important to the development of the study of social history, counts Troeltsch among those historians who found "refuge in the study of more esoteric phenomena by focusing their energies on the history of ideas and on resolving problems in the philosophy of mind and theory of history to the near-total exclusion of the material world and socioeconomic reality." See Rosenberg, "Zur sozialen Funktion," 104.

35. See chapter 2, 54–57.

36. On the triad of values, institutions, and practices, see the analysis of the antislavery movement in chapter 3, 85–96.

5
SOUL AND GIFT
The Human Being as Image and Child of God

The key thesis underlying the three historical-sociological discussions presented in this book is that we should understand the rise of human rights and the idea of universal human dignity as a process of the sacralization of the person. Inherent in this thesis is a rejection of all notions that this rise can be regarded as the product of a particular tradition, such as the Christian—a product that was more or less bound to emerge from the seed of tradition at some point in history. Traditions as such, I suggest, generate nothing. What matters is how they are appropriated by contemporary actors in their specific circumstances and amid the field of tension in which they find themselves, made up of practices, values, and institutions. Institutions and practices, however, have their own inertia, which may resist and correct actors' deviations from the spirit they embody—but only up to a certain point. Institutions drained of their "spirit" can no longer be relied upon.

We can easily find concrete examples of these propositions by examining the relationship between Christianity and human rights. There was a Christian justification for slavery. Christianity coexisted without too much trouble with torture, rejected the human rights declarations of the eighteenth century, and was even skeptical about the Universal Declaration of Human Rights of 1948. We can also point to the other side of the coin, such as Christian engagement in the abolition of torture and slavery and Christian influence on and acceptance of the human rights declarations made from the eighteenth to twentieth centuries. In all these cases, for individual Christians and sometimes even for a specific Christian community, it may have been clear what the Gospel demanded—but not to all of them, and certainly not independent of time and culture.

If tradition is not a major factor in explaining human rights, we will still do well to take a closer look at it. But we must reverse perspective.

While it is true that traditions generate nothing, they must relate in some way to any innovation. As a novel form of the sacralization of the person, the rise of human rights represents a challenge to Christianity—and to other religious and even to secular value traditions and worldviews—in light of which their adherents must inevitably reinterpret them.

In the case of human rights, in the first instance such reinterpretation relates to the foundations of political and legal thought. Here the spectrum of possible reactions extends from radical rejection to complete appropriation, which may include the invention of a tradition that declares itself the true author of the new phenomenon.[1] A few examples should suffice to demonstrate this. Catholic Christianity sharply rejected human rights in the context of its polemics against the French Revolution and associated persecution of the Church, but began to rethink its position during the period of fascism and Nazism. Philosophers such as Jacques Maritain, theologians such as the American Jesuit John Courtney Murray, and the spokespersons of numerous lay Catholic organizations played an important role in this rethinking process.[2] This went beyond the political level, centering on the question of whether—as the magisterium long asserted—human rights must really be grounded in natural law or whether in fact the crucial element was a specific understanding of human personhood. This understanding was sometimes developed within the framework of natural law and sometimes pointed beyond it.

At least in Germany, skepticism about possible proximity to (Catholic) natural law determined the initial reaction to human rights on the part of postwar Protestant theologians. For them, just as justification in terms of natural law tends to overlook the thoroughly sinful nature of the human being—which has implications for his rationality—human rights and the basic rights enshrined in the constitution might appear as a "Magna Carta of human autonomy," something unacceptable to Protestant Christians.[3] This required the development of intellectual alternatives that emphasized the break with the Lutheran faith in the state or justified human rights in Christological terms.

We find a similar spectrum of responses in other religious traditions.[4] And philosophical schools went through a similar process. Jeremy Bentham, the classical representative of utilitarianism, initially referred to human rights as "nonsense upon stilts"—a view few contemporary representatives of this school would like to be caught espousing.[5] Just like religious traditions, every secular school of thought that emphasizes a form of sacralization other than that of the person—of the nation, class, civilization, or race—must also work out its position on human rights. The sacralization of the nation may be fused with that of the person if the cause of the nation is identified with that of human rights; this happened time and again in the case of French and American nationalism.[6] German nationalism mobilized a "superior" understanding of the individual against the "Western" understanding, and thus attempted to trump human rights.[7] In Germany and elsewhere, resistance to human rights as individualistic was sometimes declared a component of national or cultural identity as well.

The idea of civilization also came into play as an alleged wellspring of human rights. This made human rights appear as a secure possession, one that entailed a moral injunction to disseminate them and introduce them to other, less valuable civilizations. If civilizations were traced back to biological foundations, this idea could also swiftly descend into racial theories and racism. We might even interpret these as pseudoscientific attempts to pull the rug from under human rights universalism once and for all.

Even the Marxist centering of political discourse on class domination, class struggle, revolution, and communist utopia offered a spectrum of possibilities. Human rights could be portrayed as a bourgeois ideological attempt to camouflage class domination and a distraction from what really matters; namely, changes in ownership of the means of production. But Marxists could also present communism as the true realization of demands for human rights: "The International Fights for the Rights of Man." This is apparent even in the arguments put forward by representatives of the Soviet bloc during the drafting process of the Universal Declaration and in the discourse of the "real existing socialist" societies.[8]

In the United States, commonly assumed to exhibit a profound sympathy for human rights universalism, there was tremendous resistance to the Universal Declaration following its adoption. One influential senator called the declaration "completely foreign to American law and tradition" and tried to prevent any attempt to align American policy with it through a constitutional amendment.[9] He only narrowly failed to do so.

I do not examine these responses and their further development in detail here. I have another aim in this chapter—namely, to discover what we can learn about the challenge to the Christian tradition triggered by the rise of human rights by examining the two components of this tradition most frequently mentioned when it is claimed that human rights are rooted in Christianity: the idea that human beings are made in the image of God and that they are the children of God.

These two components are by no means identical. Depending on denomination, one of them may be rejected, at least some of the time, and all the emphasis placed on the other.[10] This chapter does not survey the attempts by contemporary theologians or Christian philosophers to elucidate these two components of Christian thought. It does offer two suggestions of my own on how we might rearticulate these elements of tradition under contemporary intellectual conditions by building on the work of two key figures in social philosophy and sociology (William James and Talcott Parsons). The notion that we are made in the image of God becomes the idea of a divine essence in every human being: his immortal soul. The notion that we are the children of God becomes the idea that our life is a gift, which like every gift incurs certain obligations that limit our disposal over ourselves. Here, of course, the soul too is conceived as a gift; it is not acquired by the human being but created by God, who "animates" us with it.

This does not mean that my argument has covertly moved into the field of theology. I have constructed my suggestions in such a way that they do not presuppose religious faith. But they are intended at least to demonstrate to those who do not believe just what it is they do not believe. In his work on bioethics, Michael Sandel attempts to show the sensitivity to indisposability that is inherent in this idea of the gift, and the dangers that flow from its diminution—which means that its rearticulation is important to all of us, believers and nonbelievers alike.[11] In much the same way, my aim here is to critically appropriate the richness of a tradition without triumphalism, but also without resentment toward it.[12]

FROM SOUL TO SELF

Detective novels often begin with death, mostly a dramatic murder, with the rest of the book revolving around attempts to solve it.[13] These novels may be written from the perspective of an omniscient narrator or a first-person observer or other parties somehow involved in the events. Some authors have experimented with a perspective from which the perpetrator emerges as a particularly attractive or at least all-too-human being; rather than readers being confronted simply with the wicked deeds of a being very alien to them, they are indirectly confronted with their own sinister proclivities and potentialities. This not only disappoints readers' conventional expectations. On a far deeper level it threatens their basic trust in the narrator, though this trust must not be destroyed entirely if they are to have any chance of comfortably submitting themselves to depictions of wickedness and cruelty. Far less well known than such experiments (found in the books of Patricia Highsmith, for example) is another, even more audacious break with the rules of the genre and readers' expectations: a book that begins with the murder of the first-person narrator. For understandable reasons, most authors have steered clear of this possibility or have not perceived it as possible in the first place. How *are* you supposed to continue the story after such a dramatic beginning? Is the dead character to describe the background to his murder or the consequences of his death, the grief and horror of his loved ones, perhaps even their relief or barely concealed delight?

There is in fact a book that has tried to do just this. I am referring to the great Canadian writer Robertson Davies and his 1991 novel *Murther and Walking Spirits*. To the reader's amazement, the narrator is killed in the first sentence of the book; the narrator himself declares his own astonishment at this unexpected blow of fate, but immediately adds that he did not stay astonished for long. Manifestly, a narrative strategy of this kind presupposes that after being murdered the narrator somehow continues to exist and can observe the living and remember his own earlier earthly pilgrimage from the standpoint of his new existence. As virtually all religions feature ideas about a life after death, this assumption would not be viewed as sensational in any of the cultures molded by these religions. On the contrary: for most people throughout history a life after death was a certainty, more certain than most of the facts of everyday life, so certain that fear and terror or even pleasant anticipation could become key elements in people's lives. In the field of literature as well, the perspective of a soul traveling through the cosmos or through heaven and hell was widespread in Europe; we need only think of Dante, Milton, and Goethe.

Readers need have no fear that I am mentioning all of this in order to praise Robertson Davies as a Christian writer who, untouched by modern doubts, has simply held on to traditional notions of the immortality of the soul. This would be quite incorrect. In fact Davies deploys a brilliant device that does justice to our confrontation with the wide range of religious interpretive models in this "globalized" world. For him, after death the soul (and thus his narrator's ego) first enters a kind of intermediate stage in which, in Christian style, it is not yet clear what the final judgment will be, whether he faces eternal salvation in heaven, eternal damnation in hell, or temporary punishment in purgatory. Not only is this judgment yet to be made, perhaps because the heavenly court has so many cases to deal with, but it is still an entirely open question whether these ideas are correct, or whether in fact the narrator is about to be reincarnated in the form of a new earthly creature. During this stage, which I am tempted to call a postmortal transcendent waiting room, Davies's murdered first-person narrator can now observe his wife enjoying herself with his murderer, who had already been her lover and carried out the killing so that he could proceed unhindered with this relationship and in other ways.

I mention these peculiar things to bring out how tremendously important the concept of the soul was once in how human beings saw themselves, but also so as to avoid downplaying the difficulties we now have with this concept. John Locke and the empiricist school were probably the first to notice them, but it was Kant who articulated them most clearly—though these difficulties did not move either thinker to entirely abandon the notion of a soul. It was only in the nineteenth century that skepticism about the concept began to prevail. With the exception of Catholic neo-Scholasticism and certain esoteric sects such as the Theosophists, no one now defended this traditional concept with any conviction. Exponents of materialism—whether historical materialism à la Marx or medical materialism à la Rudolf Virchow—simply wanted to get rid of the notion of a soul, which they considered less than useless. Under their influence and in connection with the emerging scientific discipline of psychology, people no longer referred to the soul but to the psychical dimension. The concept of the soul was considered at best superfluous to and at worst detrimental to psychological explanations. In his extremely influential textbook *Principles of Psychology* from 1890, William James quoted an author who described the whole idea of the soul as the twisted product of a philosophical approach whose central axiom is to describe the very thing we know nothing about as the explanation of everything else.[14] It is not difficult to find similarly extreme statements about the concept of the soul in the subsequent history of science. The concept came to be seen as the epitome of all underivable *ultra qua non* concepts. The behaviorists ascribed a similar role to the concept of culture and recommended that we get rid of it as well. And when a militantly atheist neo-Pragmatist such as Richard Rorty writes that human beings are nothing but "complicated animals containing no special extra ingredient," what he has in mind is of course that special ingredient that the Christian tradition has always attributed to human beings; namely, the soul.[15]

But not all nineteenth-century thinkers who considered the concept of the soul obsolete simply proposed its banishment from scientific language. Some suggested that it could be transformed, that valuable aspects of its meaning might be salvaged by placing them on new philosophical and scientific foundations. It was these attempts to transform the concept of the soul that led to the concept of the self as used today by psychologists and sociologists. We may thus refer to a key scientific development, the shift *from soul to self*. The Pragmatists played a decisive role in this process, and the concept of the self and its development is one of the central themes of classical Pragmatism. Many authors—including me—have described the great importance of the long chapter on the self in James's *Psychology* in this respect and how it became the point of departure for the following, younger generation of Pragmatists, for thinkers such as John Dewey, George Herbert Mead, and Charles Horton Cooley. On this basis, these thinkers took fresh inspiration from the ideas of Fichte and Hegel on human intersubjectivity, developing a theory of the social constitution of the self and the foundations of a sociologically oriented social psychology.[16] There are also studies of Peirce's conception of the self and on this theme within the work of other, largely forgotten writers of the day such as James Mark Baldwin and Mary Whiton Calkins. Most interpreters, including me, have so far regarded this transformative shift from soul to self as an epochal breakthrough in the history of the social sciences, as a genuine achievement of American thought, and as having provided the impetus for important later developments such as Erik Erikson's psychology of identity and Jürgen Habermas's theory of communicative action—though this achievement was ignored entirely by the French structuralists and poststructuralists and their followers to their enduring detriment. There is no need to recapitulate this history in depth. My aim here is not to repeat this positive assessment but to provide a critical revision of this history. In common with others, I have long presented this history as one of unadulterated progress with no downside. While I am happy to stand by this evaluation of what is a considerable intellectual achievement, I now want to highlight a certain one-sidedness in this transformation of the concept of the soul into that of the self. My thesis is that the concept of the soul involves three semantic elements, but that the dominant strand of Pragmatism was concerned solely with the transformation of one of these components. The term "soul" had a richer meaning than was recognized by Pragmatist thinkers. Ignoring these other semantic components led them astray, and they paid a price for their achievement. What I propose, therefore, is that we return once again to that point in intellectual history at which Mead and Dewey distanced themselves from James. If we do so, I think we will see that James was more sensitive to these other semantic elements and tried to transform the concept of the soul in a more comprehensive and ambitious way than the younger generation of Pragmatists. So what I aim to do now is to tell this old story in a new way.[17]

There have been debates about what exactly the soul is and the character of its relationship to the body since the rise of Western philosophy in ancient Greece and throughout the history of Christian thought. These debates mostly revolved around the question of whether the soul was a sui generis substance and, if so, how this soul substance was constituted and whether it was tied to the body. In James's words (326), the soul was imagined as "a simple spiritual substance in which the various psychic faculties, operations, and affections inhere." But is an "immaterial substance" not a contradiction in terms, a square circle? In German philosophy, Kant drew a definitive line under such terminology, which he considered intellectually lazy. For him, the soul is not a substance; the roots of the supposition that it is, he thought, lie in the unwarranted application of the structure of transcendental subjectivity to an objectively given substance. It is important to note, however, that even before Kant, both the empiricist and rationalist camps put forward significant arguments that were well suited to unsettling a conception of the soul anchored in a metaphysics of substance; but these arguments were later developed in ways that differed from Kant's critique. In chapter 27 of his *Essay Concerning Human Understanding*, for example, John Locke wrote that even on the assumption that there exists such a substance that endures in identical form over time and continues to exist when one's physical existence has come to an end, this substance would be irrelevant to us (sec. 24). It would be present within us as an impersonal foreign body, so to speak, that could provide no answer to the question of immortality. Those who ask what comes after death will not be satisfied with the answer that something of their substance continues to exist, because immortality, as Locke saw, must have something to do with my most personal identity, with my deeds and experiences. Therefore, according to Locke, in addition to the soul substance there must at the very least also be a practically important nonsubstantial personal identity. We might view Locke's thinking here as a modern parallel to old theological ideas according to which the notion that the soul as such is immortal—that is, outside of its relationship to God—is heretical. And in the case of the rationalist Descartes, while his thought is generally dominated by a radical body-mind dualism and the founding of all knowledge in the self-certainty of the isolated thinking subject, this contrasts with the picture presented in the third of his *Meditations*. Here he tried to show that the subject is only spared the Sisyphean task of having to constantly reassure himself in the face of a tidal wave of doubts because he can be sure of God and this gives him a competence he could never give himself. What I want to point up here is that in the work of Locke, Descartes, and Kant we can see how an idea of subjectivity emerges out of that of the soul—an idea, however, that necessarily retains a relationship to the Creator God.

Much of the scientific psychology of the nineteenth century worked its way through the intellectual developments and alternatives of pre-Kantian and Kantian philosophy afresh on an empirical basis. Those, such as Hermann Lotze and Wilhelm Wundt, who wished to overcome the conception of the soul rooted in a metaphysics of substance without becoming materialists were faced with the problem of having to describe the soul as a given without describing it in substantial terms. Within the framework of his "voluntarist psychology," Wilhelm Wundt developed so-called actuality theory, according to which the soul is not a substance but an activity, an event. I see the tendency to fuse Pragmatist philosophy with functionalist psychology toward the end of the nineteenth century as a continuation of or parallel to Wundt's idea. If we conceive of the "psychical" realm as functioning to regulate organismic processes, we are not denying its existence, but neither are we asserting the presence of a soul substance. James dealt with these questions in his chapter on "attention," Dewey in his classical essay of 1896, "The Reflex Arc Concept in Psychology," but the most detailed philosophical discussion of this question is to be found in George Herbert Mead's 1903 text "The Definition of the Psychical"—an essay, by the way, that has yet to be printed in the United States in unabridged form since its first obscure publication. So the shift to a functionalist conception of the psychical is the consequence of a productive critique of substance metaphysics. But this can only be the first step. Such a functionalist psychology must not only reconceptualize the psychical as such, but also the unity, identity, continuity, and individuality of psychical life. How can a psychology without "immaterial substances" clarify the identity and individuality of persons?

As I mentioned earlier, the central text in the shift from soul to self was chapter 10 in James's *Principles of Psychology*. Initially, James basically uses the term "self" here in the same way that we now refer to the personality; that is, not just with reference to the way in which the person is given to herself, but in the more comprehensive sense of what goes to make up a person. James redeploys an old joke when he states that the person consists of three parts: soul, body, and clothes (280). He is quite serious about this in that he sees a person's possessions as a key means of self-expression and support; in developing our ideas, in other words, we must not precipitately detach persons from their material milieu. Alongside this kind of broadly conceived "material self," James recognizes a "social self" that he defines with reference to all the forms of recognition we receive from other people; a "spiritual self"—that is, "our ability to argue and discriminate, our moral sensibility and conscience, our indomitable will" (283); and finally the "pure ego" as the capacity to reflect on all these components of our personality and perceive our continuity over time itself.

Most important in the present context is what James calls "the self of all the other selves," people's capacity to experience themselves as the center of their own activity. James is fully aware that here he is touching on the most controversial point of all. For the "spiritualists," this self-perception as the center of activity follows quite simply from the fact of the soul, while for the materialists this self-perception is a fiction: "Some would say that it is a simple active substance, the soul, of which they are thus conscious; others, that it is nothing but a fiction, the imaginary being denoted by the pronoun I; and between these extremes of opinion all sorts of intermediaries would be found" (286). James himself tried to find a way out here by focusing on the physical dimension of the self-perception of active organisms within an environment. In this way approval and rejection, attention and exertion emerge as a fundamental layer of subjectivity. This physical dimension is far richer than Kant's transcendental ego. For James, Kant's "transcendentalism" is just a coy form of substantialism, and Kant's "ego"—he adds polemically—is just a "cheap and nasty" version of the soul concept. Viewed in this way, Kant's "ego" is a desubstantialized substance, an empty husk, incapable of capturing our physical experience of ourselves. James even prefers the old concept of the soul to this version, but like the materialists he believes that it has no scientific explanatory power whatsoever.

James's quasi-functionalist conception of the self became the point of departure for the important innovations made by Cooley and Mead. They considered it unsatisfactory that James did not consistently relate the genesis of consciousness to problematic action situations, that he treated the social self merely as one aspect of the self rather than as constitutive of all aspects, and that he failed to investigate the specific logic of interpersonal action situations in which self-reflexivity becomes functional. We might call the first point a pragmatist critique of James's focus on the "stream of consciousness," the second a call, critical of James, to examine the social constitution of the self, which means much more than just examining the self's embedding in relations of recognition. The third point may be seen as an extension of the functionalist understanding of the psychical to the logic of the constitution of the self. Mead articulated these critical points right from the start and up until his late writings, as for example in his lengthy 1929 obituary for Cooley, the other great "sociological pragmatist." To take just one example: "While James recognized early the influence of the social environment upon the individual in the formation of the personality, his psychological contribution to the social character of the self was rather in showing the spread of the self over its social environment than in the structure of the self through social interactions. The superiority of Cooley's position lies in his freedom to find in consciousness a social process going on, within which the self and the others arise."[18]

Very much in the spirit of pragmatism, but going beyond his predecessors, Mead examined this very type of action situation in which increased attention to objects in the environment is not enough to guarantee the successful continuation of action. In social situations, the actor himself is a source of stimuli for his opposite number. So he must pay attention to his own modes of action, as they trigger reactions in the other person; this makes them conditions for the continuation of his own actions. In situations of this kind, there is a functional need not just for consciousness but self-consciousness. With this analysis of self-reflexivity, Mead attempted to reconstruct the legacy of German idealism from a Pragmatist perspective.

There is no space here to provide a detailed account of his theory of communication, which was formulated with this goal in mind. But in the present context it must be underlined that Mead unambiguously views his theory of the genesis of the self as a conscious effort to help overcome the concept of the soul and naturalize traditional Christian categories in general. Again, let us take just one example: "Man's behaviour is such in his social group that he is able to become an object to himself, a fact which constitutes him a more advanced product of evolutionary development than are the lower animals. Fundamentally it is this social fact—and not his alleged possession of a soul or mind with which he, as an individual, has been mysteriously and supernaturally endowed, and with which the lower animals have not been endowed—that differentiates him from them."[19] In the work of Dewey and Mead, the theory of the self thus became part of an intellectual project of secularization.

This does not apply to James, however. As in many of his writings, here too James tries to render the two sides in the materialist-spiritualist disputes comprehensible to one another. At the end of the sixth chapter of his *Psychology*, he reveals that up until this point he has argued in quasi-materialist fashion for the very reason that he wished to convey the shortcomings of this way of thinking: "By this procedure I might perhaps force some of these materialistic minds to feel the more strongly the logical respectability of the spiritualistic position." And he adds: "The fact is that one cannot afford to despise any of these great traditional objects of belief. Whether we realize it or not, there is always a great drift of reasons, positive and negative, towing us in their direction" (181). And later in the same book James explains that while the "soul-theory" may be entirely superfluous for scientific purposes, there are other reasons, "other demands of a more practical kind," that prevent him from simply leaving things at that. He mentions two such reasons, two tasks that must be completed in order to completely transform the concept of the soul following the eclipse of the substance-metaphysical conception—and these two uncompleted tasks also provide an indication of the other two semantic components of the concept to which I alluded at the beginning. In James's language, the first of these problems still requiring resolution is that of "immortality, for which the simplicity and substantiality of the soul seem to offer a solid guarantee" (330); the "second alleged necessity for a soul-substance is our forensic responsibility before God" (331).

It would be mistaken to imagine that James was simply vacillating here, unable to choose between two options, keen to be rid of the concept of the soul for scientific reasons but wishing to retain it on religious grounds. He is well aware that the substance-metaphysical soul concept is not really well suited to answering these two religiously motivated questions. But he tries to leave these two questions open rather than ignoring them or declaring them outmoded from a secularist perspective. But what might a Pragmatist approach to these problems look like? With reference to the practical consequences of his understanding of the psychical realm for attitudes to life after death, James writes:

> The Soul, however, when closely scrutinized, guarantees no immortality of a sort *we care for*. The enjoyment of the atom-like simplicity of their substance in saecula saeculorum would not to most people seem a consummation devoutly to be wished. The substance must give rise to a stream of consciousness continuous with the present stream, in order to arouse our hope, but of this the mere persistence of the substance per se offers no guarantee. Moreover, in the general advance of our moral ideas, there has come to be something ridiculous in the way our forefathers had of grounding their hopes of immortality on the simplicity of their substance. The demand for immortality is nowadays essentially teleological.

> We believe ourselves immortal because we believe ourselves fit for immortality. (330; original emphasis)

It is hard to miss John Locke's protoexistentialist argument in this passage. Perhaps the spontaneous certainty that we are "fit for immortality" is weaker in our contemporary culture than it was in James's day. But James at least acknowledges that there is a problem here, and this distinguishes him from Dewey and Mead. In his early neo-Hegelian psychology of 1887, Dewey was still wedded to the notion of human beings' advancing self-realization, culminating in identification with the absolute person: namely, God. But in the 1890s, both Dewey and Mead began to remove our relationship to God from their constructions as a constitutive dimension of human self-realization. They resolutely accepted the consequences of these conceptual reorientations for the question of immortality. Because their thinking here was part of an intellectual project of secularization, they considered it crucial to finally overcome such illusions. Yet they failed to recognize that, quite apart from the religious questions, this was bound to saddle them with a very mundane dilemma. The problem they failed to anticipate was as follows. The concept of the soul had entailed a metaphysical guarantee of what I call the sacredness of the person; that is, the assumption of a sacred core of every human being, not acquired through one's own efforts, something that cannot be lost or destroyed. Now if the soul concept is transformed into that of the self, then people are equated with their capacity to develop self-reflexivity. In this respect, the situation is precisely parallel to a theme found in the work of Max Weber.[20] If, from a Weberian perspective, we describe the history of human rights as the "charismatization" (or "sacralization") of reason, then what happens to those who are not rational: children or the senile or mentally disabled? With reference to Dewey and Mead, we might also ask: What happens to those incapable of self-reflection?

This problem makes a second transformation necessary; namely, a theory of the processes through which sacralization occurs. Why do people experience certain things as sacred? And how do we get to a point where each person becomes sacred rather than just those who have certain capacities (such as "reason" or "self-consciousness")? The answer to these questions lies in a theory of the genesis of values, an investigation into value-constitutive experiences and especially those experiences that may give rise to an affective attachment to values rooted in moral universalism. In my book *The Genesis of Values* I tried to show that in light of his *Varieties of Religious Experience* William James should be regarded as a pioneer of such a theory, of the investigation of experiences of self-transcendence and the way in which these experiences induce commitment.[21] His theory focuses on the passive dimension of such experiences ("self-surrender," *Ergriffensein*) and on the subjective interpretation of the sources of the binding forces thus experienced. But James's approach has its limitations; these lie in his exclusive concern with the experiences of individuals "in their solitude" and in a certain neglect of the interpretive dimension; that is, the processes through which experiences are interpreted. There is no space here to repeat the argument presented in my earlier book. But I will mention that with respect to the first shortcoming I drew as a corrective on Émile Durkheim's study of the elementary forms of religious life. Durkheim focused on collective experiences, applying his insights into the dynamics of value genesis to the values of moral universalism. He spoke of the sacredness of the individual and tried to conceive of the belief in human rights as a result of the sacralization of the individual.[22]

James certainly had no comparably sophisticated theory on this topic, but remarkably he used the same expression ("the sacredness of individuality") at around the same time: namely, in 1899 in the new foreword to his book *Talks to Teachers on Psychology, and to Students on Some of Life's Ideals*.[23] Mead never went this far, and Dewey did so only in the 1930s when he wrote his book on religion (*A Common Faith*), in which, relying on James and Durkheim (!), he analyzed democracy as a complex of sacralized ideals.

So it was not just self-reflexivity but also the sacredness of the person that had to be factored in as the soul concept was transformed. Only in this way could two components of the meaning of the soul concept be incorporated into this transformation. But more than Durkheim (or Dewey and Mead), James was also sensitive to the third semantic component; namely, the potential continuity of the person beyond his physical death. Contemporary theologians refer to a "relational" anthropology rather than a metaphysics of substance as the prerequisite for a satisfactory answer to this question. Dewey and Mead were certainly exponents of a "relational" anthropology in that they conceived of the self as constituted through social relations.

But as I have mentioned, the relationship to the divine as a necessary element in human beings' relations with the world is lost in their anthropology. James is a different case again. Even when he deals with the social self, he not only scrutinizes our communication with our fellow human beings, but also prayer. Here he develops the concept of the "ideal social self," "a self that is at least *worthy* of approving recognition by the highest *possible* judging companion, if such companion there be." According to James, prayer will never be purely a thing of the past; his assumption is that we pray because "we cannot *help* praying." "The impulse to pray is a necessary consequence of the fact that whilst the innermost of the empirical selves of a man is a self of the *social* sort, it yet can find its only adequate Socius in an ideal world" (301; original emphasis).

In 1898 James published a pamphlet on the question of human immortality, his goal the relatively modest one of demonstrating that such a belief is not incompatible with a functionalist conception of the brain and that those who believe in immortality should not be put off by the idea that the hereafter may be rather overpopulated. With the first point in mind he attempted to distinguish between the "productive" and the "transmissive" functions of the brain. No scientific argument, he stated, can rule out the possibility that in the case of phenomena such as religious conversions, answered prayers and miraculous healings, premonitions, and deathbed visitations something really is happening to our consciousness that is not its own doing.[24] In my language this means that we cannot rule out scientifically the possibility that our experiences of self-transcendence represent a genuine encounter with something transcendent. And he counters the second, rather curious argument with a plea to imagine God's love and understanding as infinite, rather than judging by the yardstick of our own limited and all too easily depleted empathy and sympathy—if we wish to avoid letting "blindness lay down the law to sight."[25]

But this text imagines the human being merely as a putative, passive recipient of messages from a being that transcends the material dimension—not as its creative part. This changes in James's later writings, above all in his book *A Pluralistic Universe* from 1909. I don't think it's an exaggeration to state that one of James's key motives in this late metaphysics was to describe human beings' place in the cosmos in such a way as to render plausible the idea of immortality. Such a metaphysics must fulfill three conditions. First, it must conceive of the human self as constituted through all its relations with the world, with its fellow human beings, but also with the divine. Second, it can allow no dualism between body and soul, as if the body were no more than a shell surrounding the true personal soul. And third, it must not be deterministic, as this would entail the downgrading of human freedom of decision and the devaluation of life as mere illusion vis-à-vis eternity. These were the tasks James set himself in his late work: to set out the main features of a nonatomistic, nondualistic, strictly processual worldview. The concepts of experience and of the field (or "situation") become central here: in experience, understood in the sense of James's radical empiricism, the experiencer and what is experienced are intermeshed, just as the field includes more than just the external relations of self-contained entities identical with themselves. Such a Pragmatist metaphysics, which has also been called a "temporalistic form of personalism," replaces the soul substance with the idea of the person's constitutive relation with the divine.[26] So physical death may mean the transformation of this relation, rather than its end. The question of immortality then depends on our willingness to believe in a loving God who maintains his relationship with us after physical death. Precisely because James thinks in nondualistic terms, from this perspective God is himself reliant on his relationship with the human dimension. This is not a God who, unaffected by what we do with our freedom to be good or bad, is sufficient unto himself in the distant beyond. This is a God who has made us creative creatures. He is therefore always involved in the events of the world because our creative capacities may stand in continuity with his creation. The Promethean opposition between human and divine creation is misleading and unnecessary.

I am well aware that as they read this account of James's religiously motivated speculations some readers may have become increasingly nervous. They might say that these are wild speculations that have little in common with a rational philosophical argument and nothing at all with social science. These skeptics are right in that James never tried to provide definitive rational proof of human immortality or the existence of God or any other article of faith. His strategy was to reject scientific attempts to dispute the right to believe; by refuting such efforts he hoped to encourage the will to believe. This was his understanding of the role of Pragmatist thought in the field of religion. No one can be convinced through purely rational means to accept a religious faith in general or to consider a particular belief justified. James was simply trying to reconstruct the internal logic of religious experience and to elaborate the main features of a worldview in which this experience may coexist with science in a reciprocally fruitful manner. Ultimately, justifying this possibility of coexistence was one of the key factors motivating him to develop Pragmatism and his theory of truth.

The topic of death is often referred to as a taboo of our times. I'm not so sure about that. I tend to agree with Talcott Parsons, who once wrote that the fact that so many people rail against the taboo of death is an indication that it is no taboo at all. But it seems to me that talking about what comes after death nowadays really is taboo. The reactions one gets range from silent unease through expressions of embarrassment to vocal indignation. This was not the case among the first generation of Pragmatists. Peirce and Royce wrote about these issues, and James's contributions were clearly part of a broader discourse.[27] We often find a deep interest in cultural understandings of God, the soul, death, and the afterlife among the classical figures of sociology as well. In their sociologies of religion both Durkheim and Weber examine the subject in some depth. Other members of this classical generation went even further, dealing with these ideas and practices as more than just the object of scientific study. Max Scheler, for instance, wrote an important text, "Death and the Afterlife" ("Tod und Fortleben"), which was not published during his lifetime but which he aspired to develop into a comprehensive philosophy of death ("The Meaning of Death"). Here he dealt with the idea of a soul substance as a misguided attempt to conceptualize a fundamental form of human self-experience. Georg Simmel and Ernst Troeltsch linked the topic with the question of how we might conceive of the possibility of absolute and universal validity claims if we have a radical understanding of contingency. Troeltsch asserted that nonrelative values require a metaphysical assumption of transcendence and that carried to its logical conclusion the notion of the infinite value of the soul requires the idea of life after death.[28] And in his last book (*The View of Life*), through which he was to exercise such an influence on Heidegger, Georg Simmel explicitly linked the constitution of values with the constitution of the self. Just as enduring values emerge in particular situations under contingent circumstances, the accident of our birth is no obstacle to belief in the immortality of the soul.

As I conclude this section I want to underline that of course no one is required to share the religious or quasi-religious views of these authors. But taking them seriously can at least help us understand what meaning an old concept once had within the tradition that deployed it. And this is at the very least one prerequisite for the historical-sociological reconstruction of the genesis of the Judeo-Christian tradition and its transformation into modern value systems. These include the belief in human rights and universal human dignity—which means a belief in the sacredness of the person.

LIFE AS A GIFT

In an essay on the topic of "euthanasia," a famous and esteemed Berlin-based philosopher grapples with the traditional objections to the moral permissibility of suicide and the desire of the incurably ill for release from their suffering.[29] He highlights what he calls the "common argument" that "people should not take their own lives because life is a gift from another." But he considers this objection invalid within the framework of his own argument, which he explicitly refers to as "reason-based." For him, this objection links "a de facto restriction on action with a normative action boundary." This, he tells us, is impermissible simply on methodological grounds. If we were to adopt this approach, "we would immediately have to prohibit agriculture, hunting and fishing [as well] and strictly speaking, if we may dispose over nothing that we have not made ourselves, we couldn't even take oxygen from the air." But the fact is that "every living creature takes what it needs from nature," and despite all their autonomous productivity human beings are no exception: "We always draw on more than our own resources. This also applies to our existence. And since it is factually the case that we are able to take our own lives, we must decide whether to do so on the basis of reasons to be found within ourselves—and not inherent in the fact of mere existence."

"The fact of mere existence": to talk in this way is to fail to grasp that the crucial question is whether we can and ought to regard our lives as mere fact. Such references to *factuality* certainly contrast sharply with the idea of the *creatureliness* of human beings characteristic of the Judeo-Christian tradition. In this tradition, life is not a mere factual state of affairs, a condition of random "thrownness," but a gift. But to see life as a gift is very different from the view that merely factual limitations somehow allow normative conclusions. Even the most trivial gifts of our everyday social existence are more than just factual circumstances; they always contain within them a sense of obligation to which mere facts cannot give rise. If someone, for example, signals their acquaintance, respect, or affection in the form of a greeting, paying us attention and symbolically expressing this attention for perhaps just a brief moment, they can expect us to greet them back. Inherent in a greeting is the obligation to return it or at least to respond with a question, and this obligation is so powerful that refusing to return a greeting takes on communicative meaning. Following a greeting, we can no longer not communicate. Much the same goes for invitations, presents, and even tender caresses. All these phenomena reveal a logic of the gift that is quite different from mere factuality.

If we take the philosophical argument quoted above as symptomatic, however, many contemporary thinkers seem to have trouble taking this logic of the gift seriously and applying it to life as a whole. Our ability to formulate the idea of life as a gift under contemporary conditions in such a way that it also makes sense to the friends of "reason-based argument" is central to achieving a contemporary understanding of universal human dignity; it is equally important to distinguishing between a universalist sacralization of the person, of all persons, and the self-sacralization of the private individual—in other words, of each person in isolation.

In postmodern circles the theme of the gift has become almost fashionable, largely because of Jacques Derrida. Prominent philosophers and theologians such as Jean-Luc Marion and John Milbank have studied the logic of the gift in depth, while leading contemporary philosophers of religion such as Paul Ricoeur and Hent de Vries have built on their work. Several though not all of these authors clearly intend to contrast the logic of the gift with the logic of exchange. By reconstructing the logic of the gift, they expect to gain critical purchase on contemporary trends of all-encompassing monetarization and commodification. I will not run through these theological debates here. Instead we can change perspective by turning to sociological studies. In both empirical and normative terms, this facilitates certain productive shifts in how we look at the contemporary significance of the logic of the gift.

I should say that there is nothing artificial about returning from theology and philosophy to sociology in this context. In France at least, one classical sociological text has remained a key point of reference in the philosophical and theological literature on the gift. I am referring to *The Gift*, a 1924 book by Marcel Mauss, nephew and close collaborator of Émile Durkheim. This collated a wealth of existing ethnological studies, among others by Franz Boas on Native American tribes in the Pacific Northwest and Bronislaw Malinowski on the Polynesians and Melanesians, the famous "Argonauts of the Western Pacific." Mauss put forward the thesis that before the invention of agriculture and livestock farming the praxis of ceremonial gift exchange was a universal feature of interaction between social groups. Only with these developments did this network of reciprocal recognition, in which ancestors and spirits were included as beings inhabiting the same reality, become a system of sacrificial practices. Each sacrifice settles a debt incurred by the appropriation of natural wealth. This wealth is experienced as pregiven and is conceptualized as dependent on potentially wrathful higher beings or deities that must be placated if they are not to shut off the fountainhead of this natural bounty. This lends deep significance to the fact, often remarked upon, that sacrificial animals are always domestic and farm animals. Mauss traced the "survival of these principles" in ancient Roman, Germanic, and Hindu law and already contrasted this logic of the gift with the economic mentality of modern capitalism.

As impressive as his analyses were and however much his book retains its inspirational force, he did not manage to present the ceremonial gift with the kind of conceptual clarity that might have protected it from economistic and moralistic misconceptions. By economistic misconception I mean the notion that ritual or ceremonial gift exchange is a kind of primitive, embryonic form of goods exchange and thus of trade. As Marcel Hénaff has shown in his excellent book *The Price of Truth*, this notion is untenable simply because the profane exchange of goods always existed alongside ceremonial gift exchange, so the former could not have arisen from the latter. Yet this misconception is found even in the work of such prominent social scientists as Max Weber (in his *General Economic History* or *Wirtschaftsgeschichte*) and Karl Polanyi (in *The Great Transformation*). The moralistic misconception arises through a reversal of its economistic counterpart.

The correct observation that in ceremonial gift exchange the dominant motive is not the rational calculation of one's own utility has induced some authors to assume that it is a matter of selfless giving, of charity. A special variant, which cannot really be described as "moralistic," arose from a now-famous example in Mauss's book, the destructive potlatch. Drawing on Boas's research on the Kwakiutl of British Columbia, Mauss asserted that in some cases tribes are forced to rid themselves of everything they possess, retaining literally nothing. In this "war of property" everything is based "on the principles of antagonism and rivalry."[30] In a higher sense, "destruction" here is also tribute or expenditure. Georges Bataille and Roger Caillois built on these ideas in dramatic analyses of violence and war. But this interpretation has collapsed in light of later ethnological research, which has shown that the roots of excess and destruction lay in the specific conditions of Native American life under British colonial rule; they are by no means inherent in the phenomenon of ceremonial gift exchange as such. But the genuinely "moralistic" interpretation is not tenable either, as it fails to grasp the role of ceremonial gift exchange in constituting relationships. Against Derrida (as well as Marion), Hénaff shows convincingly that while the notion that the giver should vanish behind his gift, that he should ideally remain anonymous, may be true of certain acts of charity, it does not apply to ceremonial gift exchange. Anonymity would be an obstacle to reciprocity in the latter case.

The logic of the gift, then, is not at all a matter of the surrendering and circulation of goods. So greetings and ritual dances must also be described as gifts because, like such practices, the objects in ceremonial gift exchange are merely media for the initiation and stabilization of social relations. To illustrate this I am tempted to refer to William James's analysis of the process of falling in love. If we adopt a cold, defensive attitude and wait for others to give us sure signs of love we are likely to have a very long wait. To enter into the intersubjective process of mutual trust building we must grant others an "advance" of trust and let them know that we are doing so. Of course, we cannot conceive of modern forms of giving simply as full-fledged examples of ceremonial gift exchange à la Mauss; the Maussian version relates to interaction between groups, not individuals, and to a phenomenon that molds the entire group process rather than being relegated to the margins. On the other hand, the praxis of reciprocal giving renders the logic of the gift visible even to modern people, a logic Mauss described as a *fait social total.*

Mauss did not really tackle the transformation of the logic of the gift in later religious history. But this is of crucial importance to my topic of "life as a gift." In his late sociology of religion, Talcott Parsons, the leading sociologist of the 1950s and 1960s, placed this subsequent history center stage in his quasi-structuralist analysis of Jewish and Christian myths.[31] Drawing explicitly on Claude Lévi-Strauss's analyses of Amerindian myths, Parsons aims to identify the core of the Judeo-Christian tradition. He bases himself here on the first books of Moses (Genesis and Exodus), and on the four Gospels, "insofar as they bear on the problem of orientation to the death-life aspects of the human condition."[32] Parsons became interested in this topic due to his in-depth study of the symbolism of death in the United States and the Western world and in medical ethics. In reading these efforts toward a "sociology of Christianity" it soon becomes apparent that they also represent an attempt to grapple with what Parsons called the "expressive revolution." What he had in mind here was the hippie movement and a general renaissance of the nonrational in Western culture, the growing interest in the esoteric and in non-Western religions, and the sacralization of love, particularly its erotic variant. He even thought all of this might be the beginnings of a nascent religion, one he was rather skeptical about. He found himself confronted with the question of how exactly the idea of life as a gift, so central to Christianity, might be thought and articulated anew under conditions of great moral and expressive individuality. And this is the perspective from which I draw on his work. His studies in this field have otherwise been completely ignored by sociologists. They are equally unknown within theology, with the exception of a book by Heidelberg theologian Sigrid Brandt.[33] And I have not found a single reference to Parsons in the contemporary discourse on the logic of the gift—further testimony to the deplorable partitioning-off of disciplinary discourses.

So let's make a fresh start.[34]

Nowadays, most people view the idea of our own lives as a gift as fairly plausible only on a biological-organic level. We all know that we have not created our own physical being but instead owe our lives to an act of procreation and years of care, mostly from our parents. This gives rise to certain norms of gratitude toward our parents, family, or nation in all cultures. These days, however, this conception of life as a gift no longer finds much expression in attitudes toward death. The reason for this is that death today is often regarded merely as destruction, as annihilation, the definitive end of the person. This predominantly modern attitude is certainly not representative of most of human history. All religions emphasize—in Parsons's rather unlovely sociological language—that people are "a synthesized *combination* of a living organism and a 'personality system,'" with personality being defined as symbolically organized.[35] But if we do not reduce the person to her body, the death of the body is not necessarily the death of the person. All religions have developed relevant ideas about life after death, and some, indeed, about life before conception, in the sense of a past life. These ideas are generally connected with the concept of the soul—a soul that is assumed to be passed on to other people or beings or to live on in another dimension of reality. In all of these religious interpretive systems death may be conceptualized as the continuation of life or as a passing on of the gift of life.

To get a better idea of the specific features of the Christian attitude toward death and the idea of life as a gift we must first go back to the Jewish creation myth. As underlined above all by Gershom Scholem, it is the Jewish rather than the ancient Greek tradition that conceives of the world as created by God.[36] So ancient Judaism is characterized not just by its radical monotheism but also by the assumption that the world was created out of nothing (*creatio ex nihilo*), which stands in sharp contrast to the (Greek) notion of preexisting substance and eternal ideas. In the Jewish and Christian tradition, to the extent that it is a creation, the entire world is a gift. Even the law of the people of Israel is a gift from God to his chosen people; the people have a duty to obey the law, but the capacity to obey is once again a gift. We may therefore conceive of death as the returning of one's life to the creator of one's life and of the entire world. In ancient Judaism, however, this interpretation of death was not yet fully developed. In Parsons's words: "The biblical phrase is reception into 'the bosom of Abraham,' which we have interpreted to mean, in a sense parallel to the Chinese tradition, that the dead achieve the honorific status of ancestors in the transgenerational collectivity of 'the people.'"[37]

Christianity radicalizes this idea of a gift relationship between God and the individual. First, Jesus himself is referred to as God's only begotten son. Procreation and birth are not creation out of nothing.

Central to the myth of the Annunciation is that God is not sending an entirely divine being into the world; instead, a human being, Mary, is *giving* Jesus life on a human level. In the Gospel according to Matthew, Jesus is placed through Joseph within a genealogical tradition and at the same time introduced as the Son of God through the virgin birth. So Jesus's life is a gift from God in a far more radical sense than the life of individuals had been hitherto. God gave this life out of love for the world and for human beings. Jesus is thus the embodiment of God's love and the full realization of a life of love. This culminates in Jesus's sacrifice on the cross. For Parsons "it seems clear . . . that the primary symbolic effect of Jesus' sacrifice was the endowment of ordinary human beings with the capacity to translate their lives into gifts that simultaneously express love for other human beings (as 'neighbors') and a love for God reciprocating God's love for 'the world.' These are the two fundamental commandments of the Gospel."[38] Jesus's death is the returning of life to God. His resurrection is the overcoming of death. For Parsons, this means that death takes on a transbiological meaning because the paramount element is the giving of the gift of life to God at the end of our individual lives as an expression of our love for him. I would like to add that death already had a transbiological meaning in the Jewish creation myth, when it is introduced as punishment for the disobedience of Adam and Eve. But this transbiological meaning comes out far more clearly in the myth of the resurrection and the idea of the overcoming of death.

Two points require special emphasis here. Death is transcended in the Christian tradition, not denied. Romano Guardini provides a compelling account of this in his book *The Last Things*. On the intellectual premises of Christianity death remains sad and terrible. It would be mere kitsch to assume that anyone could ever perceive his death as entirely meaningful and devoid of any tragic sense of loss, quite apart from the fact that in many cases death comes without giving us any chance to experience it as the returning of life. Second, even—in fact especially—the death of Jesus Christ was terrible and full of despair. In the myth of the Crucifixion the Son of God is not spared death; he does not ascend triumphantly to heaven before being crucified.

In his studies Parsons describes shifts in the original myth of Christianity, mainly in the history of the West. He is interested, first, in the key transformations in the cultural symbolization of this myth and, second, in the sociostructural and organizational preconditions and consequences of these transformations. The medieval—and, we must add, Catholic—conception of the Church as the "mystical body of Christ" he interprets as a novel form of mediation between the divine and human realms. Just as the body of Christ mediated between these two dimensions, after Christ the Church does so. In this way people can partake of the divine order, and though the Church itself has a temporal and earthly dimension, as an institution it transcends this, making it timeless. In Parsons's words: "It is through symbolic identification as part of the 'body of Christ' i.e., the Church, that the individual can, even before death, participate in the 'spiritual' as distinct from the 'temporal' order. In a certain sense the old collectivity of the 'people' became the model for a spiritual collectivity, membership in which was not by kinship but by faith, that is, acceptance of Christ."[39]

The great caesura in this history of Christian symbolism was the Reformation, and Parsons is very well aware of this. In many ways all he does here is to repeat the older, influential findings of Max Weber, Ernst Troeltsch, and others. Activism and inner-worldly asceticism play as crucial a role in his work as in that of his predecessors. The dramatic nature of the switch in the understanding of the Church in the Reformation from the "mystical body of Christ" to the "community of believers" is perhaps even clearer in Parsons's work. Parsons is clear about the ambiguity of this new conception. On the one hand—in early Calvinist New England, for instance—there was a church to which only the allegedly chosen belonged, but which subjected everyone to its strict discipline. On the other hand there was a fusion of the principle of voluntary membership with that of pluralism, which institutionalized religious tolerance, the separation of church and state, and the pluralism of the denominations. Of most central importance to this transformation was the shift in the understanding of the sacraments: "The clergy were no longer manipulators of divine grace but became teachers, leaders of congregations, missionaries to the lay public exhorting it to commitment and steadfastness in the faith. To be sure, the sacraments were maintained but with profoundly altered meaning. They became merely symbolic affirmations of faith and commitment to the Christian message."[40]

The dissolution of the religious orders also had similar effects, such that the view took hold that "religious obligations in the fullest sense could be discharged by laymen and specifically in lay occupations ('Berufe') rather than by clergy in segregated monastic communities."[41] For Parsons, this shift is of tremendous importance, not because it represents a loss of status for the clergy, but because it enhanced the status of the laity. He comes to the same conclusion as Charles Taylor in his book *Sources of the Self*, that Reformation-era religious thinking made everyday life itself a value, as captured so impressively in a statement Taylor quotes from this era: "God loveth adverbs; and cares not how good, but how well."[42] While Max Weber viewed this process with deep ambivalence and discerned a first step toward secularization in the valorization of everyday life, Parsons sees this as the advancing Christianization of the world. Rather idiosyncratically and diverging from the way sociologists of religion generally use the term, he refers to this as "secularization." In his case this means a gradual process of hallowing through the inclusion and moral valorization of everything that was previously understood as the world in contrast to the spiritual order. This is far more in line with Durkheim than Weber—like Durkheim, Parsons thinks in terms of a continual sacralization of the world rather than a history of disenchantment like Weber.

Strangely, at this point Parsons probes no deeper into the connection between the Reformation theology of grace and the emerging money economy than Max Weber had done. Had he taken Marcel Mauss's work—on which he generally draws and which Max Weber did not live to see—more seriously and done more to link it with Weber's analyses, then it would have become clearer just how much the conception of grace formulated by the Reformers and especially Calvin radicalized the understanding of the gift. In any case, as we have seen, the generally monotheistic notion of a grace-dispensing God superimposes on the network of reciprocal giving the idea of a giving deity, with whom we can reciprocate only by engaging our entire person and even then only to a limited degree. Augustine went so far as to state that we cannot reciprocate at all vis-à-vis the Creator God; all we can do is show gratitude and trusting faith. But it was only during the Reformation that the idea of the absolutely sovereign God who can dispense grace as and when he chooses reached its apogee. Now any notion of a reciprocal gift-giving relationship with respect to specific issues of everyday life seemed morally reprehensible and the logic of the gift itself seemed like an obstacle to a methodical guidance of life and God-pleasing social life. This opens up a new interpretation of the dispute, so important in the German Reformation, over the so-called selling of indulgences. It now appears as a collision between a logic of the gift that was in fact being corrupted by the ascendant money economy and a radicalized and more sensitive conception of the impossibility of reciprocity in one's relationship to God. From this perspective, while Max Weber did brilliantly perceive the enormous consequences of the Reformation theology of grace for guidance of life and social relations, his indubitably anti-Catholic (and anti-Lutheran) prejudices prevented him from achieving a truly comprehensive view of this event and assessing it fairly. Though Mauss allows a different perspective, Parsons did not fully exploit his work in this respect.

This throws up the question of the pro- or antieconomic character of the logic of the gift and the overall question of the precise normative implications of the idea that life is a gift. Parsons follows Mauss when he assumes that a gift relationship leads beyond mere direct reciprocity and connects people more closely, because it engenders a diffuse sense of obligation and a generalized expectation of reciprocity between them. Where a gift relationship exists, there is no need for immediate reciprocity. Gratification may even circulate in social structures, because an actor can count on the satisfaction of his needs even when this does not come directly from the person for whom he has done something. Giving creates an obligation to reciprocate, and both Parsons and Mauss are surely right to assume that this is the foundation of a social life that cannot develop on the basis of mere calculating, direct reciprocity. But can we really apply Mauss's analysis of the gift in this way to the idea of life as a gift, as Parsons did time and again in his late work? At first sight, the only difference appears to be one of scale. While all gifts produce more or less diffuse obligations of reciprocity, the gift of life is one of such enormous magnitude that it is impossible to reciprocate through one single action; only the "fullness of a complete life . . . constitutes a full reciprocation of the original gift of life."[43] With these words Parsons does in fact apply Mauss's theory to the analysis of Christian symbolism. The trouble with this line of thought is that in our lives some gifts are unwelcome; they may be completely abhorrent to us, particularly if we sense that the giver is giving only in order to obligate us in some way or to compel us into a permanent relationship with him. We may feel quite oppressed by such a gift and by the obligations entailed in this act of giving. Parsons himself mentions that such obligations are a burden and may be perceived as "tyrannical," and that some people may regard their lives as a shabby and niggardly gift if they consist largely of misery, want, and suffering. In his book *Funktion der Religion* (*Function of Religion*) from 1977, Niklas Luhmann went one step further, expressing his views in a way I am tempted to describe as blasphemous, since here God is ascribed diabolical qualities: "This gift puts us in a condition of permanent gratitude and permanent debt. To give in this way is at the very least morally ambivalent. We might see this as good, as life is a good thing, but on the other hand it is malicious cunning to place the recipient in permanent debt from which he is unable to free himself."[44] Luhmann tries to find a way out of this dilemma by introducing higher levels of reflection; he suggests that we receive our lives not for the sake of reciprocity but in order to be free and to decide whether we wish to adhere to the norm of reciprocity or not. For Luhmann, then, contingency remains the last word, particularly with respect to religion, even the despair of Jesus Christ on the cross. I don't think that Parsons was as keenly aware of this dilemma as Luhmann; he certainly didn't think in terms of a malicious God. But it seems to me that both Parsons and Luhmann fail to grasp a crucial attribute of Christian teaching, one that inevitably has to be added to the assumption of a benevolent God.

This consists in the complex interweaving of love and justice that arises from the Christian conception of a loving God. Christianity did not replace the principle of justice with that of love. Derrida fails to grasp this when he asserts that the gift transcends the constraints of exchange entirely, indeed "crazily" (John O'Neill). Christianity instead acknowledges both principles and the fact that they belong to different dimensions and cannot easily be translated one into the other. The easiest way to explain what I mean by this is to refer to the Sermon on the Mount, as presented for example in the Gospel according to Luke ("Sermon on the Plain"). Here we find in immediate proximity the Golden Rule and the commandment to love one's enemy. The Golden Rule is the moral expression of the principle of reciprocity, while the new message goes beyond reciprocity, in fact criticizes the principle of reciprocity. If we view this commandment of love itself as a moral principle, then we end up faced with all the difficulties and paradoxes that have been discussed at least since Kant. How can love be commanded in the first place, and how can we regard our life as a gift without the feeling that we are the object of "malicious cunning" on the part of the giver? The answer given by Max Scheler and Paul Ricoeur is that love is not part of the moral dimension.[45] In this interpretation of the Christian tradition, God loves human beings and his entire creation, Jesus Christ is the embodiment of a superabundance of divine love, and we human beings are invited to follow Christ and emulate him. But we are not subject to a commandment that demands obedience and feelings of love that we do not possess, feelings we must honor against our spontaneous impulses. And because love is part of a supramoral dimension, it can never replace the principles of the organization of social life such as the principle of justice. It can only reinterpret the rules of morality and empower us to act morally: love may stabilize our commitment to these rules, facilitate mercy, generosity, and humility, and prevent a relapse into calculating-utilitarian reciprocity. A reformulation of the idea of life as a gift in keeping with our times must incorporate this full meaning of the Christian concept of love and of the relationship between love and justice.

But this emphasis on the balance between love and justice and resistance to what Weber would have called the "acosmism of love" also means that the logic of the gift should not be deployed against a calculating conception of justice, as if it required the stigmatization of money, the denigration of economic action, and a reversal of modern processes of differentiation. Rather, what we are dealing with here is a relationship of indissoluble tension. We do not have to choose between *either* the logic of the gift *or* the logic of goods exchange. Instead, we must develop or preserve social forms in which we can make well-founded decisions as to which logic should apply in which fields and to what degree. This is what Michael Walzer means when he refers to "spheres of justice," and Marcel Hénaff builds on his ideas when he underlines the emancipatory role of money in his reconstruction of the logic of the gift. In earlier works I myself have expressed a similar idea in referring to the "democratization of the question of differentiation."[46] This means that there must be limits to monetarization and commodification, but these limits do not expose money and commodities as such as problematic. Rather, the real limit emerges in all those cases where only free giving allows the meaning of a given act to come to fruition. Love and friendship are the most common examples. But the same also applies to truth; this is why Hénaff's book is called *The Price of Truth*. So to conceive of life itself as a gift is one of the most effective ways of protecting it from instrumentalization. In this sense, the idea of life as a gift entails the ideas of universal human dignity and inalienable human rights.

Very little attention is now paid to the fact that historic human rights declarations made clear reference to notions of gift and creation. When we hear that "all men are created equal," we are much more aware of the "equal" than the "created." But, as Wolfgang Vögele has shown, up to and including the present day we find numerous references to inalienable rights as a gift with which God himself and not the modern state has endowed us.[47] This fact is an expression of a widespread fear among the authors of human rights declarations that a merely human positing would inevitably be less stable than a divine one. And this is surely correct. But the problem is that presumably every assertion about a divine positing is a human assertion. I make this sobering point not in order to question this divine positing but to question the self-certainty with which we talk about it. So I am against any sweeping assertions that only belief in our immortal soul and acceptance of our creatureliness allow human rights and universal human dignity to be firmly anchored in people's minds. Politically and morally Christians should not rule out the possibility of achieving a genuine consensus of values with those who do not share this basic precept of Christian belief. None of my remarks on life as a gift—or those on the concept of the soul—constitutes proof or an attempt to prove that we *must* believe in immortality and a creator. In the spirit of Pragmatism, my aim was merely to demonstrate that such a belief is not antithetical to reason. For me, the belief in life as a gift and in an immortal soul is no illusionary attempt to dress up the harsh factuality of our existence; instead, on the basis of trust in God, it allows believers to dedicate themselves to the dignity of all people and to take the risky step of participating in creative processes that depend on such belief. Those who do not share this belief must show how they can deploy their own intellectual resources to justify the idea of indisposability and endow it with motivating force.

NOTES

1. For a study of the Catholic-personalist human rights discourse of the twentieth century informed by this perspective, see Moyn, "Personalism, Community and the Origins of Human Rights."

2. Maritain, *Rights of Man and Natural Law*. On John C. Murray and his book *We Hold These Truths*, see Vögele, *Menschenwürde zwischen Recht und Theologie*, 180–83. As early as 1937 Pope Pius XI was making statements that defended human rights in personalist and natural-law terms. See Moyn, *Last Utopia*, 50.

3. Quotation from a speech by the German federal justice minister Gustav Heinemann on December 22, 1967, on receiving an honorary doctorate from the theology faculty of the University of Bonn. The full text can be found in Heinemann, "Rechtsstaat als theologisches Problem," here 34 (quoted in Vögele, *Menschenwürde zwischen Recht und Theologie*, 397). I hasten to add that Heinemann was arguing *against* the suspicions of Protestant theologians.

4. Islam is currently of greatest public interest in this respect. See, e.g., Krämer, "Contest of Values" and *Gottes Staat als Republik*.

5. Bentham, "Anarchical Fallacies," 523.

6. See, e.g., Durkheim, "Germany above All." For a discussion of this text, see Joas, *War and Modernity*, 69–70. For an examination of American missionary universalism that is still of much value today, see Krakau, *Missionsbewußtsein und Völkerrechtsdoktrin*.

7. Joas, "Deutsche Idee von der Freiheit?"

8. For further information, see Simpson, *Human Rights and the End of Empire*, and Amos, "Embracing and Contesting."

9. More on this in chapter 6. For the quotation from Senator John Bricker (R-OH), see Lauren, *Evolution of International Human Rights*, 246.

10. Leiner, "Menschenwürde und Reformation." Of the vast theological literature on the notion of humans as the children of God and as made in the image of God and their connection with human rights, I shall mention just two particularly valuable titles: Lutterbach, *Gotteskindschaft*; Angenendt, *Toleranz und Gewalt*, esp. 110–21. On the history of the Catholic critique of human rights, see Isensee, "Katholische Kritik an den Menschenrechten."

11. Sandel, *Case against Perfection*.

12. In this vein, see my review of Avishai Margalit: Joas, "Decency, Justice, Dignity."

13. This section is a revised version of my essay of the same name (in German, "Von der Seele zum Selbst").

14. James, *Principles of Psychology*, 329. Page references for quotations from this book are subsequently given in parentheses in the text.

15. Rorty, "Response to Richard Bernstein," 70.

16. Joas, *George Herbert Mead*.

17. Klaus Oehler is one of the few interpreters of Pragmatism in Germany to take James's religious motives entirely seriously. See, e.g., his book *Sachen und Zeichen*, 46–49.

18. Mead, "Cooley's Contribution to American Social Thought," xxix. For an excellent account of Cooley and the questions dealt with here, see Schubert, *Demokratische Identität*, and his introduction to Cooley, *On Self and Social Organization*.

19. Mead, *Mind, Self and Society*, 137 n. 1.

20. See Joas, "Max Weber and the Origins of Human Rights," and chap. 1 in this book.

21. Joas, *Genesis of Values*, esp. chap. 3.

22. See chap. 2 in the present book. Durkheim himself develops a theory concerning the genesis of the soul concept in his great work on the sociology of religion from 1912. See Durkheim, *Elementary Forms of the Religious Life*, 240–69.

23. James, *Talks to Teachers on Psychology*, v.

24. James, "Human Immortality," 93.

25. Ibid., 101.

26. Capek, "Reappearance of the Self," 544. The most thorough study of these questions is Fontinell, *Self, God, and Immortality*. Excellent too are Pihlström, "William James on Death, Mortality, and Immortality"; Seibert, *Religion im Denken von William James.*

27. Peirce, "Immortality in the Light of Synechism"; Royce, *Conception of Immortality.*

28. Troeltsch, "Der christliche Seelenbegriff."

29. This section is a revised version of Joas, "Logik der Gabe." The essay referred to is Gerhardt, "Letzte Hilfe."

30. Mauss, *Gift*, 47.

31. See esp. Parsons, *Action Theory and the Human Condition.*

32. Ibid., 266.

33. Brandt, *Religiöses Handeln in der modernen Welt.*

34. In what follows I draw on the ideas developed in an earlier essay: Joas, "Gift of Life."

35. Parsons, *Action Theory and the Human Condition*, 331; original emphasis.

36. Scholem, "Schöpfung aus Nichts."

37. Parsons, *Action Theory and the Human Condition*, 274.

38. Ibid., 274–75.

39. Ibid., 273.

40. Ibid., 306.

41. Ibid.

42. Taylor, *Sources of the Self*, 211–33, here 224.

43. Parsons, *Action Theory and the Human Condition*, 267.

44. Luhmann, *Funktion der Religion*, 209–10.

45. See Scheler, *Formalism in Ethics*, esp. 220–26; Ricoeur, "Love and Justice." See also Joas, *Genesis of Values*, esp. chaps. 6 and 10.

46. Walzer, *Spheres of Justice*; Joas, *Creativity of Action*, 223–44.

47. Vögele, *Menschenwürde zwischen Recht und Theologie.*

6
VALUE GENERALIZATION
The Universal Declaration of Human Rights and the Plurality of Cultures

So far in my attempt to construct an affirmative genealogy of human rights I have placed great emphasis on the importance of subjective certainty, the sense of self-evidence and affective intensity of the kind characteristic of the sacred. I have portrayed the genesis and development of human rights as a history of the relocating of such self-evidence, a process that straddles the spheres of practices, values, and institutions. So experiences are an important driving force in this history—everyday experiences, but above all experiences that transcend the everyday, that fill actors with enthusiasm or affect them profoundly as their horror transforms their personality against their will.

Empirically speaking subjective self-evidence is a key hallmark of value commitments; but it is not an argument that can be put forward to convince others. People may share a sense of self-evidence; this sense may even be taken for granted culturally. Shifts in this sense of self-evidence may also be common to a large number of people. Then the Zeitgeist has changed; something that was until recently perceived as deviant may now seem exemplary. But for those who probe their own conscience or seek answers from others a cultural commonality, old or new, is not a justification. And often one person's subjective sense of self-evidence diverges from another's or collides with it.

How then do we deal with such disagreement when it comes to values? There is a wide range of options. Since it is not values, value systems, or religions that act, but only ever people and groups of people, we may band together to carry out joint actions even if our values differ. We may also decide not to act jointly and merely to tolerate other people in a positive sense, their values seeming to us alien or incomprehensible. We may also agree on certain areas of common ground, leaving everything else up in the air. We may take on something from others and incorporate it into our own value systems.

Initially it may seem like a foreign body, but over the course of time, through gradual adaptations of our beliefs, it may become an organic component. Finally, by engaging with others we may discover surprising commonalities that prompt us to reformulate our own values and breathe new life into our own traditions.

In this concluding chapter I aim to show that amid the plurality of competing value systems it is possible to reach agreement on new areas of common ground, and that the Universal Declaration of Human Rights of 1948 is the successful result of such agreement. To convey the character of this process I use the term "value generalization." This term was developed decades ago in one of the most ambitious theories of social change, but it seems to me to have great significance to moral philosophy as well. The importance of this term and the associated concept lies in a field that we might call the logic of communication about values. I believe that this logic contrasts markedly with that of a rational-argumentative discourse in the strict sense, but it is not the mere collision of differing values or identities or cultures either. Because I view values here as the articulation of experiences, they do not, as in the case of an irrational decisionism, appear as the result of a baseless choice that we have no way of rendering intersubjectively plausible. I aim to demonstrate the fruitfulness of this concept in three stages: following some remarks on the limits of purely rational discourse, I introduce and explain the concept of value generalization before applying it to the genesis of the Universal Declaration of Human Rights.

To prevent misunderstandings, I should add straight away that my aim here is to demonstrate a possibility—I do not naively assume that value discrepancies can always be harmoniously resolved. To object to this concept by pointing out that conflicts frequently occur is no more compelling than to assail a theory of rational argument on the basis that many people put forward unsound arguments. Every possibility, of course, entails certain preconditions. So I will also be asking which conditions were necessary to the Universal Declaration of Human Rights in the years following the Second World War.

COMMUNICATION ABOUT VALUES

Why do we need a theory of the specific logic inherent in our communication about values?[1] Why should we not be satisfied with the nuanced discourse theory of morality set out by Jürgen Habermas, Karl-Otto Apel, and their students? Inspired mainly by the founder of American Pragmatism, Charles Sanders Peirce, as well as by Stephen Toulmin and others, these thinkers have developed a comprehensive model of rational-argumentative discourse about cognitive, normative, and other validity claims. The basic idea here is that the point of departure for every rational discourse lies in speech acts in which a speaker pursues the illocutionary goal of convincing the listener that his implicit or explicit validity claim is justified. The listener is expected not just to listen but to accept the validity claim or to put forward good reasons why she cannot do so or can do so only partially. Should the listener express dissent, the first speaker is now confronted with an alternative validity claim. Now it is he who must either accept this claim or provide reasons why he cannot. In successful cases, this process of back-and-forth leads to the progressive mutual modification of these validity claims by means of reasons. In the absence of temporal or other external restrictions, such a rational, argument-based discourse may lead to an "organic" conclusion in which the participants find themselves, uncoerced, in a situation of self-generated consensus.

The exponents of this model are all aware that the above account is an idealization of real-life processes of argumentation. But they regard such idealization not as worthless abstraction, but as a regulative idea that guides and ought to guide us in the empirical world as we engage in argument with others. So these thinkers cannot, I believe, be accused of naive idealization, of ignoring the fact that real debates often fail to conform to their model.

But this does not mean that there is no more to say about discourses and their place within moral philosophy. This model tells us nothing about what motivates us to enter into such a discourse in the first place or about why we feel obligated to honor the outcome in our actions. The relationship between a discursive situation unencumbered by any pressure to act and situations in which the discursively achieved results are "applied" requires further clarification, as does the exact difference between different types of validity claim and their specific modes of discursive verification.[2] These questions must be left to one side here. All I want to establish for now is whether such a purely rational discourse about values is possible, and if it is not, whether the only alternative is pure decisionism and confrontation.

The sense that there must be a third way is broadly shared. It is the basis of the praxis of interreligious dialogue. Jürgen Habermas himself concedes that when it comes to values it is impossible to make as clean a distinction between questions of genesis and validity as it supposedly is with respect to cognitive and normative validity claims—an insight that prompted me to develop the idea of an "affirmative genealogy" in the present context.[3] But for him all this means is that values are inevitably particular and cannot be subject to the kind of universalization that he considers possible in the case of cognitive and normative validity claims. For him, moreover, the particularity of values means the particularism of values, so logically there can be no universalist values. The only hope of universalization thus lies in the spheres of law and normative morality. Yet this is unconvincing, both philosophically and historically. The fact that the carriers of values are particular individuals and groups does not mean that the addressees of their value orientation can also only be particular individuals and groups.[4] On the contrary, in historical terms we can in fact precisely localize the genesis of such universalist values—in connection with notions of transcendence in the so-called Axial Age.[5] Because Habermas makes these implausible assumptions, he has not even attempted to elaborate a specific logic of communication about values.

Three specific features of communication about values seem to me to be critical:

First, to talk about values presupposes that we take account of the affective intensity of our commitment to them. We can of course reformulate all values in propositional form as assertions that something is good or evil/bad. And it is beyond dispute that religions and secular worldviews include a wealth of factual claims such as that Jesus was resurrected or that Muhammad was a prophet. But our commitment to values differs from a commitment to purely cognitive validity claims. We "have" values in a different way than opinions; this is what the term "value commitment" expresses. If we wish to get at the character of values, we must take seriously this aspect of commitment. We can do this if we first clarify what commitment means by considering our commitment to other people. How do we react if asked why we love a particular person, such as a wife, son, or close friends? I suggest that when it comes to love and friendship we have no trouble grasping intuitively how inappropriate it is to list a person's specific attributes, such as their appearance or talents, or even specific achievements and accolades that may well suffice as explanation in many cases. It is certainly possible to list attributes in this way, and no doubt our love rests partly on cognitive assumptions about the character and conduct of a loved person in the past, present, and future. So we can try to explain our commitment in dialogue with others. But here our expectation of the listener is quite different than that to which discourse theory refers. We neither expect nor even intend to convince the listener in such a way that he comes to share our feelings or promptly develops a fondness for the person whose lovability we are describing. So the aim here can only be plausibility, not consensus. This may seem a modest goal. But such communication involves exploring deep-seated feelings and experiences, so it may be more sophisticated and richer than rational argument.

Because values without commitment are mere assertions, but values with commitment cannot be dealt with in the same way as mere assertions, the first key characteristic of the logic of communication about them is consideration of how our commitment to them is constituted.

The second key difference between regular discursively raised validity claims and values lies in the status of negation. It has often been remarked that the refutation of a cognitive statement within a religious worldview rarely diminishes believers' commitment to their faith. From the perspective of believers, many elements of faith are often flexible, in fact replaceable. This is because they did not become committed through a process of discursive persuasion. From an empiricist standpoint, believers must therefore appear blinkered and dogmatic, unwilling to abandon their faith in the face of scientific progress and enlightened thinking. But this perception rests on the false idea that faith is a matter of believing in the truth of a system of propositions.

At least since the posthumous publication of Ludwig Wittgenstein's reflections *On Certainty* in 1969, a process of rethinking has begun within the tradition of analytical philosophy that draws on his work. Evidently, all cognitive systems of reference rest upon "certainties," which are constitutive even of all specific doubts and possible procedures of falsification. So these certainties cannot be fallible in the same sense as each individual proposition within a given referential system. Building on the work of Wittgenstein, various authors have tried to show that religious convictions cannot be reduced to cognitive-propositional elements; but this does not mean that they consist only of expressive-regulative ones.[6] Religious convictions are not immune to communicative questioning; but this must be appropriate to their status and not reduce them to cognitions (or norms).

In the case of value commitments, we tend to react to others' questioning of them not with arguments but by disparaging the questioner. Because for us the good has the quality of subjective self-evidence, those who do not share our views are themselves relegated to the sphere of the bad.[7] The second difference from the discourse model thus derives from the binding aspect of values, but relates not to the conditions of their constitution, but their negation.

Third, taking account of the constitution of value commitments and the specific features of negation gives rise to another difference. Values cannot simply be discussed in an atomistic way, as if they were no more than discrete, self-contained opinions. In connection with a thought experiment about whether we subject mere preferences to a moral judgment, Hilary Putnam has pointed out that value judgments form groups or clusters and that we judge as morally neutral only those preferences that are not related to other preferences that we view as morally relevant.[8]

I believe this plausible idea must be extended to include the temporal dimension. Value judgments point to histories. We explain our value commitments but at the same time we defend them by narrating how we or others arrived at them and what happens when these values are flouted. So biographical, historical, and mythological narratives are not illustrations to didactic ends but a necessary feature of communication about values. It is enough here to refer back to the detailed rationale for an affirmative genealogy in the fourth chapter of this book as an appropriate way of justifying values.

THE CONCEPT OF VALUE GENERALIZATION

Beyond this attempt to shed light on possible ways of communicating about values, we require an understanding of how through such processes of communication values can be transformed to make them universalist. At the start of this chapter I identified the concept of value generalization as well suited to this. It comes from the work of Talcott Parsons, the most influential American sociologist in the decades following the Second World War.[9] In response to the many critics who claimed that his so-called structural-functional theory was incapable of explaining social change, Parsons applied his theory of the four basic functions that each social system must fulfill to the field of "social dynamics." He identified these four functions as adaptation to the system environment, achievement of system goals, integration of system elements, and maintenance of the value patterns constitutive of the system's identity. From this perspective, social change too occurs in four forms: as an increase in system adaptability, internal system differentiation, the increasingly total integration of members of society, and as value generalization.

The concept of values had played a crucial role in Parsons's work from the outset. But for a long time he "treated institutionalized value-patterns as a primary, indeed in one special respect the most important single structural component of social systems." Such values and value systems, he thought, had a "considerable stability transcending the shorter-run change in the structure of particular societies—meaning time periods up to several centuries." He increasingly came to realize, however, that processes of differentiation cannot advance without influencing the dimension of institutionalized values in significant ways. This prompted him to put forward the fundamental thesis: "The more differentiated the system, the higher the level of generality at which the value-pattern must be 'couched' if it is to legitimate the more specified values of all of the differentiated parts of the social system."[10] Elsewhere he writes that "when the network of socially structured situations becomes more complex, the value pattern itself must be couched at a higher level of generality in order to ensure social stability."[11]

If we look at Parsons's examples, it is clear that he was very much thinking of the distinction between church and state and the institutionalization of a moral conception of community within a society, a conception that "both cuts across 'denominational' lines—in the more narrowly religious sense—and those of ethnic culture." Here "cuts across"—and this can be viewed as the definition of value generalization—means "the inclusion, under a single legitimizing value-pattern, of components which are not only diverse and differentiated from each other, but many of which have, historically, claimed some sort of an 'absolutistic' monopoly of moral legitimacy."[12]

Parsons is well aware that such value generalization is a process that extends across many stages and is frequently conflictual. Some groups will protest against "any alteration of their concrete commitments," viewing such change as "a surrender of integrity to illegitimate interests," which Parsons describes as a "fundamentalist" response.[13] Others will deride these fundamentalists and call for more radical innovation, questioning the value of the differentiation that has already occurred.

For Parsons, this idea of value generalization was a contribution to an empirical theory of social change. But on closer inspection we can also make out a slight ambiguity with respect to the empirical or normative status of his thought. In his autobiography he refers to value generalization as "the mode of change required to complete such a phase for the system, if it is to have the prospect of future viability."[14] He believed that value generalization became necessary as a result of the industrial, democratic, and educational revolutions. But what exactly does it mean when we describe a change as necessary? It has always been one of the key weaknesses of functionalist thought to derive a process from a functional requirement. Why should the necessary in fact occur? Here Parsons succumbed to a kind of evolutionist optimism that no longer seems plausible after the twentieth century. To make the concept of value generalization productive, we must detach it from this functionalist framework.

This is just what Jürgen Habermas did in his interpretation of Parsons in *The Theory of Communicative Action*. Beyond a mere critique of functionalism, Habermas presents a trenchant argument that makes neglect of possible tensions between the different dimensions of social change seem typical of harmonious conceptions of social change.[15] It is not just that value generalization is not the simple result of differentiation processes. There may even be huge tensions between advancing differentiation and specific forms of value generalization.

While I believe this critique is correct, Habermas's intention here is clearly very different from mine. For him, value generalization leads to a decoupling of communicative action from all specific binding patterns of action.[16] On this view, social integration is increasingly achieved through rational discourse, with religiously anchored mutual understanding playing an ever-smaller role. This is what he calls the "linguistification of the sacred"—one of the most radical theories of secularization ever conceived. Conversely, what Parsons had in mind when he developed the idea of value generalization was that value traditions may develop a more general, and mostly more abstract understanding of their content, without being entirely uprooted from the specific traditions and experiences that are the source of affective binding force for the actors involved.

Value generalization does not intellectualize value traditions. Stripped of their affective dimension, they would be quite sterile. But through this process of generalization, people who feel bound to a tradition find new ways to articulate it by engaging with social change or the representatives of other traditions. If this occurs on both sides of a process of engagement involving different value traditions it may lead to a new and authentic sense of commonality. So value generalization is neither a consensus achieved through rational-argumentative discourse nor merely a decision to embrace peaceful coexistence despite insurmountable value differences. Again, it is evident that the result of successful communication about values is both more and less than the result of rational discourse: though we do not reach total consensus, we can achieve the dynamic, mutual modification of our own traditions as well as finding stimuli for their renewal.

In addition to Parsons, a wide range of thinkers has put forward ideas of this kind. The best-known example at present is the thought of John Rawls. Subsequent to his epochal *Theory of Justice* from 1971, he made room within his evolving intellectual framework for a plurality of "comprehensive doctrines" and their "overlapping consensus."[17] This is undoubtedly similar to Parsons, but Parsons's sociological conception seems to me superior to Rawls's philosophical one, for two reasons. First, Parsons's conception does not envisage a static constellation of coexisting elements but rather a dynamic process of mutual modification. Second, rather than restricting communication to political or constitutional principles, it pays attention to the deeper layers of value systems and religions.[18] The "overlapping consensus" is attained by omitting questions, while value generalization is geared toward the very thing that Rawls omits.

However this may be in the detail, it would seem that every theoretical attempt that neither aims at incontestable ethical foundations such as natural law nor assumes that it is impossible for the representatives of differing values or value systems to talk to one another rationally must include an intellectual equivalent of Parsons's idea of value generalization. In terms of my attempt to shed light on the genesis of the Universal Declaration of Human Rights of 1948, the most useful idea of all seems to be that of Parsons, despite the fact that it was initially geared toward the challenges to a value system arising from advancing functional differentiation rather than the encounter between a number of different value systems.

THE UNIVERSAL DECLARATION OF HUMAN RIGHTS: GENESIS AND CONSEQUENCES

As with the historical issues dealt with so far in this book—the origins of the human rights declarations of the late eighteenth century and the processes that led to the abolition of torture and slavery—this is not the place for a broad narrative account. Once again my sole aim is to show that certain powerful ideas held by the general public have long been refuted by serious researchers. This also allows me to demonstrate that a narrative that we might refer to as the "sacralization of the person" is well suited to synthesizing our historical knowledge of the origins of the 1948 declaration. Here my emphasis is on how we might reconcile fundamentally different cultural traditions, ones featuring "sacralities" that at first sight appear to differ greatly.

In 2002 American political scientist Susan Waltz identified four persistent myths that dominate popular understanding of the Universal Declaration of Human Rights.[19] These are her four myths: that the declaration was entirely a reaction to the Holocaust; that most of the work was done by the major powers of the United States, Great Britain, and the Soviet Union; that the text of the declaration was composed by a clearly identifiable individual; and that the success of the declaration is owed chiefly to the United States. And these myths are in fact very hard to dislodge. I aim to refute them here by attempting to answer three questions. I first examine the background to the declaration, which allows us to gain a realistic sense of its relation to Nazism and its crimes. Above all, though, I then scrutinize the collective process through which the declaration was composed by a diverse group of authors and the successful case of "value generalization" that this entailed. Finally, I outline the historical window of opportunity in which the declaration was drafted in all its ambivalence.[20]

While it is true that rejection of Nazism and the belligerent and inhuman policies of Hitler's Germany helped achieve the consensus needed to compose the declaration, it would be anachronistic to think mainly in terms of the mass murder of Jews. The world was unaware of the full extent of the Holocaust during the war, but efforts toward a human rights declaration were made before the war was over. After President Roosevelt's State of the Union address on January 6, 1941, at the latest, human rights were a recognizable element of American policy, and from January 1, 1942, they were also part of the Allies' war aims.[21] This does not mean that they appeared in every document or were adhered to without deviation. This is hardly surprising, as evident from a moment's reflection on the human rights situation in Stalin's Soviet Union, Great Britain's determination to retain its colonial empire, and official race discrimination in the American South. None of the three major powers intended to forgo one iota of their own national sovereignty after the war because of human rights. The American leadership was nonetheless willing to grant human rights such importance because of the pressure exerted mainly by American nongovernmental organizations and small countries. A wide variety of national and international organizations and individuals put forward proposals through publications, petitions to the American Department of State, and in other ways. These recommendations came from Catholics, Protestants, and Jews, lawyers, diplomats, and peace activists. It appears that a broad movement gained traction during the war because President Roosevelt made achieving its aims seem a realistic possibility.

But this movement had formed long before the war. Over the last few years, a number of historians have tried to create the impression that, after the revolutions in the late eighteenth century, human rights discourse had largely disappeared—or at least been completely marginalized by other key sociopolitical concepts of the European-dominated world such as "civilization," "race," "nation," and "class."[22] The understandable reason why they come to this conclusion is the wish to counter historical teleologies that imply the continuous unfolding of an idea conceived at a given point in time, and instead to emphasize contingency and conflict within the history of human rights. But they seem to me to be overstating the case, and even to contradict themselves. The great controversies over Georg Jellinek's book and publication of the groundbreaking interpretation of human rights by Émile Durkheim informed by the sacredness of the person—both of which received so much attention in the first two chapters of this book—occurred in the late nineteenth century. It is true that the nationalism of the First World War repressed this discourse, but it grew again after the war—in the shape of very different national variants.[23] Restrictions on civil liberties in the war were in fact one of the key factors stimulating renewed intellectual and organizational efforts in many countries.[24] The interwar period was replete with such efforts. This is particularly apparent if we eschew a Eurocentric perspective and take account of the discourse of black Americans and the fight against lynching in the United States, resistance to the increasingly comprehensive racial segregation in South Africa, Latin American reactions to the Spanish Civil War, and then responses to the Nazi persecution of the Jews from the 1930s.[25] There is dispute over the extent to which we ought to describe efforts to achieve collective self-determination as part of the discourse of human rights. In the interwar period the League of Nations had certainly installed a regime of national self-determination and protection for ethnic minorities in Central and Eastern Europe, but only there: not in the Western states, not for the people of the Ottoman Empire, and certainly not in the colonies. Not every argument for national self-determination and not every anticolonial struggle should be viewed as part of the history of human rights; but to sweepingly exclude them from this history is also unconvincing.

Further, in the nineteenth century human rights discourse had already spread to Asia, Latin America, and Africa, and it was embraced with great enthusiasm in countries such as China—to which cultural essentialists still impute an inability to grasp even the concept of human rights.[26] The fight against slavery, attempts to protect the Christians in the Ottoman Empire, and of course the emergence of an international movement for the rights of women are rightly listed, but it would be just as true to point out that there were no comparable movements or campaigns against the extermination of Native Americans, the pogroms of Jews in Russia, or colonialism as such.[27] Colonialists misused certain movements to further their own ends, the most cynical example probably being the Belgian king Leopold II, who justified his colonization of the Congo by claiming it would eliminate the (Arab) slave trade.[28]

So—and this is why I have mentioned these things—it is not true that the human rights discourse, after subsiding for 150 years, sprang anew from the reaction to Nazism or the Holocaust. Though many of the publications and petitions during the war and many of the initiatives and blueprints in the interwar period had no demonstrable influence on the Universal Declaration of Human Rights of 1948, the declaration nonetheless has a long and deep prehistory. It is also hard to imagine its success after 1948 without the panoply of jumping-off points generated by this prehistory. This very prehistory shows that it would be difficult to regard a single culture, religion, or philosophy as the sole basis for the declaration.

The diversity of its authors, and contributors' conscious decision not to insist on their specific version of a justification, make it particularly clear that this document was a result of value generalization. But as I have said, to see this we must first dispel the myth of sole authorship. Two individuals have at times been claimed to have done all or most of the work: former American first lady Eleanor Roosevelt and French jurist René Cassin, who was in fact awarded the 1968 Nobel Peace Prize for it. As far as Eleanor Roosevelt is concerned, there is universal agreement among researchers that while she moderated the process of composition with great diplomatic skill and therefore contributed to its success, she can in no way be considered the key intellectual driving force. René Cassin is a different case in that his legal expertise seemed to predestine him for the role of author and there exists a draft in his handwriting very similar to the final text of the declaration. But this handwritten text, as we now know, is itself a copy, which has led to the opposing claim that Cassin is not only not the father of the declaration, but that he entered the delivery room after the baby had been born.[29] Cassin came from a Jewish family, his father secular-republican, his mother religious. Seriously wounded in the First World War, he was one of the founders of the French veterans' movement, which was oriented toward peace. Through his role there and in the international veterans' movement, he became a member of the French delegation to the League of Nations, a position he held from 1924 to 1938. At the time of France's defeat in the Second World War he was a legal adviser at the ministry of the interior. He resolved to join the resistance organized by Charles de Gaulle, and fled to London in 1940, where he played an important role both in legal and propaganda terms. He was appointed French delegate to the commission charged with composing the declaration. While human rights were often proclaimed a part of French national identity, it is not clear that they enjoyed this status within the ideas of the resistance or Cassin's thinking on a personal level. He by no means entered the negotiations with a well-prepared conception. His role seems to have been more that of a legally trained logical systematizer than a man of ideas. Given his strong secularist tendencies, it is interesting to note his openness to religious influences. As Cassin himself stated, Angelo Roncalli, later Pope John XXIII, who was so important in opening the Catholic Church to human rights, met with him discreetly several times in autumn 1948, as then nuncio in France, to express his support.[30]

But a text without a clear main author must still have been authored by someone. The commission was made up of delegates from eighteen countries. The extent to which they were bound by instructions from their national governments, or received such instructions at all, seems to have varied greatly. Some—such as the Lebanese and Chinese representatives—appear to have acted largely independently. Researchers underline the important editorial role of the commission secretary, the Canadian John Humphrey. But two individuals are highlighted as particularly influential intellectually—and their contributions have scarcely penetrated the public consciousness. These were the representatives of Lebanon and China referred to above, Charles Malik and Peng-chun Chang.

Charles Malik, an Arab and recognized as a spokesman for the Arab world, particularly on the question of Palestine, was an Orthodox Christian. He studied at the American University in Beirut and gained a PhD in philosophy at Harvard supervised by Alfred North Whitehead before further studies at the University of Freiburg under Martin Heidegger, where in 1935 he was beaten up by Nazis who mistook him for a Jew. As diplomat and philosopher he was doubly qualified for his role. His personal orientation is often described as "Thomist." But it seems more pertinent to emphasize that he had a personalist rather than individualist understanding of human rights and human dignity.[31]

Peng-chun Chang was an even more remarkable figure. He was a philosopher and educationalist, dramatist, literary critic, and diplomat. His background, to which he frequently referred, was Confucian. Through an American scholarship he was able to obtain his PhD at the Columbia Teachers' College in 1921 under the great American Pragmatist philosopher and educationalist John Dewey. At the time of the Japanese invasion of China in 1937 he held a senior academic post. He joined the resistance against the Japanese and, after escaping from the occupiers, strove to bring the so-called Rape of Nanking to the world's attention.[32] As ambassador in Turkey he gave lectures comparing Confucianism and Islam; as ambassador in Chile he came into contact with the lively human rights discourse in Latin America. During the negotiations he constantly warned against any narrowly rationalist foundation for human rights and against the idea that any particular religious tradition should receive special emphasis within it. The synthesis of justificatory traditions was one of his key concerns.

I will not list all the actors involved by name, partly because most of the others played a less significant role than these two figures. But it is important to mention Indian delegate Hansa Mehta, thanks to whom the language of the declaration is gender neutral (not "all men" but "all human beings"), and Hernan Santa Cruz, Chilean judge, childhood friend of Salvador Allende, and especially engaged in efforts to ensure the mention of socioeconomic rights.

The involvement of these actors already gives us an idea of the diverse range of intellectual and cultural traditions involved. The schema Western/non-Western is incapable of capturing this diversity. The Western powers were not politically united (especially with regard to the colonial question), and their representatives also differed in philosophical and religious terms. There was certainly no opposing non-Western consensus. Here the spectrum ranged from Stalinists to representatives of the other world religions. Even more important than the diversity represented on the commission was the more or less conscious decision by the leading actors to agree on an internally logical text but not on its derivation and justification. The UN Educational, Scientific, and Cultural Organization (UNESCO) had appointed a group of esteemed philosophers in 1947 to discuss the theoretical foundations of human rights. But the resulting publication was simply ignored by the commission concerned with the declaration. It was vital that their work *not* revolve around philosophical justification. This attitude toward the group of philosophers was unfair in the sense that they had come to the same conclusion themselves. In the words of Jacques Maritain, the only expedient way of reaching an agreement was "not on the basis of common speculative ideas, but on common practical ideas, not on the affirmation of one and the same conception of the world, of man, and of knowledge, but upon the affirmation of a single body of beliefs for guidance in action."[33]

This was most impressively evident at those points in the debates where concepts were consciously avoided that would have made agreement impossible for a group of thinkers or believers. The text therefore makes mention neither of God nor of any normatively substantial concept of nature.[34] On this basis, Johannes Morsink, who has written a detailed and impressive account of the negotiations, justifies describing the declaration as secular. This is correct if it means that a religiously founded declaration must contain a reference to God. But it is not correct if it means that a religious justification was not permitted in the Universal Declaration and that a justification anchored in a purely secular worldview or philosophy was inserted instead. This is by no means the case. In the words of Charles Malik, one of its key authors, the declaration is a "composite synthesis," the result of a "dynamic process in which many minds, interests, backgrounds, legal systems and ideological persuasions played their respective determining roles"—the result of a successful process of value generalization.[35]

We should, however, resist any temptation to idealize this process. There were of course many "disagreements, misunderstandings, personal quirks, national rivalries, and colonial resentments."[36] Given that agreement was ultimately reached, it seems unproductive to focus on these. More important is the fact that the agreement had a major shortcoming right from the outset. What was agreed was merely a declaration that was entirely or largely legally nonbinding. No implementation procedures were provided for. Neither the Soviet Union nor the US Senate would have signed up to such procedures, and the representatives of the American government quickly made this abundantly clear to Eleanor Roosevelt. Was the declaration's nonbinding nature the high price of agreement? This at least seemed to be what those states that voted in favor, and even more those who abstained, were hoping. The Soviet Union and its allies-of-necessity, plus South Africa (which was intensifying its policy of apartheid the same year) and Saudi Arabia, abstained when the UN General Assembly voted on the declaration (the latter as the only Muslim-majority state to do so). Neither the issue of the position of women nor that of conversion from Islam prevented the other states with large Muslim populations from voting in favor.[37] This is not the place to clarify the extent to which and for whom opportunist political motives were chiefly responsible for assent. But it is clear that the declaration was not a Western imposition. Particularly in the United States, up to the highest levels of government the declaration quickly inspired strong resistance as a dangerous document anchored in a state socialist mindset.[38]

No doubt in line with the intentions of its authors, but quite against those of most of the governments involved, the 1948 declaration became a key reference text for political struggles and the point of departure for legal regulations. "It has come to achieve a significance it was carefully designed not to possess at the time."[39]

This emphasis on the intended status of the declaration ushers in a process of disillusionment that deepens the moment we take a closer look at the window of opportunity within which the declaration became possible. How could the individuals involved possibly have had so much influence and room for maneuver? In the interval between the end of the Second World War and the definitive onset of the Cold War, the governments of the victorious powers became victims of their own self-presentation. When they set about reining in the pathos of universal human rights, it quickly unleashed a storm of criticism from nongovernmental organizations and other disappointed parties. Nonetheless, it seemed politically harmless to agree to a mere declaration. Yet here we are confronted with another perplexing fact. The Declaration of Human Rights seemed to help neither the colonized nor the millions of people driven from their homelands toward the end of the Second World War and thereafter within the framework of a policy of ethnic expulsion and resettlement in Eastern and East-Central Europe initiated by the Soviet Union but approved by the Allies. This problem is particularly apparent when we consider two individuals. Edvard Beneš, president of the Czechoslovak government in exile and postwar regime, had championed human rights as early as the 1920s. During the war he worked in a range of ways for an internationally binding guarantee of human rights.[40] Through the decrees named after him, he was largely responsible for the expulsion of Germans and Hungarians from Czechoslovak territory after the war. The other individual is Jan Smuts, who served twice as prime minister of South Africa and was the figure mainly responsible for the racist policy of apartheid. In 1945, incomprehensibly, he was entrusted with the honorable task of drafting the preamble to the Charter of the United Nations, for which he quickly found the right tone, referring to the "sanctity and ultimate value of human personality" and so on.[41] Were these two individuals simply contemptible hypocrites or did they have at hand interpretations of the world—peace through separation of peoples, personality development in the context of strict racial segregation—that allowed them to delude themselves that human rights were compatible with ethnic expulsion or racial segregation?[42] Whatever the truth may be with regard to these two individual cases, it is clear that the deliberate lack of protection for ethnic minorities in the declaration actually increased states' room for maneuver compared with the League of Nations period and worsened the protection of minorities.[43] "Behind the smokescreen of the rights of the individual . . . the corpse of the League's minority policy could be safely buried."[44] It is true that the Third Reich abused regulations governing minorities, but does this justify what happened after 1945?

Fortunately, the period following the adoption of the Universal Declaration on December 10, 1948, showed that values and a declaration of rights based on a process of value generalization can have a substantial influence on intellectual debates, lived practices, and both legal and political institutions. I will not go into this subsequent history with all its own contingencies here. Again, this was not a process of maturation that unfolded as a matter of course, the efflorescence of an idea that could not be held down. Many factors made this text into the towering monument it was to become.

Let us now turn our attention away from affirmative genealogy, from the past, to future objectives. I have already discussed how the sacralization of the person had constantly to compete with sacralizations of other secular entities such as the nation, and I have mentioned the risk of human rights becoming an ideological element in a new process of social self-sacralization through national, cultural, or religious triumphalism.[45] The achievements of the sacralization of the person are by no means comfortingly secure, nor can we assume that they will be more widely disseminated in the future. If we take obstacles and threats seriously it is evident that, in terms of my triad of practices, values, and institutions, the achievements of the sacralization of the person can be secured only if three things occur. In the sphere of practice, there must be greater sensitivity to experiences of injustice and violence and their articulation. In the field of values, the need is for the argumentational justification of the universal validity claim, though—as I have tried to show—this can only be achieved through the incorporation of a relevant narrative into that argumentation. And on the level of institutions we need both national and global processes of codification so that people from very different cultures can invoke the same rights. None of these three spheres takes priority in all circumstances. In the long term, human rights and the sacralization of the person will have a chance only through a combination of all three: if human rights are supported by institutions and civil society, defended through argument, and incarnated in the practices of everyday life.

NOTES

1. The first two sections of this chapter are based in part on Joas, "Value Generalization."

2. I list and discuss these problems of discourse theory in depth in the final chapter of my book *The Genesis of Values*, 161–66.

3. Habermas, *Between Facts and Norms*, 163. On affirmative genealogy, see chap. 4 of this book.

4. See Joas, *Genesis of Values*, 182–86, and esp. Bernstein, "Retrieval of the Democratic Ethos."

5. Drawing on the work of Karl Jaspers, this refers to the period 800–200 BC. See Jaspers, *Origin and Goal of History*. For a sociological take on this, see esp. the important subsequent works by Shmuel Eisenstadt and Robert N. Bellah: Eisenstadt, "Axial Age in World History"; Bellah, "What Is Axial about the Axial Age?"; Bellah and Joas, *Axial Age and Its Consequences*.

6. See the contributions in Joas, *Was sind religiöse Überzeugungen?*

7. Williams, *Ethics and the Limits of Philosophy*, 185.

8. Putnam, *Reason, Truth and History*, 154–55. On Putnam and the questions discussed here, see Joas, "Values versus Norms."

9. On Parsons's impressive oeuvre, which is largely ignored in contemporary American sociology, see Joas and Knöbl, *Social Theory*, 20–93.

10 The most detailed account of the notion of value generalization is in Parsons, "Comparative Studies and Evolutionary Change"; see 307.

11. Parsons, *System of Modern Societies*, 27.

12. Parsons, "Comparative Studies on Evolutionary Change," 308.

13. Ibid., 311.

14. Parsons, "On Building Social System Theory," 51.

15. Habermas, *Theory of Communicative Action*, 179.

16. Ibid., 180.

17. Rawls, *Political Liberalism*, 133–72.

18. Like other contemporary legal theorists such as Ronald Dworkin, Winfried Brugger has distinguished between several levels of generality in the articulation of values; like me, he has therefore attempted to reflect on a form of communication about values that remains alive to the experiential foundations of our value commitments. See Brugger, *Liberalismus, Pluralismus, Kommunitarismus*; Dworkin, *Taking Rights Seriously*.

19. Waltz, "Reclaiming and Rebuilding."

20. My account here is based on the following texts, each excellent in its own way: Morsink, *Universal Declaration of Human Rights*; Lauren, *Evolution of International Human Rights*; Glendon, *World Made New*; Simpson, *Human Rights and the End of Empire*. The essays of Susan Waltz are also indispensable. In addition to the text cited in the preceding note, see esp. "Universal Human Rights" and "Universalizing Human Rights." Of the German literature, I shall refer here only to Vögele, *Menschenwürde zwischen Recht und Theologie*, 197–235; Kaufmann, *Entstehung sozialer Grundrechte*. Further references are given as I develop my argument.

21. For a concise survey of the prehistory (up to 1945), see Burgers, "Road to San Francisco."

22. Such historians include Cmiel, "Recent History of Human Rights"; Moyn, *Last Utopia*; Geyer, "Disappearance of Human Rights post 1800"; Afshari, "On Historiography of Human Rights." This list of dominant concepts comes from Hoffmann, "Introduction," 1.

23. Hoffmann mentions (ibid., 10) the reversal of the development that set in with the Dreyfus scandal (in France), but does not go on to discuss what happened (internationally) after 1918. In Germany—to take one example—Ernst Troeltsch published his lecture "The Ideas of Natural Law and Humanity in World Politics," in which he initiated the combining of the Western tradition of human rights with the German "expressivist" tradition of individuality, making this one of the most important philosophical texts on the topic of human rights. See on this text Joas, "Deutsche Idee von der Freiheit?"

24. A wealth of information on this can be found in Lauren, *Evolution of International Human Rights*, e.g., 106–38, which refers to Carl von Ossietzky.

25. Again, Lauren provides a wealth of relevant references. But this is a research field that has yet to be properly cultivated.

26. See esp. the book by Marina Svensson, *Debating Human Rights in China*. She points out that Jellinek's book had been translated into Chinese by 1908. A Japanese translation appeared in 1929. (I have Pekka Korhonen of the University of Jyväskylä to thank for this information.)

27. Cmiel, "Recent History of Human Rights," 127.

28. Hochschild, *King Leopold's Ghost*.

29. Morsink, *Universal Declaration of Human Rights*, 29. Astonishingly, the thesis of Cassin's authorship and thus the French-republican origins of the declaration appears again, with no refutation of the latest research, in Winter, *Dreams of Peace and Freedom*, 99–120.

30. Glendon, *World Made New*, 132; Vögele, *Menschenwürde zwischen Recht und Theologie*, 220.

31. Glendon, *World Made New*, 227.

32. I take most of this information from Glendon, *World Made New*.

33. Maritain, quoted in Glendon, *World Made New*, 77–78.

34. Morsink, *Universal Declaration of Human Rights*, 284–90.

35. The first quotation comes from Glendon, *World Made New*, 164; the second from Vögele, *Menschenwürde zwischen Recht und Theologie*, 235.

36. Glendon, *World Made New*, 50.

37. For an excellent treatment of this topic, see Waltz, "Universal Human Rights." On the conduct of the Soviet Union, see Amos, "Embracing and Contesting."

38. See the quotations from Secretary of State John Foster Dulles from 1953 and from the president of the American Bar Association, Frank E. Holman, from January 1949 in Glendon, *World Made New*, 205 and 199. Republican senator John Bricker from Ohio went even further, attempting to amend the Constitution to prohibit any restriction on sovereignty. See Simpson, *Human Rights and the End of Empire*, 461.

39. Simpson, *Human Rights and the End of Empire*, 11.

40. Ibid., 160–61, with references to his relevant publications and activities.

41. On Smuts, see the study by Mark Mazower, "Jan Smuts and Imperial Internationalism."

42. Simpson (*Human Rights and the End of Empire*, 161) even believes that "enthusiasm for human rights and hypocrisy not uncommonly go hand in hand."

43. See ibid., 442, on the arguments made in association with this decision.

44. Mazower, "Strange Triumph of Human Rights," 389. By the same author, see also the important essays "International Civilization?"; "End of Civilization and the Rise of Human Rights."

45. See the fourth section ("Threats") in chap. 2 of this book and the conclusion of chap. 3.

BIBLIOGRAPHY

Afshari, Reza. "On Historiography of Human Rights: Reflections on P. G. Lauren's *The Evolution of International Human Rights.*" *Human Rights Quarterly* 29 (2007): 1–67.

Alexander, Jeffrey. "On the Social Construction of Moral Universals: The 'Holocaust' from War Crime to Trauma Drama." *European Journal of Social Theory* 5 (2002): 5–85.

Alexander, Jeffrey, et al. *Cultural Trauma and Collective Identity.* Berkeley: University of California Press, 2004.

Amos, Jennifer. "Embracing and Contesting: The Soviet Union and the Universal Declaration of Human Rights, 1948–1958." In Hoffmann, *Human Rights in the Twentieth Century*, 147–65.

Anderson, Frank Maloy. *The Constitution and Other Select Documents Illustrative of the History of France, 1789–1907.* New York: Russell & Russell, 1908.

Angenendt, Arnold. *Toleranz und Gewalt: Das Christentum zwischen Bibel und Schwert.* Münster: Aschendorff, 2008.

Arendt, Hannah. *Origins of Totalitarianism* (1951). New York: Harcourt, 1973.

Baberowski, Jörg, and Anselm Doering-Manteuffel. *Ordnung durch Terror: Gewaltexzesse und Vernichtung im nationalsozialistischen und im stalinistischen Imperium.* Bonn: Dietz, 2006.

Beccaria, Cesare. *On Crimes and Punishments.* Cambridge: Cambridge University Press, 1995. Originally published as *Dei delitti e delle penne* (1764).

———. *Über Verbrechen und Strafen.* With a foreword by Wilhelm Alff. Frankfurt am Main: Insel, 1998. Originally published as *Dei delitti e delle penne* (1776 ed.).

Bellah, Robert N. "Durkheim and Ritual." In *The Cambridge Companion to Durkheim*, edited by Jeffrey Alexander and Philip Smith, 183–210. Cambridge: Cambridge University Press, 2005.

———. Introduction to *On Morality and Society*, by Émile Durkheim, i–lv. Chicago: University of Chicago Press, 1973.

———. "What Is Axial about the Axial Age?" *Archives européennes de sociologie* 46 (2005): 69–90.

Bellah, Robert N., and Hans Joas, eds. *The Axial Age and Its Consequences.* Cambridge, MA: Harvard University Press, 2012.

Bender, Thomas, ed. *The Antislavery Debate: Capitalism and Abolitionism as a Problem in Historical Interpretation*. Berkeley: University of California Press, 1992.

Bendix, Reinhard, and Guenther Roth. *Scholarship and Partisanship: Essays on Max Weber*. Berkeley: University of California Press, 1971.

Bentham, Jeremy. "Anarchical Fallacies: Being an Examination of the Declaration of Rights Issued during the French Revolution" (1792). In *The Works of Jeremy Bentham*, 11 vols., 2:489–534. Edinburgh: William Tate, 1838–43.

Bernstein, Richard. "The Retrieval of the Democratic Ethos." *Cardozo Law Review* 17 (1996): 1127–46.

Birnbaum, Pierre. *Geography of Hope: Exile, the Enlightenment, Disassimilation*. Stanford, CA: Stanford University Press, 2004. Originally published as *Géographie de l'espoir: L'exil, les lumières, la désassimilation* (2004).

Boutmy, Émile. "La déclaration des droits de l'homme et du citoyen et M. Jellinek." *Annales des sciences politiques* 17 (1902): 415–43.

———. "Die *Erklärung der Menschen- und Bürgerrechte* und Georg Jellinek." In Schnur, *Zur Geschichte der Erklärung der Menschenrechte*, 78–112.

Branch, Taylor. *Parting the Waters: America in the King Years, 1954–63*. New York: Simon & Schuster, 1988.

Brandt, Sigrid. *Religiöses Handeln in der modernen Welt: Talcott Parsons' Religionssoziologie im Rahmen seiner Handlungs- und Systemtheorie*. Frankfurt am Main: Suhrkamp, 1993.

Breuer, Stefan. "Das Charisma der Vernunft." In *Charisma: Theorie, Religion, Politik*, edited by Winfried Gebhardt et al., 154–84. Berlin: de Gruyter, 1993.

———. *Georg Jellinek und Max Weber: Von der sozialen zur soziologischen Staatslehre*. Baden-Baden: Nomos, 1999.

Brown, Christopher Leslie. "Christianity and the Campaign against Slavery and the Slave Trade." In Brown and Tackett, *Enlightenment, Reawakening and Revolution*, 517–35. Cambridge: Cambridge University Press, 2006.

Brown, Stewart J., and Timothy Tackett, eds. *Enlightenment, Reawakening and Revolution, 1660–1815*. Vol. 7 of *The Cambridge History of Christianity*. Cambridge: Cambridge University Press, 2006.

Brugger, Winfried. "Historismus und Pragmatismus in Georg Jellineks *Erklärung der Menschen- und Bürgerrechte*." In Hollstein, Jung, and Knöbl, *Handlung und Erfahrung*, 217–46.

———. *Liberalismus, Pluralismus, Kommunitarismus: Studien zur Legitimation des Grundgesetzes*. Baden-Baden: Nomos, 1999.

———. *Menschenrechtsethos und Verantwortungspolitik: Max Webers Beitrag zur Analyse und Begründung der Menschenrechte*. Freiburg im Breisgau: Alber, 1980.

———. "Sozialwissenschaftliche Analyse und menschenrechtliches Begründungsdenken: Eine Skizze im Anschluß an Max Webers Werk." *Rechtstheorie* 11 (1980): 356–77.

Burgers, Jan Herman. "The Road to San Francisco: The Revival of the Human Rights Idea in the Twentieth Century." *Human Rights Quarterly* 14 (1992): 447–77.

Capek, Milic. "The Reappearance of the Self in the Last Philosophy of William James." *Philosophical Review* 62 (1953): 526–44.

Cassirer, Ernst. *The Philosophy of the Enlightenment.* Princeton, NJ: Princeton University Press, 2009. Originally published as *Die Philosophie der Aufklärung* (1932).

Cho, Joanne Miyang. "The German Debate over Civilization: Troeltsch's Europeanism and Jaspers' Cosmopolitanism." *History of European Ideas* 25 (1999): 305–19.

Cmiel, Kenneth. "The Recent History of Human Rights." *American Historical Review* 109 (2004): 117–35.

Colliot-Thélène, Catherine. "Les modes de justification des droits subjectifs." In *Études wéberiennes: Rationalités, histoires, droits*, 259–78. Paris: Presses universitaires de France, 2001.

Colpe, Carsten, ed. *Die Diskussion um das "Heilige."* Darmstadt: WBG, 1977.

———. *Über das Heilige: Versuch, seiner Verkennung kritisch vorzubeugen.* Frankfurt am Main: Hain, 1990.

Davies, Robertson. *Murther and Walking Spirits.* New York: Viking, 1991.

Davis, David Brion. *Inhuman Bondage: The Rise and Fall of Slavery in the New World.* Oxford: Oxford University Press, 2006.

Davis, Derek H. "Religious Dimensions of the Declaration of Independence: Fact and Fiction." *Journal of Church and State* 36 (1994): 469–82.

Dewey, John. "The Reflex Arc Concept in Psychology" (1896). In *The Early Works*, 5:96–110. Carbondale: Southern Illinois University Press, 1972.

Dilthey, Wilhelm. "Rede zum 70. Geburtstag (1903)." In *Gesammelte Schriften*, 5:7–9. Leipzig: Teubner, 1924.

Döblin, Alfred. *Tales of a Long Night.* New York: Fromm, 1984. Originally published as *Hamlet, oder Die lange Nacht nimmt ein Ende* (1956).

Donzelot, Jacques. "Die Mißgeschicke der Theorie: Über Michel Foucaults 'Überwachen und Strafen.'" In *Denken und Existenz bei Michel Foucault*, edited by Wilhelm Schmid, 140–58. Frankfurt am Main: Suhrkamp, 1991.

Drescher, Seymour. "Trends in der Historiographie des Abolitionismus." *Geschichte und Gesellschaft* 16 (1990): 187–211.

Durkheim, Émile. "Anti-Semitism and Social Crisis." *Sociological Theory* 26 (2008): 321–23. Originally published as "Antisémitisme et crise sociale," in *Enquête sur l'antisémitisme*, edited by Henri Dagan, 59–63 (1899).

———. *The Division of Labour in Society.* New York: Free Press, 1997. Originally published as *De la division du travail social* (1893).

———. *The Elementary Forms of Religious Life.* Oxford: Oxford University Press, 2008. Originally published as *Les formes élémentaires de la vie religieuse* (1912).

———. *The Evolution of Educational Thought*. London: Routledge, 2006. Originally published as *L'évolution pédagogique en France* (1938).

———. "Germany above All: German Mentality and War." In *Studies and Documents on the War*. Paris: Armand Colin, 1915. Originally published as "L'Allemagne au-dessus de tout" (1915).

———. "Individualism and the Intellectuals." In *Durkheim on Religion*, edited by W. S. F. Pickering, 59–73. London: Routledge, 1975. Originally published as "L'individualisme et les intellectuels" (1898).

———. "Introduction to Ethics." In *Durkheim: Essays on Morals and Education*, edited by W. S. F. Pickering, 77–98. London: Routledge, 2005. Originally published as *Introduction à la morale* (1917).

———. *Professional Ethics and Civic Morals*. London: Routledge, 1991. Originally published as *Leçons de sociologie: Physique des moeurs et du droit* (1922).

———. "Sacré." *Bulletin de la Société française de philosophie* 15 (1917): 1–2.

———. *Textes*, 3 vols., edited by Victor Karady. Paris: Minuit, 1975.

———. "Two Laws of Penal Evolution." In *Émile Durkheim on Institutional Analysis*, edited by Mark Traugott, 153–79. Chicago: University of Chicago Press, 1994. Originally published as *Deux lois de l'évolution pénale* (1899/1900).

Dworkin, Ronald. *Life's Dominion: An Argument about Abortion, Euthanasia, and Individual Freedom*. New York: Knopf, 1993.

———. *Taking Rights Seriously*. London: Duckworth, 1977.

Eisenstadt, Shmuel. "The Axial Age in World History." In Joas and Wiegandt, *Cultural Values of Europe*, 22–42.

Ellingson, Stephen. "Understanding the Dialectic of Discourse and Collective Action: Public Debate and Rioting in Antebellum Cincinnati." *American Journal of Sociology* 101 (1995): 100–144.

Ferro, Marc, ed. *Le livre noir du colonialisme: XVIe–XXIe siècle; De l'extermination à la repentance*. Paris: Laffont, 2003.

Filloux, Jean-Claude. "Personne et sacré chez Durkheim." *Archives de sciences sociales des religions* 35, no. 69 (1990): 41–53.

Fontinell, Eugene. *Self, God, and Immortality: A Jamesian Investigation*. Philadelphia: Temple University Press, 1986.

Forst, Rainer. *Toleranz im Konflikt: Geschichte, Gehalt und Gegenwart eines umstrittenen Begriffs*. Frankfurt am Main: Suhrkamp, 2003.

Foucault, Michel. *Discipline and Punish: The Birth of the Prison*. London: Allen Lane, 1977. Originally published as *Surveiller et punir: Naissance de la prison* (1975).

Fournier, Marcel. *Émile Durkheim (1858–1917)*. Paris: Fayard, 2007.

Furet, François, and Mona Ozouf, eds. *A Critical Dictionary of the French Revolution*. Cambridge, MA: Harvard University Press, 1989. Originally published as *Dictionnaire critique de la Révolution française* (1988).

Gadamer, Hans-Georg. *Truth and Method*. London: Sheed & Ward, 1989. Originally published as *Wahrheit und Methode: Grundzüge einer philosophischen Hermeneutik* (1960).

Garland, David. *Punishment and Modern Society: A Study in Social Theory*. Chicago: University of Chicago Press, 1990.

Gauchet, Marcel. "Á la recherche d'une autre histoire de la folie." In *Dialogue avec l'insensé: Á la recherche d'une autre histoire de la folie*, edited by Gladys Swain, ix–lviii. Paris: Gallimard, 1994.

———. *La révolution des droits de l'homme*. Paris: Gallimard, 1989.

———. "Rights of Man." In Furet and Ozouf, *Critical Dictionary of the French Revolution*, 818–28. Originally published as "Droits de l'homme."

Gay, Peter. *The Enlightenment: An Interpretation*. Vol. 1, *The Rise of Modern Paganism*. New York: Norton, 1966.

Gephart, Werner. *Gesellschaftstheorie und Recht: Das Recht im soziologischen Diskurs der Moderne*. Frankfurt am Main: Suhrkamp, 1993.

Gerhardt, Volker. "Letzte Hilfe." *Frankfurter Allgemeine Zeitung*, September 19, 2003, 8.

Gestrich, Andreas. "Die Antisklavereibewegung im ausgehenden 18. und 19. Jahrhundert: Forschungsstand und Forschungsperspektiven." In *Unfreie Arbeits- und Lebensverhältnisse von der Antike bis in die Gegenwart: Eine Einführung*, edited by Elisabeth Herrmann-Otto, 237–57. Hildesheim: Olms, 2005.

Geyer, Michael. "The Disappearance of Human Rights post 1800: With an Eye on the Situation post 2000." Unpublished manuscript, Department of History, University of Chicago, 2009.

Ghosh, Peter. "Max Weber and Georg Jellinek: Two Divergent Conceptions of Law." *Saeculum* 59 (2008): 299–347.

Glendon, Mary Ann. *A World Made New: Eleanor Roosevelt and the Universal Declaration of Human Rights*. New York: Random House, 2001.

Graf, Friedrich Wilhelm. "Puritanische Sektenfreiheit versus lutherische Volkskirche: Zum Einfluß Georg Jellineks auf religionsdiagnostische Deutungsmuster Max Webers und Ernst Troeltschs." *Zeitschrift für neuere Theologiegeschichte* 9 (2002): 42–69.

Grimm, Dieter. "Europäisches Naturrecht und amerikanische Revolution." *Ius Commune: Veröffentlichungen des Max-Planck-Instituts für Europäische Rechtsgeschichte* 3 (1970): 120–51.

Guardini, Romano. *The Last Things: Concerning Death, Purification after Death, Resurrection, Judgement and Eternity*. London: Burns & Oates, 1954. Originally published as *Die letzten Dinge: Die christliche Lehre vom Tode* (1952).

Guyer, Paul. "From a Practical Point of View: Kant's Conception of a Postulate of Pure Practical Reason." In Guyer, *Kant on Freedom, Law, and Happiness*, 333–71.

———. *Kant on Freedom, Law, and Happiness*. Cambridge: Cambridge University Press, 2000.

Habermas, Jürgen. *Between Facts and Norms: Contributions to a Discourse Theory of Law and Democracy*. Cambridge, MA: MIT Press, 1996. Originally published as *Faktizität und Geltung: Beiträge zur Diskurstheorie des Rechts und des demokratischen Rechtsstaats* (1992).

———. *The Inclusion of the Other: Studies in Political Theory*. Cambridge, MA: MIT Press, 1998. Originally published as *Die Einbeziehung des Anderen: Studien zur politischen Theorie* (1996).

———. *The Theory of Communicative Action*. Vol. 2, *Lifeworld and System: A Critique of Functionalist Reason*. London: Heinemann, 1984–87. Originally published as *Theorie des kommunikativen Handelns*. Vol. 2, *Zur Kritik der funktionalistischen Vernunft* (1981).

Hall, Timothy L. *Separating Church and State: Roger Williams and Religious Liberty*. Chicago: University of Illinois Press, 1998.

Hamburger, Philip. *Separation of Church and State*. Cambridge, MA: Harvard University Press, 2002.

Haskell, Thomas. "Capitalism and the Origins of the Humanitarian Sensibility." In *Objectivity Is Not Neutrality: Explanatory Schemes in History*, 235–79. Baltimore: Johns Hopkins University Press, 1998.

Heinemann, Gustav. "Der Rechtsstaat als theologisches Problem." In *Unser Grundgesetz ist ein großes Angebot: Rechtspolitische Schriften*, edited by Jürgen Schmude, 26–36. Munich: Kaiser, 1989.

Hénaff, Marcel. *The Price of Truth: Gift, Money and Philosophy*. Stanford, CA: Stanford University Press, 2010. Originally published as *Le prix de la vérité: Le don, l'argent, la philosophie* (2002).

Hochschild, Adam. *King Leopold's Ghost: A Story of Greed, Terror and Heroism in Colonial Africa*. Boston: Mifflin, 1998.

Hoffmann, Stefan-Ludwig, ed. *Human Rights in the Twentieth Century*. Cambridge: Cambridge University Press, 2010. Originally published as *Moralpolitik: Geschichte der Menschenrechte im 20. Jahrhundert* (2010).

———. "Introduction: Genealogies of Human Rights." In Hoffmann, *Human Rights in the Twentieth Century*, 1–26. Originally published as "Einführung: Zur Genealogie der Menschenrechte."

Hofmann, Hasso. "Zur Herkunft der Menschenrechtserklärungen." *Juristische Schulung* 28 (1988): 841–48.

Hollstein, Bettina, Matthias Jung, and Wolfgang Knöbl, eds. *Handlung und Erfahrung: Das Erbe von Pragmatismus und Historismus und die Zukunft der Sozialtheorie*. Frankfurt am Main: Campus, 2011.

Honneth, Axel. *The Critique of Power: Reflective Stages in a Critical Social Theory*. Cambridge, MA: MIT Press, 1991. Originally published as *Kritik der Macht: Reflexionsstufen einer kritischen Gesellschaftstheorie* (1986).

Hoye, William J. *Demokratie und Christentum: Die christliche Verantwortung für demokratische Prinzipien*. Münster: Aschendorff, 1999.

Hübinger, Gangolf. "Staatstheorie und Politik als Wissenschaft im Kaiserreich: Georg Jellinek, Otto Hintze, Max Weber." In *Politik, Philosophie, Praxis: Festschrift für Wilhelm Hennis*, edited by Hans Maier et al., 143–61. Stuttgart: Klett-Cotta, 1988.

Hunt, Lynn, ed. *The French Revolution and Human Rights: A Brief Documentary History*. Boston: Bedford, 1996.

———. "Introduction: The Revolutionary Origins of Human Rights." In Hunt, *French Revolution and Human Rights*, 1–32.

———. *Inventing Human Rights*. New York: Norton, 2007.

———. "The Paradoxical Origins of Human Rights." In *Human Rights and Revolutions*, edited by Jeffrey Wasserstrom et al., 3–17. Lanham, MD: Rowman & Littlefield, 2000.

———. "The Sacred and the French Revolution." In *Durkheimian Sociology: Cultural Studies*, edited by Jeffrey C. Alexander, 25–43. Cambridge: Cambridge University Press, 1988.

Isensee, Josef. "Die katholische Kritik an den Menschenrechten: Der liberale Freiheitsentwurf in der Sicht der Päpste des 19. Jahrhunderts." In *Menschenrechte und Menschenwürde: Historische Voraussetzungen—säkulare Gewalt—christliches Verständnis*, edited by Ernst-Wolfgang Böckenförde and Robert Spaemann, 138–74 (plus discussion, 175–81). Stuttgart: Klett-Cotta, 1987.

Jaeger, Friedrich. "Ernst Troeltsch und John Dewey: Religionsphilosophie im Umfeld von Historismus und Pragmatismus." In Hollstein, Jung, and Knöbl, *Handlung und Erfahrung*, 107–30.

James, Henry, ed. *The Letters of William James*. 2 vols. Boston: Atlantic Monthly Press, 1920.

James, William. "Bain and Renouvier" (1876). In *Essays, Comments, and Reviews*, 321–24. Cambridge, MA: Harvard University Press, 1987.

———. "Human Immortality" (1898). In *Essays in Religion and Morality*, 75–101. Cambridge, MA: Harvard University Press, 1982.

———. *The Principles of Psychology* (1890). Cambridge, MA: Harvard University Press, 1981.

———. *Talks to Teachers on Psychology; and to Students on Some of Life's Ideals* (1899). New York: Holt, 1910.

———. "The Will to Believe" (1897). In *The Will to Believe and Other Essays in Popular Philosophy*, 1–31. London: Longmans Green, 1905.

Jaspers, Karl. *The Origin and Goal of History*. New Haven, CT: Yale University Press, 1953. Originally published as *Vom Ursprung und Ziel der Geschichte* (1949).

Jellinek, Georg. "Antwort an Boutmy." In Schnur, *Zur Geschichte der Erklärung der Menschenrechte*, 113–28.

———. *The Declaration of the Rights of Man and of Citizens: A Contribution to Modern Constitutional History*. Westport, CT: Hyperion, 1979.

———. *Die Erklärung der Menschen- und Bürgerrechte: Ein Beitrag zur modernen Verfassungsgeschichte*, 3rd ed. Munich: Duncker & Humblot, 1919.

———. "Réponse à M. Boutmy." *Revue du droit public et de la science politique* 18 (1902): 385–400.

Joas, Hans. *The Creativity of Action*. Cambridge: Polity, 1996. Originally published as *Die Kreativität des Handelns* (1992).

———. "Cultural Trauma? On the Most Recent Turn in Jeffrey Alexander's Cultural Sociology." *European Journal of Social Theory* 8 (2005): 365–74. Originally published as "Gibt es kulturelle Traumata? Zur jüngsten Wendung der Kultursoziologie von Jeffrey Alexander" (2005).

———. "Decency, Justice, Dignity: On Avishai Margalit." In Joas, *Do We Need Religion?* 115–24.

———. "Eine deutsche Idee von der Freiheit? Cassirer und Troeltsch zwischen Deutschland und dem Westen." In *Sozialphilosophie und Kritik*, edited by Rainer Forst et al., 288–316. Frankfurt am Main: Suhrkamp, 2009.

———. *Do We Need Religion?* Boulder, CO: Paradigm, 2008. Originally published as *Braucht der Mensch Religion? Über Erfahrungen der Selbsttranszendenz* (2004).

———. *The Genesis of Values*. Cambridge: Polity, 2000. Originally published as *Die Entstehung der Werte* (1997).

———. *George Herbert Mead: A Contemporary Reexamination of His Thought*. Cambridge MA: MIT Press, 1997. Originally published as *Praktische Intersubjektivität: Die Entwicklung des Werkes von George Herbert Mead* (1989).

———. "The Gift of Life: Parsons' Late Sociology of Religion." *Journal of Classical Sociology* 1 (2001): 127–41.

———. "Globalisierung und Wertentstehung—Oder: Warum Marx und Engels doch nicht recht hatten." *Berliner Journal für Soziologie* 8 (1998): 329–32.

———. "Human Dignity: The Religion of Modernity?" In Joas, *Do We Need Religion?* 133–47. Originally published as "Der Glaube an die Menschenwürde als Religion der Moderne?"

———. "Die Logik der Gabe und das Postulat der Menschenwürde." In *Gott, Geld und Gabe* (2004 supplement to the *Berliner Theologische Zeitschrift*), edited by Christof Gestrich, 16–27. Berlin: Wichern, 2004.

———. "Max Weber and the Origins of Human Rights: A Study of Cultural Innovation." In *Max Weber's Economy and Society: A Critical Companion*, edited by Charles Camic, Philip Gorski, and David Trubek, 366–82. Stanford, CA: Stanford University Press, 2005.

———. "Mit prophetischem Schwung: Rezension zu Tine Stein, *Himmlische Quellen und irdisches Recht.*" *Frankfurter Allgemeine Zeitung*, December 14, 2007, 37.

———. "Morality in the Age of Contingency." *Acta Sociologica* 47 (2004): 392–99. Originally published as "Wertevermittlung in einer fragmentierten Gesellschaft" (2002).

———. "Punishment and Respect." *Journal of Classical Sociology* 8 (2008): 159–77. Originally published as "Strafe und Respekt" (2006).

———. "Review of William S. Pickering, *Durkheim's Sociology of Religion.*" *American Journal of Sociology* 92 (1986): 740–41.

———. "Sociology and the Sacred." In Joas, *Do We Need Religion?* 51–64. Originally published as "Die Soziologie und das Heilige."

———. "Value Generalization: Limitations and Possibilities of a Communication about Values." *Zeitschrift für Wirtschafts- und Unternehmensethik* 9 (2008): 8–96.

———. "Values versus Norms: A Pragmatist Account of Moral Objectivity." *Hedgehog Review* 3 (2001): 42–56. Also published as "Werte versus Normen: Das Problem der moralischen Objektivität bei Putnam, Habermas und den klassischen Pragmatisten" (2002).

———. "Von der Seele zum Selbst." In *Pragmata: Festschrift für Klaus Oehler*, edited by Kai-Michael Hingst and Maria Liatsi, 216–29. Tübingen: Narr, 2008.

———. *War and Modernity.* Cambridge: Polity, 2003. Originally published as *Kriege und Werte: Studien zur Gewaltgeschichte des 20. Jahrhunderts* (2000).

———, ed. *Was sind religiöse Überzeugungen?* Göttingen: Wallstein, 2003.

Joas, Hans, and Wolfgang Knöbl. *Social Theory*. Cambridge: Cambridge University Press, 2009. Originally published as *Sozialtheorie* (2004).

Joas, Hans, and Klaus Wiegandt, eds. *The Cultural Values of Europe.* Liverpool: Liverpool University Press, 2009. Originally published as *Die kulturellen Werte Europas* (2005).

Kalupner, Sibylle. "Vom Schutz der Ehre zum Schutz körperlicher Unversehrtheit: Die Entdeckung des Körpers im modernen Strafrecht." *Paragrana* 15 (2004): 114–35.

Kansteiner, Wulf. "Menschheitstrauma, Holocausttrauma, kulturelles Trauma: Eine kritische Genealogie der philosophischen, psychologischen und kulturwissenschaftlichen Traumaforschung seit 1945." In *Handbuch der Kulturwissenschaften*, 3 vols., edited by Friedrich Jaeger and Jörn Rüsen, 3:109–38. Stuttgart: Metzler, 2004.

Kant, Immanuel. *Groundwork of the Metaphysics of Morals.* Cambridge: Cambridge University Press, 1998. Originally published as *Grundlegung zur Metaphysik der Sitten* (1785).

Karsenti, Bruno. *La société en personnes: Études durkheimiennes.* Paris: Economica, 2006.

Kaufmann, Franz Xaver. *Die Entstehung sozialer Grundrechte und die wohlfahrtsstaatliche Entwicklung.* Paderborn: Schöningh, 2003.

Keck, Margaret E., and Kathryn Sikkink. *Activists beyond Borders: Advocacy Networks in International Politics.* Ithaca, NY: Cornell University Press, 1998.

Kelly, Duncan. "Revisiting the Rights of Man: Georg Jellinek on Rights and the State." *Law and History Review* 22 (2004): 493–530.

Kersten, Jens. *Georg Jellinek und die klassische Staatslehre*. Tübingen: Mohr, 2000.

Kiesel, Helmuth. *Literarische Trauerarbeit: Das Exil- und Spätwerk Alfred Döblins*. Tübingen: Niemeyer, 1986.

King, Henry Churchill. *Theology and the Social Consciousness: A Study of the Relations of the Social Consciousness to Theology*. London: Hodder & Stoughton, 1902.

King, Martin Luther. "The Ethical Demands of Integration" (1962). In *A Testament of Hope*, 118–19. New York: Harper Collins, 1991.

Knöbl, Wolfgang. "Makrotheorie zwischen Pragmatismus und Historismus." In Hollstein, Jung, and Knöbl, *Handlung und Erfahrung*, 273–315.

Kohen, Ari. *In Defense of Human Rights: A Non-religious Grounding in a Pluralistic World*. London: Routledge, 2007.

König, Matthias. *Menschenrechte bei Durkheim und Weber*. Frankfurt am Main: Campus 2002.

Krakau, Knud. *Missionsbewußtsein und Völkerrechtsdoktrin in den Vereinigten Staaten von Amerika*. Frankfurt am Main: Metzner, 1967.

Krämer, Gudrun. "The Contest of Values: Notes on Contemporary Islamic Discourse." In Joas and Wiegandt, *Cultural Values of Europe*, 338–56.

———. *Gottes Staat als Republik: Reflexionen zeitgenössischer Muslime zu Islam, Menschenrechten und Demokratie*. Baden-Baden: Nomos, 1999.

Langbein, John. *Torture and the Law of Proof*. Chicago: University of Chicago Press, 1977.

Laqueur, Thomas W. "Bodies, Details, and the Humanitarian Narrative." In *The New Cultural History*, edited by Lynn Hunt, 176–204. Berkeley: University of California Press, 1989.

Lauren, Paul Gordon. *The Evolution of International Human Rights: Visions Seen*. Philadelphia: University of Pennsylvania Press, 1998.

Lauterpacht, Hersh. *An International Bill of the Rights of Man*. New York: Columbia University Press, 1945.

Leiner, Martin. "Menschenwürde und Reformation." In *Des Menschen Würde—entdeckt und erfunden im Humanismus der italienischen Renaissance*, edited by Rolf Groeschner et al., 49–62. Tübingen: Mohr, 2008.

Léonard, Jacques. "L'historien et le philosophe." *Annales historiques de la révolution française* 49 (1977): 163–81.

Leys, Ruth. *Trauma: A Genealogy*. Chicago: University of Chicago Press, 2000.

Luhmann, Niklas. *Funktion der Religion*. Frankfurt am Main: Suhrkamp, 1977.

Lutterbach, Hubertus. *Gotteskindschaft: Kultur- und Sozialgeschichte eines christlichen Ideals*. Freiburg im Breisgau: Herder, 2003.

MacIntyre, Alasdair. *After Virtue*. London: Duckworth, 2007.

———. *Three Rival Versions of Moral Enquiry: Encyclopaedia, Genealogy, and Tradition*. Notre Dame, IN: University of Notre Dame Press, 1990.

Maier, Pauline. *American Scripture: Making the Declaration of Independence*. New York: Knopf, 1997.

Malinowski, Stephan, and Robert Gerwarth. "Der Holocaust als 'kolonialer Genozid'? Europäische Kolonialgewalt und nationalsozialistischer Vernichtungskrieg." *Geschichte und Gesellschaft* 33 (2007): 439–66.

Mann, Michael. *The Dark Side of Democracy: Explaining Ethnic Cleansing*. Cambridge: Cambridge University Press, 2005.

Mannheim, Karl. "Historicism." In *Essays on the Sociology of Knowledge*, 84–133. London: Routledge, 1952. Originally published as "Historismus" (1924).

Maritain, Jacques. *The Rights of Man and Natural Law*. London: Geoffrey Bles, 1944. Originally published as *Les droits de l'homme et la loi naturelle* (1942).

Marske, Charles. "Durkheim's 'Cult of the Individual' and the Moral Reconstitution of Society." *Sociological Theory* 5 (1987): 1–14.

Marty, Martin. "The American Revolution and Religion, 1765–1815." In Brown and Tackett, *Enlightenment, Reawakening and Revolution*, 497–516.

Mauss, Marcel. "A Category of the Human Mind: The Notion of Person, the Notion of Self" (1938). In *The Category of the Person: Anthropology, Philosophy, History*, edited by Michael Carrithers, Steven Collins, and Steven Lukes, 1–25. Cambridge: Cambridge University Press, 1985.

———. *The Gift: Forms and Functions of Exchange in Archaic Societies*. London: Routledge, 2001. Originally published as *Essai sur le don: Forme et raison de l'échange dans les sociétés archaïques* (1925).

Mayer, Henry. *All on Fire: William Lloyd Garrison and the Abolition of Slavery*. New York: St. Martin's Press, 1998.

Mazower, Mark. "The End of Civilization and the Rise of Human Rights: The Mid-Twentieth Century Disjuncture." In Hoffmann, *Human Rights in the Twentieth Century*, 29–61.

———. "An International Civilization? Empire, Internationalism and the Crisis of the Mid-Twentieth Century." *International Affairs* 82 (2006): 533–66.

———. "Jan Smuts and Imperial Internationalism." In *No Enchanted Palace: The End of Empire and the Ideological Origins of the United Nations*, 28–65. Princeton, NJ: Princeton University Press, 2009.

———. "The Strange Triumph of Human Rights, 1933–1950." *Historical Journal* 47 (2004): 379–98.

———. "Violence and the State in the Twentieth Century." *American Historical Review* 107 (2002): 1158–78.

McLeod, Hugh. *Religion and the People of Western Europe, 1789–1989*, 2nd ed. Oxford: Oxford University Press, 1997.

McLoughlin, William G. *Revival, Awakenings, and Reform: An Essay on Religion and Social Change in America, 1607–1977*. Chicago: University of Chicago Press, 1978.

Mead, George Herbert. "Cooley's Contribution to American Social Thought" (1930). In *Human Nature and the Social Order*, by Charles Horton Cooley, xxi–xxxviii. New Brunswick, NJ: Transaction, 1964.

———. "The Definition of the Psychical." In *Decennial Publications of the University of Chicago*, ser. 1, 3:77–112. Chicago: University of Chicago Press, 1903.

———. *Mind, Self and Society*. Chicago: University of Chicago Press, 1934.

———. "The Objective Reality of Perspectives." In *Proceedings of the Sixth International Conference of Philosophy*, edited by E. S. Brightman, 75–85. New York: Longmans, Green & Co., 1927.

———. *Philosophy of the Present*. LaSalle, IL: Open Court, 1932.

———. "The Psychology of Punitive Justice." *American Journal of Sociology* 23 (1917/18): 577–602.

Melot, Romain. "La notion de droit subjectif dans l'oeuvre de Max Weber." Mémoire de DEA, Paris-Sorbonne University, 2000.

Mills, C. Wright, and H. H. Gerth, eds. *From Max Weber: Essays in Sociology*. London: Routledge, 2007.

Molendijk, Arie L. "The Notion of the Sacred." In *Holy Ground: Re-inventing Ritual Space in Modern Western Culture*, edited by Molendijk and Paul Post, 55–89. Leuven: Peeters, 2010.

Mommsen, Wolfgang. "Einleitung." In *Zur Russischen Revolution von 1905*, by Max Weber, 1–54. Tübingen: Mohr, 1989.

Morsink, Johannes. *The Universal Declaration of Human Rights: Origins, Drafting, and Intent*. Philadelphia: University of Pennsylvania Press, 1999.

———. "World War Two and the Universal Declaration." *Human Rights Quarterly* 15 (1993): 357–405.

Moyn, Samuel. *The Last Utopia: Human Rights in History*. Cambridge, MA: Harvard University Press, 2010.

———. "Personalism, Community and the Origins of Human Rights." In Hoffmann, *Human Rights in the Twentieth Century*, 85–106.

Murray, John C. *We Hold These Truths: Catholic Reflections on the American Proposition*. New York: Sheed & Ward, 1960.

Nelson, Benjamin. "Max Weber, Ernst Troeltsch, Georg Jellinek as Comparative Historical Sociologists." *Sociological Analysis* 36 (1975): 229–40.

Nietzsche, Friedrich. "The Use and Abuse of History." In *The Untimely Meditations* (*Thoughts Out of Season*, pts. 1 and 2), 96–133. Lawrence, KS: Digireads: 2010. Originally published as "Vom Nutzen und Nachteil der Historie für das Leben," in *Unzeitgemäße Betrachtungen: Zweites Stück* (1874).

Nussbaum, Martha C. *Liberty of Conscience: In Defense of America's Tradition of Religious Equality*. New York: Basic, 2008.

Oehler, Klaus. *Sachen und Zeichen: Zur Philosophie des Pragmatismus*. Frankfurt am Main: Klostermann, 1995.

Osterhammel, Jürgen. *Die Verwandlung der Welt: Eine Geschichte des 19. Jahrhunderts*. Munich: Beck, 2009.

Otto, Rudolf. *The Idea of the Holy: An Inquiry into the Non-rational Factor in the Idea of the Divine and Its Relation to the Rational*. Oxford: Oxford University Press, 1950. Originally published as *Das Heilige: Über das Irrationale in der Idee des Göttlichen und sein Verhältnis zum Rationalen* (1917).

Ouédraogo, Jean Martin. "Sociologie religieuse et modernité politique chez Max Weber." *Revue européenne des sciences sociales* 34 (1996): 25–49.

Owen, David. *Nietzsche's "Genealogy of Morality."* Stocksfield: Acumen, 2007.

Ozouf, Mona. "De-Christianization." In Furet and Ozouf, *Critical Dictionary of the French Revolution*, 20–32. Originally published as "Déchristianisation."

———. "Revolutionary Religion." In Furet and Ozouf, *Critical Dictionary of the French Revolution*, 560–70.

Parsons, Talcott. *Action Theory and the Human Condition*. New York: Free Press, 1978.

———. "Comparative Studies and Evolutionary Change." In Parsons, *Social Systems and the Evolution of Action Theory*, 279–320.

———. "On Building Social System Theory: A Personal History." In *Social Systems and the Evolution of Action Theory*, 22–76.

———. *Social Systems and the Evolution of Action Theory*. New York: Free Press, 1977.

———. *The System of Modern Societies*. Englewood Cliffs, NJ: Prentice-Hall, 1971.

Paul, Garrett E. "*Der Historismus* in North America." In *Ernst Troeltsch's "Historismus*," vol. 11 of *Troeltsch-Studien*, edited by Friedrich Wilhelm Graf, 200–217. Gütersloh: Gütersloher Verlagshaus, 2000.

Peirce, Charles S. "Immortality in the Light of Synechism" (1893). In *The Essential Peirce*, vol. 2, *1893–1913*, 1–3. Bloomington: Indiana University Press, 1998.

Perry, Michael. *The Idea of Human Rights: Four Inquiries*. Oxford: Oxford University Press, 1998.

Pettenkofer, Andreas. "Protest als ritualgestützte Glückserfahrung." In Pettenkofer, *Radikaler Protest*, 209–48.

———. *Radikaler Protest: Zur soziologischen Theorie politischer Bewegungen*. Frankfurt am Main: Campus, 2010.

Pickering, William S., ed. *Durkheim: Essays on Morals and Education*. London: Routledge, 2005.

———, ed. *Durkheim on Religion*. London: Routledge, 1975.

———. *Durkheim's Sociology of Religion*. London: Routledge, 1984.

Pihlström, Sami. "William James on Death, Mortality, and Immortality." *Transactions of the Charles Sanders Peirce Society* 38 (2002): 605–28.

Pipes, Richard. "Max Weber und Russland." *Außenpolitik* 6 (1955): 627–39.

———. *Struve: Liberal on the Left, 1870–1905*. Cambridge, MA: Harvard University Press, 1970.

Putnam, Hilary. *The Collapse of the Fact/Value Dichotomy*. Cambridge, MA: Harvard University Press, 2002.

———. *Reason, Truth and History*. Cambridge: Cambridge University Press, 1991.

Ramp, William. "Durkheim and Foucault on the Genesis of the Disciplinary Society." In *Durkheim and Foucault*, edited by Mark Cladis, 71–103. Oxford: Durkheim Press, 1999.

Rawls, John. *Political Liberalism*. New York: Columbia University Press, 1996.

Reiner, Robert. "Crime, Law and Deviance: The Durkheim Legacy." In *Durkheim and Modern Sociology*, by Reiner et al., 175–201. Cambridge: Cambridge University Press, 1984.

Reinhard, Marcel. *Paris pendant la Révolution*. 2 vols. Paris: Centre de documentation universitaire, 1966.

Rendtorff, Trutz. "Geschichte durch Geschichte überwinden: Beobachtungen zur methodischen Struktur des Historismus." In *"Geschichte durch Geschichte überwinden": Ernst Troeltsch in Berlin*, vol. 1 of *Troeltsch-Studien*, new ser., edited by Friedrich Wilhelm Graf, 285–325. Gütersloh: Gütersloher Verlagshaus, 2006.

Resick, Patricia A. *Stress and Trauma*. Hove: Psychology Press, 2000.

Ricoeur, Paul. "Love and Justice." In *Paul Ricoeur: The Hermeneutics of Action*, edited by Richard Kearney, 23–39. London: Sage, 1996.

———. *Oneself as Another*. Chicago: University of Chicago Press, 1994. Originally published as *Soi-même comme un autre* (1990).

Rohls, Jan. *Protestantische Theologie der Neuzeit*. Vol. 2, *Das 20. Jahrhundert*. Tübingen: Mohr, 1997.

Rorty, Richard. "Human Rights, Rationality and Sentimentality" (1993). In *Truth and Progress*, 167–85. Cambridge: Cambridge University Press, 1998.

———. "Response to Richard Bernstein." In *Rorty and Pragmatism: The Philosopher Responds to His Critics*, edited by Herman J. Saatkamp, 68–71. Nashville, TN: Vanderbilt University Press, 1995.

Rosenberg, Hans. "Zur sozialen Funktion der Agrarpolitik im Zweiten Reich." In *Machteliten und Wirtschaftskonjunkturen*, 102–17. Göttingen: Vandenhoeck & Ruprecht, 1978.

Roth, Guenther. *Politische Herrschaft und persönliche Freiheit*. Heidelberg: Suhrkamp, 1987.

Royce, Josiah. *The Conception of Immortality* (1899). New York: Greenwood, 1968.

Ruddies, Hartmut. "'Geschichte durch Geschichte überwinden': Historismuskonzept und Geschichtsdeutung bei Ernst Troeltsch." In *Die Historismusdebatte in der Weimarer Republik*, edited by Wolfgang Bialas and Gérard Raulet, 198–217. Frankfurt am Main: Lang, 1996.

Saar, Martin. *Genealogie als Kritik: Geschichte und Theorie des Subjekts nach Nietzsche und Foucault*. Frankfurt am Main: Campus, 2007.

Samwer, Sigmar-Jürgen. *Die französische Erklärung der Menschen- und Bürgerrechte von 1789/91*. Hamburg: Hansischer Gildenverlag, 1970.

Sandel, Michael. *The Case against Perfection: Ethics in the Age of Genetic Engineering*. Cambridge, MA: Harvard University Press, 2007.

Sander, Gabriele. *Alfred Döblin*. Stuttgart: Reclam, 2001.

Sandweg, Jürgen. *Rationales Naturrecht als revolutionäre Praxis: Untersuchungen zur "Erklärung der Menschen- und Bürgerrechte" von 1789*. Berlin: Duncker & Humblot, 1972.

Scheler, Max. *Formalism in Ethics and Non-formal Ethics of Values*. Evanston, IL: Northwestern University Press, 1973. Originally published as *Der Formalismus in der Ethik und die materiale Werteethik* (1916).

———. "Tod und Fortleben." In *Schriften aus dem Nachlaß*, vol. 1, *Zur Ethik und Erkenntnislehre*, 9–64. Bern: Francke, 1957.

Schluchter, Wolfgang. *The Rise of Western Rationalism: Max Weber's Developmental History*. Berkeley: University of California Press, 1981. Originally published as *Die Entwicklung des okzidentalen Rationalismus* (1979).

———. "The Sociology of Law as an Empirical Theory of Validity." *Journal of Classical Sociology* 2 (2002): 257–80. Originally published as "Rechtssoziologie als empirische Geltungstheorie" (2000).

Schmale, Wolfgang. *Archäologie der Grund- und Menschenrechte in der Frühen Neuzeit*. Munich: Oldenbourg, 1997.

Schmoeckel, Matthias. *Humanität und Staatsraison: Die Abschaffung der Folter in Europa und die Entwicklung des gemeinen Strafprozeß- und Beweisrechts seit dem hohen Mittelalter*. Cologne: Böhlau, 2000.

Schneewind, Jerome B. "Autonomy, Obligation, and Virtue: An Overview of Kant's Moral Philosophy." In *The Cambridge Companion to Kant*, edited by Paul Guyer, 309–41. Cambridge: Cambridge University Press, 1992.

Schnur, Roman, ed. *Zur Geschichte der Erklärung der Menschenrechte*. Darmstadt: WBG, 1964.

Scholem, Gershom. "Schöpfung aus Nichts und Selbstverschränkung Gottes." In *Über einige Grundbegriffe des Judentums*, 53–89. Frankfurt am Main: Suhrkamp, 1970.

Schubert, Hans-Joachim. *Demokratische Identität: Der soziologische Pragmatismus von Charles Horton Cooley*. Frankfurt am Main: Suhrkamp, 1995.

———. Introduction. In *On Self and Social Organization*, by Charles Horton Cooley, 1–31. Chicago: University of Chicago Press, 1998.

Schwöbel, Christoph. "'Die Idee des Aufbaus heißt Geschichte durch Geschichte überwinden': Theologischer Wahrheitsanspruch und das Problem des sogenannten Historismus." In *Ernst Troeltsch's "Historismus,"* vol. 11 of

Troeltsch-Studien, edited by Friedrich Wilhelm Graf, 261–84. Gütersloh: Gütersloher Verlagshaus, 2003.

Seibert, Christoph. *Religion im Denken von William James: Eine Interpretation seiner Philosophie*. Tübingen: Mohr, 2009.

Sellmann, Matthias. *Religion und soziale Ordnung: Gesellschaftstheoretische Analysen*. Frankfurt am Main: Campus, 2007.

Sheehan, Jonathan. "Enlightenment, Religion, and the Enigma of Secularization." *American Historical Review* 108 (2003): 1061–80.

Sieberg, Herward. "Französische Revolution und die Sklavenfrage in Westindien." *Geschichte in Wissenschaft und Unterricht* 42 (1991): 405–16.

Simmel, Georg. *The View of Life: Four Metaphysical Essays*. Chicago: University of Chicago Press, 2010. Originally published as *Lebensanschauung: Vier metaphysische Kapitel* (1918).

Simpson, Alfred W. Brian. *Human Rights and the End of Empire: Britain and the Genesis of the European Convention*. Oxford: Oxford University Press, 2001.

Smith, Philip. "Meaning and Military Power: Moving on from Foucault." *Journal of Power* 1 (2008): 275–93.

———. *Punishment and Culture*. Chicago: University of Chicago Press, 2008.

Sorkin, David. *The Religious Enlightenment: Protestants, Jews, and Catholics from London to Vienna*. Princeton, NJ: Princeton University Press, 2008.

Spranger, Eduard. "Das Historismusproblem an der Universität Berlin seit 1900." In *Studium Berolinense: Aufsätze und Beiträge zu Problemen der Wissenschaft und zur Geschichte der Friedrich-Wilhelms-Universität zu Berlin*, edited by Hans Leussink et al., 425–43. Berlin: de Gruyter, 1960.

Stackhouse, Max. *Creeds, Society, and Human Rights*. Grand Rapids, MI: Eeerdmans, 1984.

Stein, Tine. *Himmlische Quellen und irdisches Recht: Religiöse Voraussetzungen des freiheitlichen Verfassungsstaates*. Frankfurt am Main: Campus, 2007.

Stolleis, Michael. "Georg Jellineks Beitrag zur Entwicklung der Menschen- und Bürgerrechte." In *Georg Jellinek: Beiträge zu Leben und Werk*, edited by Stanley L. Paulson and Martin Schulte, 103–16. Tübingen: Mohr, 2000.

Svensson, Marina. *Debating Human Rights in China: A Conceptual and Political History*. Lanham, MD: Rowman & Littlefield, 2002.

Tackett, Timothy. "The French Revolution and Religion to 1794." In Brown and Tackett, *Enlightenment, Reawakening and Revolution*, 536–55.

Tarot, Camille. "Émile Durkheim and After: The War over the Sacred in French Sociology in the 20th Century." *Distinktion* 19 (2009): 11–30.

———. *Le symbolique et le sacré: Théories de la religion*. Paris: Découverte, 2008.

Taylor, Charles. *A Secular Age*. Cambridge, MA: Harvard University Press, 2007.

———. *Sources of the Self: The Making of the Modern Identity*. Cambridge: Cambridge University Press, 1992.

Tétaz, Jean-Marc. "Identité culturelle et réflexion critique: Le problème de l'universalité des droits de l'homme aux prises avec l'affirmation culturaliste. La stratégie argumentative d'Ernst Troeltsch." *Études théologiques et religieuses* 74 (1999): 213–33.

Thomas, Günter. *Implizite Religion: Theoriegeschichtliche und theoretische Untersuchungen zum Problem ihrer Identifikation.* Würzburg: Ergon, 2001.

Tilly, Charles. "Comment on Young: Buried Gold." *American Sociological Review* 67 (2002): 689–92.

Tiryakian, Edward. *For Durkheim: Essays in Historical and Cultural Sociology.* Farnham: Ashgate, 2009.

Tocqueville, Alexis de. *The Ancien Régime and the Revolution.* London: Penguin, 2008. Originally published as *L'Ancien Régime et la Révolution* (1856).

Tole, Lise Ann. "Durkheim on Religion and Moral Community in Modernity." *Sociological Inquiry* 63 (1993): 1–29.

Touraine, Alain. *Critique of Modernity.* Oxford: Blackwell, 1995. Originally published as *Critique de la modernité* (1992).

Troeltsch, Ernst. *Aufsätze zur Geistesgeschichte und Religionssoziologie*, edited by Hans Baron. Tübingen: Mohr, 1925.

———. *Christian Thought: Its History and Application.* London: University of London Press, 1923. Reprinted in Troeltsch, *Fünf Vorträge zu Religion und Geschichtsphilosophie*, 133–203. Originally published as *Der Historismus und seine Überwindung* (Berlin: Heise, 1924).

———. "Der christliche Seelenbegriff." In *Glaubenslehre*, 279–325. Munich: Duncker & Humblot, 1925.

———. *Fünf Vorträge zu Religion und Geschichtsphilosophie für England und Schottland.* Vol. 17 of *Kritische Gesamtausgabe*, edited by Gangolf Hübinger. Berlin: de Gruyter, 2006. Originally published as *Der Historismus und seine Überwindung* (1924).

———. *Der Historismus und seine Probleme* (1922), vols. 16.1 and 16.2 of *Kritische Gesamtausgabe.* Berlin: de Gruyter, 2008.

———. *Der Historismus und seine Überwindung.* Berlin: Heise, 1924.

———. "The Ideas of Natural Law and Humanity in World Politics" (1923). In Otto Gierke, *Natural Law and the Theory of Society, 1500–1800*, 201–22. Boston: Beacon Press, 1957.

———. "Naturrecht und Humanität in der Weltpolitik" (1923). In *Schriften zur Politik und Kulturphilosophie, 1918–23*, vol. 15 of *Kritische Gesamtausgabe*, 493–512. Berlin: de Gruyter, 2002.

———. "Politik, Patriotismus, Religion." In *Der Historismus und seine Überwindung*, 84–103.

———. "Rezension von Jellineks 'Ausgewählte Schriften und Reden.'" *Zeitschrift für das Privat- und öffentliche Recht in der Gegenwart* 39 (1912): 273–78.

———. *The Social Teaching of the Christian Churches.* London: Allen & Unwin, 1950. Originally published as *Die Soziallehren der christlichen Kirchen und Gruppen* (1912).

———. "Die Zufälligkeit der Geschichtswahrheiten" (1923). In *Schriften zur Politik und Kulturphilosophie, 1918–1923*, vol. 15 of *Kritische Gesamtausgabe*, 551–67. Berlin: de Gruyter, 2008.

Van Kley, Dale K. "Christianity as Casualty and Chrysalis of Modernity: The Problem of Dechristianization in the French Revolution." *American Historical Review* 108 (2003): 1081–104.

Vögele, Wolfgang. *Menschenwürde zwischen Recht und Theologie: Begründungen von Menschenrechten in der Perspektive öffentlicher Theologie.* Gütersloh: Gütersloher Verlagshaus, 2000.

Waltz, Susan. "Reclaiming and Rebuilding the History of the Universal Declaration of Human Rights." *Third World Quarterly* 23 (2002): 437–48.

———. "Universal Human Rights: The Contribution of Muslim States." *Human Rights Quarterly* 26 (2004): 799–844.

———. "Universalizing Human Rights: The Role of Small States in the Construction of the Universal Declaration of Human Rights." *Human Rights Quarterly* 23 (2001): 44–72.

Walzer, Michael. *Spheres of Justice.* Oxford: Robertson, 1983.

Weber, Marianne. *Max Weber: A Biography.* New Brunswick, NJ: Transaction, 1975. Originally published as *Max Weber: Ein Lebensbild* (1950).

Weber, Max. *Economy and Society.* 3 vols. New York: Bedminster Press, 1922. Originally published as *Wirtschaft und Gesellschaft* (Tübingen: Mohr, 1922).

———. "Religious Groups (The Sociology of Religion)." In *Economy and Society*, 399–634. Berkeley: University of California Press, 1992. Originally published as "Religionssoziologie: Typen religiöser Vergemeinschaftung," in *Wirtschaft und Gesellschaft* (1922).

Wells, Gordon, and Peter Baehr. "Editors' Introduction." In Wells and Baehr, *Max Weber*, 1–39.

———, eds. *Max Weber: The Russian Revolutions.* Ithaca, NY: Cornell University Press, 1995.

Williams, Bernard. *Ethics and the Limits of Philosophy.* London: Fontana, 1985.

Williams, Eric. *Capitalism and Slavery.* Chapel Hill: University of North Carolina Press, 1944.

Winter, Jay. *Dreams of Peace and Freedom: Utopian Moments in the Twentieth Century.* New Haven, CT: Yale University Press, 2006.

Wittgenstein, Ludwig. *On Certainty* (1969). Oxford: Blackwell, 1974.

Young, Michael P. *Bearing Witness against Sin: The Evangelical Birth of the American Social Movement.* Chicago: University of Chicago Press, 2006.

———. "Confessional Protest: The Religious Birth of U.S. National Social Movements." *American Sociological Review* 67 (2002): 660–88.

———. "Reply to Tilly: Contention and Confession." *American Sociological Review* 67 (2002): 693–95.

Zagorin, Perez. "Christianity and Freedom: In Response to Martha C. Nussbaum, 'Liberty of Conscience.'" *New York Review of Books*, September 25, 2008, 97.

———. *How the Idea of Religious Toleration Came to the West*. Princeton, NJ: Princeton University Press, 2003.

Zimmerer, Jürgen. *Von Windhuk nach Auschwitz: Beiträge zum Verhältnis von Kolonialismus und Holocaust*. Münster: Lit, 2007.

INDEX

CPSIA information can be obtained
at www.ICGtesting.com
Printed in the USA
BVOW10s0803090617
486345BV00001B/17/P